W9-COE-411

Hawaii's Incredible Anna

Hawaii's Incredible Anna

by

Ruth M. Tabrah

PRESS PACIFICA

Library of Congress Cataloging-in-Publication Data

Tabrah, Ruth M., 1921–
    Hawaii's incredible Anna.

    Includes index.
    1. Perry-Fiske, Anna Lindsey.   2. Hawaii—
Biography.   3. Hawaii—Social life and customs.
4. Ranch life—Hawaii.   I. Title.
DU627.7.P47T33   1987   996.9'04   86-30648
ISBN O-916630-53-6

Cover design and illustrations by Judy Hancock.

Copyright 1987 Ruth M. Tabrah.

All rights reserved.

Typeset by The Last Word, Kailua, HI

Manufactured by Kingsport Press, Kingsport, TN

Available from:
Pacific Trade Group, P.O. Box 668, Pearl City, HI 96782

This book is lovingly dedicated to my parents
William and Mary Lindsey
whose zest for life, work and giving has been my lifelong inspiration –

Anna Lindsey Perry-Fiske

Author's Note
and Acknowledgements

THIS IS ANNA'S story as she has told it to me over several years of intensive interviews. Other recollections and reminiscences were added by those of her friends and family whom I interviewed, including many like former Judge Nelson Doi who had been Anna's admiring adversary on the other side of a court case. I wish to thank Richard Lindsey and Judy Hancock in particular, Monty Richards, Richard Penhallow, Richard and Nancy Frazier, John Ushijima, Federal Judge Martin Pence, Yutaka Kimura, Julia and Tommy Rodenhurst, the late Bill Bryan, Irma Bryan, the late Brother Low, Budger Ruddle, Ronald Tooman, Bernard Nogues, William 'Bull' Awaa and Nelson Doi for their interviews.

I am particularly indebted to Maxine Hughes whose voluminous output of articles about Anna and her activities, published for more than thirty years in the *Hilo Tribune-Herald* (now *Hawaii Tribune-Herald)*and *The Orchid Isle* was extraordinarily helpful to me. I am also grateful to *Honolulu Advertiser* staff writer Mary Cooke for the insights in her numerous features on Anna and on 'Old Hawaii on Horseback'. As always, the patient and hardworking librarians of the Hawaii-Pacific room of the main branch of Hawaii State Library, and the staff of Hawaii State Archives have been of tremendous research assistance.

To all of these, and to the many others who helped give me an understanding of Hawaii's incredible Anna, my heartfelt mahalo. As a personal history this is, of course, told from Anna's point of view of how and why things were as they seemed to her. One's life is one's own very intimate portrait, painted here as she looks back on it, and as those who know her best remember how things were. Her memories in this book are not intended to be a scholarly history nor a formal biography. They are rather the portrait of a remarkable woman and the very special Hawaii in which she worked and lived. No defamation of anyone's character or anyone's memory has been intended and should not be inferred.

In her artwork and the photographs she has assembled to illustrate this book, Judy Hancock has done a superb job of acquainting readers pictorially with "Hawaii's Incredible Anna". It has been most inspiring to work with her, and with publisher Jane Pultz of Press Pacifica on this very special contribution to Hawaiiana.

Ruth Tabrah
Honolulu, January 1987

FOREWORD

THIS IS THE story of Anna Lindsey Perry-Fiske, a truly remarkable woman of Hawaiian, English, and German Jewish ancestry who has lived an exciting and most unusual life in one of Hawaii's very special places – Waimea-Kohala, in the heart of the Big Island's *paniolo* country.

The title of her biography expresses exactly what she is – HAWAII'S INCREDIBLE ANNA. She is a tough, shrewd, hard-working cowboy and, at the same time, a strikingly beautiful, elegantly groomed great lady. To see her sitting at the captain's table on a cruise ship, dressed in a gold lame dinner gown, a white fox fur around her shoulders, a diamond tiara sparkling on the coronet of her dark hair, one would never guess that, at various times in her life, Anna has been a racing jockey, a butcher, and a truck driver. Throughout the islands of this fiftieth state, Anna's cattle-breeding expertise, and her fabulous black-tie dinner parties have both brought her reknown. For hundreds of thousands of parade-goers – in Hawaii, at the Tournament of Roses in Pasadena, at the Calgary Stampede and the Lethbridge, Alberta Centennial celebration of the Royal Canadian Mounted Police, Anna will always be remembered as the Queen of the Pa'u Riders.

At an age when most women and men sit back in retirement, this incredible Anna is still a ranch owner, ranch boss, cattle buyer, business woman, and glamourous hostess. As she has been for all of her long life, Anna is a vibrant, charming and caring person who can, at the same time, be a formidable adversary when the occasion arises. She enjoys a well-deserved reputation of being a most powerful persuader when it comes to raising funds for charitable causes and she herself is a most generous benefactress. Her "Old Hawaii on Horseback", a spectacular pageant presented on the spacious front lawns of her ranch house, has long been one of the nation's most successful fund raisers for the American Heart Association.

Anna's diminutive size and dainty, well-manicured hands are deceptive. She is a dynamo of energy – a strong, self-reliant woman who never considered being female an obstacle. With unflagging confidence and verve, Anna Perry-Fiske has made a name for herself in business and politics. She is both indomitable and assuredly feminine, surpassing most men with her stamina, gutsiness, and courage. With grit and determination, almost always on her own, she has coped with hard times, divorce, family crises, despair over a much loved *hanai* (adopted) child, and the everyday adversities of making a cattle ranch succeed in this highly competitive world. Her life has never been easy.

Of late years, Anna has survived injuries that would have led anyone else to hang up their saddle for good – but her belief in herself, and her deep Christian faith, have sustained her. All these many facets of Anna Lindsey Perry-Fiske's strong character makes hers the story of a life of challenge and amazing resilience, of living through failure to achieve success. She has always been at the crest of the waves of change that have washed through this twentieth century and thus her biography is rich in Hawaiiana and the anecdotes that make history vivid.

Hers is also a feminist story, although Anna has never thought of herself as such. Those with concern for the emergence of women enjoying equal status with men will find that in her own decisive way Anna Lindsey Perry-Fiske has set a pattern that young feminists can envy – and emulate. Not only has she pioneered in the development of Hawaii's modern ranching industry. She has earned the respect of women and men alike for her business acumen, her talent for innovation in cattle raising, range, and ranch management, and her political savvy as she has already won their admiration for her great beauty and charm.

How did all this come to be?

"It was my parents," Anna acknowledges. "My mother made me the lady that I am, and my father made me the man I am today!"

Contents

Waimea

THE ANCIENT HAWAIIAN name of the Big Island's South Kohala region where Anna Lindsey Perry-Fiske has spent most of her life is Waimea. Newcomers may refer to the area as Kamuela, but as Anna keeps reminding everyone, that is only the name of the post office in Waimea.

Anna is a tiny, dark-haired dynamo of a woman whose beautiful features and expressive brown eyes convey in a most appealing way the varied lineage of her ancestry– Hawaiian, English, German Jewish. It is a blend that gave her a soft heart, an impulse to generosity, a resolve and courage, and an out-spoken independence. It is because of her long, impassioned fight to respect and preserve the Hawaiian-ness that her home region's traditional name expresses, that today on official maps and road signs this high green country stretching from the summits of the Kohala Mountains to the flanks of Mauna Kea still bears its traditional name – Waimea.

According to Pukui-Elbert's Hawaiian-English Dictionary, the meaning of Waimea is 'reddish water'. The area's many streams, which bring down the run-off from the heavy rainfall at the summit of the Kohala Mountains, are often tinged a reddish champagne color from the spores of tree ferns that thrive in the high rain forests. Such is the color of Waiauea

1

stream, which runs across Anna Ranch, a lush spread of sloping green pastures above what oldtimers in Waimea know as the Government Road. The ranch was once her father's, but when he died, after a long illness, and Anna became its manager, she was faced with the almost insurmountable task of bringing the place back from the brink of failure. Over the more than forty years of her ownership and personal, hard-working management, it has become a showplace.

Anna and her story are strictly twentieth century, but her roots in Waimea and the development of the area as *paniolo* country in which her grandfather, Tom Lindsey, was a pioneer rancher, are an essential background. So, first, we must go back two hundred years, to the beginnings of Hawaii's contacts with the outside world.

The first foreigner to describe the countryside where Anna Ranch is located was the British explorer, Lord George Vancouver, who had visited Hawaii with Cook's expedition in 1778-9. In 1792, 1793, and 1794 Vancouver returned with his own expedition. His 1792 visit was brief but in 1793 and 1794 he spent a great deal of time with King Kamehameha I on the Big Island.

The pig, the dog, and the rat were the islands' only indigenous animals. Taro, bananas, and sweet potatoes were the major food crops. Vancouver was anxious to introduce a variety of domestic animals and new food plants from which he felt the Hawaiians might benefit, and which would be a future resource for provisioning foreign ship visitors. To this end – as had Cook to Niihau – he brought a few goats and some geese, and a variety of seeds and seedlings. In 1794 he brought five cows and a bull as special gifts for King Kamehameha. Vancouver anchored at the hot, arid South Kohala port of Kawaihae. From that village, he walked eleven miles upcountry to Waimea where, so he had been told, there was a much cooler climate, more rainfall, and grassland. In short, a place where cattle might thrive. Some of Anna's Hawaiian forebears, who were *alii*, Polynesians of high rank and chiefly status, probably were on hand when Vancouver made his historic personal survey of the area.

The 2500 foot plus elevation of Waimea gives it a bracing climate. Trade winds clouds often hover on the summits of the Kohalas, and wreath the majestic 13,784 foot height of Mauna Kea.

Sun-struck mists often blow down across Waimea. Sometimes, in Hawaii's mild tropical winter, the area sits shrouded in chilly gray fog. On other days, rain slashes in heavy, almost horizontal gusts across these slopes. But there are days when the sky above Waimea is a clear bright blue – a big sky filled with the changing drama of scudding white cumulus clouds. The hills are a vivid green. All the great mountains are visible. The spectacular view carries the eye down over the dry sweep of lower elevations to the lava cliffs and white sand beaches of the South Kohala coastline and the deep dark blue of the sea.

It must have been on such a bright day that Vancouver first saw the place where Anna lives now. He wrote later in his journal that Waimea was an "upland plain, very rich and productive, occupying a space of several miles in extent and winding at the foot of lofty mountains . . far into the country." Vancouver convinced King Kamehameha that the five cows and bull he had brought from Senor Quadra's ranch in Monterey, California, be driven up to Waimea, where there was "a great tract of luxuriant natural pasturage." To prevent Hawaiians from slaughtering the cattle to see how the meat of these new animals might taste, Vancouver persuaded King Kamehameha I to declare a royal kapu. For the next ten years, any Hawaiian who harmed these horned cattle would lose his own life. With a decade of protection, Vancouver was confident that the five cows and a bull would "increase and multiply".

They were lean, slab-sided animals, black longhorns small in stature with shaggy heads and large eyes. Like the Hawaiians themselves, the ancestors of these cattle had a long history of migration. In Spain, they had been black Moorish cattle whose descendants are still to be seen today in Spanish bullfight rings. Centuries ago such lean longhorns were shipped to the West Indies and, later, from there to California. Thanks to Kamehameha's royal kapu, the longhorns brought from California to Hawaii by Vancouver in 1794 increased and multiplied to such an extent that within thirty years large herds of wild cattle roamed the Waimea hillsides and the slopes of Mauna Kea.

The wild bullocks were a menace to travelers going overland to Hilo on trails along the eight thousand foot elevation of Mauna Kea. Many were attacked and gored. The situation was such that by 1830 King Kamehameha III began to try to eradicate the wild longhorns by offering a generous cash bounty for each hide brought to his agent at Kawaihae. It was not an entirely compassionate gesture on the part of this youngest son of Kamehameha I. Hides brought a good price at South American ports, and the royal treasury enjoyed a profit from the venture. The problem soon became one of more demand than bounty hunters working on foot could supply.

Horses had been introduced to Hawaii in 1803 and riding was, by 1830, a sport at which Hawaiians excelled and about which they were much enthused. Realizing that more cattle could be roped and slaughtered from horseback, the King imported three *vaqueros* from Mexico to teach the Hawaiians of Waimea their cowboy arts.

Paniolo – the Hawaiian word for cowboy – leaped into the language when, in answer to the Hawaiians' question as to what the vaqueros called themselves, Kussuth, Luzada and Ramon answered: "Espanol". The *paniolo* who for years have helped Anna Perry-Fiske with her seasonal jobs of branding and driving cattle still show that long ago influence of the vaqueros in their jingling spurs, their hand-wrought bits and hand-braided rawhide ropes. The uniquely Hawaiian touch of the *paniolo* is that on the hatband of his cowboy hat he wears either a lei of fresh flowers, a lei of dried flowers, or one of feathers woven in the style of the ancient Hawaiian feather capes once worn by the *alii*.

About the same time that these first cowboys arrived to begin teaching cattle roping skills to the Hawaiian bounty hunters, other foreigners began flocking to Waimea to kill wild cattle and collect the cash bounty for the hides. There was no attempt made to use the meat on the carcass of the slaughtered animals then. Bounty hunters like former Australian colonist Jim Fay, and Hawaii's Governor Kuakini, brother of the powerful Queen Kaahumanu, were interested only in the hides. No less a person than Rev. Hiram Bingham, head of the American Mission that since 1820 had been trying to christianize the Hawaiians, visited Waimea in 1830 and recorded in his journal that he had seen "several striking exhibitions of seizing wild cattle, chasing them on horseback, and throwing the lassos over their horns ... and subdueing or killing these mountain -fed animals."

'Subdueing' was an alternative already explored by an ex-seaman from Massachusetts, John Palmer Parker. A few years previously he had been given a tract of land in North Kohala by Kamehameha I. There he had built a corral and experimented with trying to domesticate a few wild longhorns. He was successful enough so that when he married a Waimea chiefess, and moved his operation to her extensive lands at Mana in South Kohala, Parker continued his experiment. In 1840, the number of whaling ships stopping to provision in Hawaii had increased to such an extent that the demand for salted and dried beef made the meat of the wild longhorns more profitable than hides and tallow. Since ship visitors were not likely to wait for a hunter to go kill a few longhorns while they were in port, ranches like John Parker's became feasible. Soon others began to follow his lead.

A tremendous impetus to the growth of ranching, as it was to the development of Hawaii's vast sugar cane plantations, was the Great *Mahele* which between 1846 and 1854 modernized and westernized Hawaii's traditional feudal system of land tenure. Now Hawaiians could have title to their lands without fear a chief would arbitrarily decide to give the land to somebody else. Under the new system, foreigners could also buy or lease land and among those who did was Anna's great-great grandfather Jim Fay, who married a Hawaiian *alii* and established the first sawmill in South Kohala – *Pali Huki Papa*, 'the place where they drag the wood.' It was a prosperous venture. No longer were Hawaiians building grass houses as they had for centuries. Probably no previously isolated culture was ever more quick and eager to adopt new and different ideas. Hawaiians soon saw that wooden or stone walls kept out Waimea's cold winter winds and rain far more effectively than pili grass thatch. The lumber from Jim Fay's mill found a ready market.

Jim Fay and his Hawaiian wife had one child, a daughter, Mary Fay, a girl of unusual intelligence and extraordinary beauty. When she was old enough, her proud parents sent her to Honolulu to attend school. Nothing but the best for their daughter! As her parents had hoped, Mary Fay excelled in her studies. She was also a popular girl, always in demand to attend the balls and picnics given by Honolulu society to entertain officers from visiting foreign ships.

One day a British man-o-war anchored in Honolulu harbor. As usual, Mary Fay was one of the beauties selected to attend a ball given for its officers. At sixteen she had enjoyed many such parties, and been admired by many escorts. But this occasion was different. She found herself swept off her feet by the attentions of a handsome young officer, George Kingston Lindsey. He launched an impetuous and successful courtship. Against the strong objections of her parents, who did not want her either to marry a British officer or to marry so young, the pair eloped. A family legend is that George Kingston Lindsey and Mary Fay went out to sea on a sailing ship to get married since Jim Fay had alerted all his friends and the sheriff in Honolulu to prevent anyone on Oahu from marrying them.

It was the custom in England at that time for an officer to be able to buy his way out of the navy. This George Lindsey did, and as he had promised his young wife, he returned to Waimea to live. There, soon after the birth of their son, Mary Fay's devoted husband became seriously ill. Consumption was the great killer of youth in the nineteenth century. Hoping that he might be cured if he returned to England, George Lindsey left Hawaii. But in England neither treatment nor cure was yet available. On his deathbed, he begged his brother, Thomas Weston Lindsey, to promise he would go to Hawaii and look after George's wife and son.

It was a promise to which Thomas Weston Lindsey was faithful. He sailed for Hawaii, went to Waimea and there – as had his late brother – Thomas Weston Lindsey fell madly in love with the beautiful Mary Fay. He married his brother's young widow and adopted their son. During the many years of their life together, he and Mary Fay Lindsey had a large family of eleven children. Anna's grandfather, Thomas Lindsey, was one of their sons.

Anna has many memories of this paternal grandfather, and of his spacious koa home that once stood where there is today a small, picturesque red house with white gingerbread trim, which was built for one of the sons of Richard Smart, owner of Parker Ranch. In the years when Tom Lindsey's koa home was on this site, Anna spent many happy hours visiting her grand-parents. She likes to describe the unusual French windows of her grandfather's koa home, and the flower boxes under those windows which her paternal grandmother, the former Betsy Fredenberg of Maui, kept filled with masses of colorful blooms. Through this grandmother Anna received another strain of *alii* lineage – that of High Chief Kalakaua ehu a Kama.

Anna's father, William Miller Seymour Lindsey, although his parents each were of part-Hawaiian ancestry, had beautiful blue eyes. He had been sent first to St. Louis College in Honolulu to be educated and later transferred to the fine new institution established by the legacy of Princess Bernice Pauahi Bishop – Kamehameha Schools. A handsome young man whose ambi-tion was to be a rancher like his father, William Lindsey returned to Waimea after graduation and acquired a small place of his own-the nucleus of the acreage that is now Anna Ranch.

In the late 1890's, when young William Lindsey graduated from Kamehameha and returned to Waimea to live, he often helped his father with cattle drives. Tom Lindsey always marketed his beef on the hoof in Hilo. At that time there were two routes from Waimea. One was the old wagon road along Keanakolu on the slopes of Mauna Kea, and then down through the saddle between that mountain and Mauna Loa. The other was a two day trip along the Hamakua Coast, stopping over-night at Paauilo Plantation to rest the cattle and horses.

One of the stories Anna remembers being told by her grand-father Tom Lindsey is of how he solved a problem in safely driving his cattle on past Paauilo. At the turn of the century that plantation had begun to employ Puerto Ricans who emigrated to Hawaii after the Spanish-American war and the devastation of epidemics, famine, and hurricanes on their home island. The first time he drove his cattle through Paauilo after the Puerto Ricans arrived, Tom Lindsey encountered near disaster. His Waimea steers were used to seeing cowboys on horseback but they panicked at the sight of these Puerto Ricans walking along the road. The cattle stampeded into the canefields. It took the better part of the day to round them up and continue on to Hilo.

What to do to prevent stampedes on future drives through that plantation? Tom Lindsey devised an ingenuous solution.

Anna chuckles as she tells how he met with the Puerto Ricans and arranged a signal with them. Each time he approached Paauilo with his cattle he would ride well ahead of the herd, cracking his big bullwhip. When the pedestrians heard this, they would head for the canefields and hide there until the cattle were safely driven past. "Everybody who wasn't in on the fact this was a pre-arranged signal thought my grandfather was a mean man to do this!" says Anna. "But he and the Puerto Ricans understood what the sound of that bullwhip meant and he never had a problem getting his cattle through Paauilo after that!"

Hilo, the destination of these cattle drives, was then a town whose entire bayfront was a broad black sand beach, popular for picnicking, swimming, surfing and racing one's horse. Front Street, which edged this beach, was unpaved. When Hilo people saw clouds of dust approaching the town they'd say, "Here comes Tom Lindsey with his cattle again!" But, in the late 1890's it was often William Lindsey bringing his father's cattle to Hilo. On one of these trips, the young rancher happened to meet Mary Rosenberg, a vivacious, dark-eyed part-Hawaiian school teacher with whom he immediately fell in love.

Like William Lindsey, Mary Rosenberg was then in her early twenties. Like him too she had grown up in a large, well-to-do family. Mary Rosenberg was an extremely attractive young woman with an independent spirit and air of self-reliance that William Lindsey liked. She loved horses and riding. Most of the school teachers who had country teaching jobs a short distance from Hilo depended on a helper to groom and saddle their horses for them. Not Mary Rosenberg! She always groomed and saddled her own horse, took off his saddle when she got to school and then put the horse out to pasture until the close of the school day. At dismissal time she brought the horse in herself, saddled up, and rode home.

It took no more than three trips to Hilo for William Lindsey to court her. Mary Rosenberg was quick to decide that he was the man with whom she wished to share her life. At a picnic at Hilo's famed Rainbow Falls, where she wove a white ginger lei for him to wear on his hat, William Lindsey proposed and Mary accepted.

Mary Rosenberg Lindsey gave her daughter Anna both

European and Hawaiian proud lineages. Anna's maternal grandfather, William Leonard Rosenberg, was from a prominent
German-Jewish family in Stuttgart and Gluckstadt, people of
such high standing that they were "von" Rosenberg, according
to one genealogy. Anna's grandfather – whom she always refers
to as Grandpa Rose – had emigrated to Hawaii some time before
he applied for and was granted citizenship in the Kingdom of
Hawaii. That document, signed November 18, 1850 by Kamehameha III, reveals that William Leonard Rose, as he now chose
to call himself, was then thirty-three years old. He was a skilled
coppersmith and tinsmith who began a new industry in Hilo,
a community that in the mid-nineteenth century had a large
German population. In 1868, at the age of fifty-one, William
Rosenberg married a fifteen-year old Hawaiian girl, Kanaina,
who was the descendant of the great chief Nohomulani, through
the same line as King Lunalilo, that gentle monarch who ruled
Hawaiii for just one year before his death. It was Lunalilo's father,
Charles Kanaina, who asked Anna's maternal great-
grandparents, Kamakahai and Kaaikumoku, to name their
daughter Kanaina after him when she was born in the Puna
district of the Big Island on May 6, 1853.

Kanaina Rosenberg brought a dowry of rich lands to her
marriage. Her husband was already affluent from his pioneering blacksmithing and iron works business. The thirty-six year
difference in their ages seems not to have mattered. Theirs was
a happy union. Anna's mother, Mary Leialoha Rosenberg was
the sixth child and fourth daughter in their family of ten children.
At the time of her marriage to William Lindsey, Mary Rosenberg's
parents owned an entire business block in downtown Hilo. Their
spacious home occupied a site where the Palace Theater now
stands. Later, they moved to a home on Reed's Bay which was
then accessible only by boat from Hilo town. The properties
which Anna's grandmother, Kanaina Rosenberg (also known
as Kanaina Rose) owned included this prime Reed's Bay
frontage and a substantial portion of what is today Hilo's bayfront
resort area.

For Mary Rosenberg Lindsey life on her husband's Waimea
ranch was a great adventure. Although, in contrast to Hilo,
it was an isolated rural area, she never felt anything but

enthusiasm and aloha for her new home. Her first child, William Miller Seymour Lindsey, Jr. – whom everyone called Bill – was born in the small cottage which, in later years, was remodeled and extended to its present spacious size. When she was well along in her second pregnancy, Mary Lindsey chose to go with toddler Bill to Hilo to be with her mother until the new baby was born. So it was in Hilo that Anna Leialoha Lindsey, William and Mary Lindsey's only daughter, was born on February 20th, 1900. Anna was only two weeks old when her mother tucked her into a saddle bag for her first horseback ride home to the ranch in Waimea.

In 1902 the William Lindsey family was completed with the birth of their third child, Anna's younger brother Charles. Anna still remembers what fun she and her two brothers had on the days when Mary Lindsey did the laundry. In those days, the ranch house did not have the convenience of a wash house as home laundries in Hawaii were then called. What Mary Lindsey put to use was an *auwai*, a ditch that carried a stream of clean, cool fresh water across the Lindsey's front lawn from its neighbor, the home of the manager of the ranch that John Palmer Parker had founded, and that had become the largest singly owned cattle ranch in the world.

In the *auwai* that ran from there through her place, Mary Lindsey had placed a large flat rock on which, Anna remembers, her mother did the weekly washing. Mrs. Lindsey would pound the clothes clean on the rock, rinsing them in the fresh flowing water while Anna and her two brothers played in the stream, having a wonderful wet time. "We didn't know there was any other way to do the laundry!" Anna recollects.

Then as now, the upper boundary of this ranch where Anna was to spend most of her life was at the summit forest. From there, William Lindsey's broad acreage continued down over the slopes of the Kohala Mountains, to the government road. That ranch still has today the sense of enormous space and serenity that Anna remembers from her earliest childhood. The view is a vast panorama of distant ocean, cloistering mountains, and the ever-changing cloud-studded dome of the big Hawaiian sky. From the old Government Road, which is now Highway 19, passersby today enjoy the panorama of Anna's big white ranch house with its blue and white striped awnings, its expanse of green lawns and formal gardens, the white outbuildings and fences, and the arched white gates in the roadside stone wall boundary where, in summer, night-blooming cereus thrive and in winter poinsettias are a swath of bright red blossoms across the entire frontage.

Not visible from the highway are the upper slopes of Anna Ranch, one of Anna's favorite places. For her, to ride horseback over these upper slopes, reveling in the crisp air, has always been one of the most exhilarating experiences imaginable. All around is the scenic sweep of mountains. On a clear day she can see the nearly fourteen thousand foot summits of Mauna Kea and Mauna Loa, which are often snowcapped in winter. To the south she can see Kona's slumbering 8700-foot volcano, Hualalai. Below her are the dry lower slopes of Lalamilo, the indentations of the Kawaihae coastline and the gleaming buildings of Kawaihae's deepwater modern harbor edged by the shimmering blue of the sea.

To ride through this spectacular countryside in any kind of weather has always been what Anna loved best. From her high South Kohala pastures of Keawewai across the slopes of Anna Ranch and on beyond the village to her pastures beyond Puukapu– this has been her territory, her working place, the source of much of her delight and joy in life. Her childhood, until the age of 9, was spent here.

A Tomboy and a Lady

IN ANNA'S CHILDHOOD her father's herd of cattle were lean, slab-sided longhorns much like their ancestors – the gifts that Lord Vancouver had brought long ago to Kamehameha I.

As his family and its needs grew, William Lindsey had expanded his ranch acreage, buying or leasing more pastures in the Waimea area and increasing the size of his herd. For most men, running the ranch would in itself have been a full-time job, but William Lindsey was energetic and ambitious. Anna recalls that he not only took care of his own spread, but also was deputy sheriff of the South Kohala district. Some of her earliest memories are of her father going out politicking for votes for Sheriff Sam Pua, under whom he served as deputy. Later, William Lindsey took on a third job – as assistant manager of Parker Ranch.

With all this to do, he needed and got the full support of his family. From William Lindsey's side there was never a division of "the boys do this, and Anna, you're a girl so you do that". He gave his daughter exactly the same training, and expected from her the same results as he did from his two sons. To his delighted surprise, Anna showed more interest, and far more aptitude at ranching, than did either of her brothers. From an early age she loved to ride, rope, help mend fences and set fence posts. She was – in the saddle – a genuine tomboy.

When she got off her horse and walked in the house, however, she met her mother's expectations that she would learn and practice to perfection all the skills of being a homemaker and a socially adept female. Mary Lindsey saw to it that her daughter became accomplished in all the domestic arts, including those of sewing and such fancy work as embroidery and cutwork. From the age of three, Anna was trained in everything either a good cowboy or a genteel young lady could be expected to know and do. Thus to ride out with her father early each morning became as natural a part of little Anna's day as was her late afternoon stint in the kitchen where she learned from her mother how to set a table with good linen, fine silver, and water goblets.

Mary Lindsey made it a habit to set a formal dinner table for her family every night, and to train her daughter to do the same. After dinner, Anna would stand on a stool so she could reach the sink to help her mother wash the dishes. Neither parent criticized or complained about each other's expectations of Anna. It was their mutual understanding, which Anna never heard discussed or argued about, that their daughter would excel in what each thought important.

She had no idea she was being brought up differently from most girls. Riding the range and helping in the kitchen were, for her, normal activities. She loved everything she was given a chance to do out on the ranch, in the household, and in the wide world of Waimea village where she remembers first being driven in her mother's buckboard. Occasionally, in those early years, Anna's horizons were extended beyond her home district. Every once in a while she would go with her mother on the long trip to Hilo to visit Grandma Rose (as Anna called her maternal grandmother). Grandpa Rose had died before Anna was born.

Anna could never forget one particular trip when she was staying with her mother in Grandma Rose's home on Reed's Bay. That morning, when they got up, Mary Lindsey dressed Anna first, as she usually did, and then proceeded to get dressed herself. Anna was eager to go wherever it was they were heading that day and so, without anyone noticing, she ran downstairs and outside. A wide lawn was all that separated the house from the bayfront. There, in deep water off a small dock, the rowboat that was their transport to Hilo town was tied up. Anna headed straight for that boat!

Minutes later, Mary Lindsey happened to look out of the window and saw Anna's head bobbing in the water alongside the boat. Her tiny hands were clenched on the gunwhales. She had fallen into the water. All that saved her from being drowned was the uncommon good sense for a three year old to grab the edge of the rowboat and hang on, not panicking, until someone noticed her plight.

A far shorter journey, on which Anna was frequently taken by her parents, was the trip in the family surrey from Waimea to North Kohala, seventeen miles over the twists and turns of the Mountain Road. That windward district was where Hawaii's first king, Kamehameha I, was born and where he grew to manhood. In Anna's childhood it was a busy place with its five plantations. The main village, Kapaau, boasted a drug store and soda fountain! Anna was four the year her parents decided to take the family to a Christmas party in North Kohala. It was held in Iole, the old mission compound, at the Kohala Girls' School, a boarding seminary which had been founded by pioneer missionary Elias Bond in 1874.

Until that Christmas party in Kohala, Anna had never seen a Santa Claus. Tradition in the Lindsey household was that on Christmas eve the three children were tucked into bed early. After they were asleep, their parents trimmed the tree and put out the presents for them. At midnight, they woke Anna and her two brothers, saying, "Ah! You missed him! Santa has just left – and look what he brought for you!"

There was a delicious mystery about those Christmases. Anna remembers yearning to stay awake so she could see Santa Claus. The Christmas party at Kohala Girls School was her first chance – but at the sight of him, dressed in a red suit and fitted with a long white beard, Anna was terrified. She spent the entire evening hiding under one of the desks in the classroom where the party was being held.

In general, North Kohala was not Anna's favorite. Each trip she dreaded the place where they must pass the painted bronze statue of King Kamehameha. To her, that immense stern figure with its haughty gaze was as scary as had been the Christmas party Santa Claus. So that she might avoid the piercing gaze of the statue's eyes, Anna would hide on the floor of her mother's surrey whenever they drove past. Kamehameha I was a close relative of one of her ancestors on her mother's side, and undeniably a great King who united all the islands of Hawaii under his rule, but Anna was always afraid of that tall bronze figure.

It was on one of these trips to Kohala that Anna had her first taste of *ulu* poi– poi made from steamed breadfruit. The rule in the Lindsey family was never to make a face no matter how much you might dislike something. However, Anna remembers her father telling with much amusement about the occasion when he took her to visit a family in Kohala where breadfruit poi was served. "I saw them all eating it – so I took a spoonful and gave it to Anna," he said. "She swallowed it, but you should have seen her face!" For *ulu* poi, William Lindsey understood, one has to acquire a very special taste.

Poi pounded from the ripe, purplish, steamed taro, and prepared as her mother prepared poi, was one of Anna's favorite foods. Poi was a favorite on the family table. When Mary Lindsey gave one of her lavish *pa'ina,* her Hawaiian dinner parties, she always served individual bowls of poi to accompany the succulent kalua pig that was the main course. Mary Lindsey loved to give parties. She would have the whole family help move the furniture out of the living room and set up tables and benches enough to seat all of the guests she had invited.

With Anna at her side helping, Mary Lindsey would cover and transform the wooden tables with ti leaves and palapalai fern. On these fragrant green covers she would make continuous long centerpieces of flowers from her garden – gardenias, roses, hibiscus – whatever happened to be in bloom. Her *pa'ina* were memorable dinner parties. She never used the term luau – which to her meant simply the leaves of the taro plant, an essential ingredient of many of the Hawaiian delicacies on her *pa'ina* menu.

When she served kalua pig for the family only, Mary Lindsey took pride in preparing the pig herself for the imu, the Hawaiian earth oven where the pig is cooked in a wrapping of clean ti leaves in the steam and heat from porous, white-hot lava stones. To heat the stones, a fire of either mamane, kiawe, or ohia wood was kept burning in the imu pit for at least three hours. The hot stones were placed in the front shoulder and abdominal cavities of the pig before it was lowered onto a layer of shredded banana trunk, banana leaves, and ti leaves, that had been carefully placed over more hot stones lining the oval imu pit. A covering of ti leaves, and clean, dampened burlap sacks were then placed over the pig. The oven was sealed with a layer of earth about eighteen inches deep. If even a faint thread of steam was seen escaping from the dampened imu, more earth was tamped on to plug the vent.

For her *pa'ina,* Anna's mother always had friends to help kalua a pig. To cook a three hundred pounder in the imu took seven hours. When she fixed a suckling pig for the family, however, it would be well cooked in as little as three hours.

Mary Lindsey always dressed the suckling pigs for the imu herself. For this purpose she used one of her husband's old razors – a necessity to properly shave the skin so not a single hair remained. William Lindsey had lost a thumb and it was difficult for him to use the straight razor favored by men of that era. As a result, it was his wife who shaved him, and who kept the old razors to use when a pig must be dressed – another skill she taught her daughter.

Anna always had a pretty new dress to wear when her mother gave a *pa'ina.* Mary Lindsey was an expert seamstress with a flair for design. Not only did she create fashionable party dresses for her daughter. She also made Anna tailored divided skirts that came just to the tops of her boots. With each of these outfits, she made Anna a little matching cap.

Mary Lindsey was a loving and yet a stern mother, who never objected to Anna's ranch activities with her father – so long as she had fulfilled the household duties expected of her. These, Mary Lindsey insisted, had to be done to perfection – or else! "One time," Anna remembers, "it would be mother calling me in when I was in the saddle and ready to go. She'd noticed I hadn't cleaned my hairbrush properly that morning. I had to get down off my horse, run inside, and pull the last few stray hairs out of that brush! Another time, it was that my bedspread hadn't been pulled down straight on one side. But lucky for me,

Anna's mother's family circa 1880's. Left to right, Pauline Rose, husband George Rutman, Louisa, Charles, Edmund and Otto Rose; Mrs. Kanaina Rose; Emma Rose (seated); William Leonard Rosenberg (Rose); Anna's mother, Mary; unknown boy, Anna's namesake – Anna Rose.

Kanaina Rose, Anna's maternal grandmother.

William Leonard Rose, Anna's maternal grandfather.

The William Lindseys, circa 1910– Bill, Charles, Mary, Anna, and William.

Charles, circa 1920.

Bill, 1920's.

Anna at nine.

William Miller Seymour Lindsey, Anna's father.

Mary Rosenberg Lindsey, Anna's mother.

my father was patient. He always waited for me!" Anna would ride the ranch all day with her father and brothers, but as soon as they reached the home corral, she would have to hurry to bathe and change clothes to help her mother finish preparing and serving the evening meal.

One of William Lindsey's several enterprises was a slaughterhouse at Ahualoa, an upland community between Waimea and the windward plantation community of Honokaa. Anna always looked forward to going with her father on his trips to Ahualoa, but it was an extra early start on such days. Anna knew that if she wasn't ready on time, he simply couldn't wait for her. She got the habit of secretly getting all dressed the night before – then no matter how early, she was always ready. This prompt but somewhat tousled beginning to the day led Mary Lindsey to check up on her daughter the night before one Ahualoa excursion was to take place.

"There I was! Discovered!" Anna laughs, reminiscing about her mother finding her sound asleep under the covers, all dressed in riding skirt, shirt, sweater – even with boots on and laced. "She made me get up, undress, and put on my nightgown before I could go back to sleep! I sure had to rush to get ready to go next morning, I tell you!"

When Anna was old enough to start school, she walked the mile from the ranch to the government school house with her big brother, Bill. Later, when he was old enough, Charles came along with them. The village of Waimea, where the schoolhouse was located, was in those years strictly a rural place. A wooden bridge spanned the stream that still runs through the heart of modern Waimea. Trees were everywhere. On her way home from school, Anna liked to walk slowly past Akona Store and Restaurant, the favorite *pau hana* (after work) gathering place of Parker Ranch cowboys.

Early mornings, before driving cattle down the slopes to Kawaihae for shipment to Honolulu, Parker Ranch cowboys were provided a hearty pre-dawn breakfast in Akona's Restaurant. Akona's also packed the lunch that went along in the cowboys' saddle bags. Often, when Anna passed Akona's in the afternoon, the hitching posts in front of the store and restaurant would have a number of spirited cowboy horses tied to them.

On the occasions when there was no school, and Anna rode into the village, her favorite treat was to go buy boiled peanuts from the Chinese store which was on the far side of the village, where the Mormon church now stands.

It was in these earliest years that Anna learned Hawaiian. Her father spoke the language well, but he never used anything other than English at home with his children. It was the cowboys who taught Anna her Hawaiian vocabulary. She took great delight in going down to the village to visit the saddle shop of a Hawaiian named Puna, who spoke Hawaiian beautifully. Everyone went to Puna to have saddles made. There in his shop, under the shade of great trees, with the sharp, good smell of leather all around her, Anna would sit and talk to the old saddle maker in Hawaiian. Puna called her *''Keike wahine akamai oe!''* – "Smart little girl!"

Anna was also called *akamai* by her teacher at the elementary school in the village. *Akamai* as well was her creative solution to wanting to walk home from school faster than her brother Bill could or would go. Bill was a very fat little boy who always complained that the mile from school going home was far longer than the mile from home to school. He would lag along, trying Anna's patience. Often Bill would just lie down beside the road and refuse to go on. In those days many Waimea farmers and ranchers owned buckboards which they would drive down to Kawaihae to buy loads of fish. Their route, along the government road, led past the Lindsey ranch which was about a quarter-mile from the juncture where one fork of the road led along the mountainside to North Kohala and the other led down to the coast at Kawaihae.

Anna hit upon the idea of hailing one of these passing wagons and persuading them to give her fat brother a ride home. Once Bill was hoisted up into the buckboard, she and skinny Charles would skip and run what always seemed to them the very short mile home.

Saturday was a school holiday when Anna was often invited to visit her friend Thelma Parker, the heiress of Parker Ranch, whose mother was a close friend of Anna's mother. Thelma was a teenager, and Anna no more than six years old when these visits began. She remembers Thelma was an extraordinarily beautiful and softspoken girl. Thelma evidently liked Anna's company for when she was at Puuopelu, the Parker home, she would send her driver, Kiau Kailikini, and the Parker Ranch surrey, to pick Anna up on Saturday mornings.

In the Parker ranch house living room was a grand piano with enormous fat legs. Thelma loved to play and Anna would sit on the bench next to her friend, listening intently for as long as the music continued. When the swimming pool at Puuopelu was built, Thelma and Anna were the first to christen it. Sometimes the two girls would go out riding together until lunchtime. Her older friend did not have Anna's abundant energy. Thelma was not well even then and so after lunch they would go to Thelma's room. Thelma would nap on her bed, and Anna would lie quietly on the other bed waiting for her friend to wake up.

These intimate times ended when Thelma married Mr. Smart, whom Anna remembers as a strikingly handsome young man. It was a big wedding, the reception held at Puuopelu with tables laden even more lavishly than Anna had seen at her mother's finest *pa'ina*.

In those years, the sociability of Waimea was one in which the whole family participated. On no occasion were children left at home. They went along with their parents to parties and social evenings, the littlest ones falling asleep when they got too tired. Anna and her two brothers always went with their parents to Waimea's frequent dances and shows. Mary Rosenberg Lindsey was in charge of putting on the particularly popular entertainment of tableaux. Anna was usually in these. She remembers one tableau her mother produced and directed which portrayed each of the islands. Anna, in a white dress and wearing fine shell leis, represented Ni'ihau.

Carrying out the philosophy by which he taught her how to be a rancher, Anna's father gave her equal access to the sports which her brothers and their friends enjoyed. From the time she could heft a bat, Anna was the only girl included in the baseball games for which her father was informal coach and umpire. William Seymour also taught his daughter how to shoot marbles. She became a champion, beating her brothers every time. Each day she would take her winnings to the attic and hide the marbles under a loose board in the floor.

"Show me how many you won today, Anna," her father would ask. Anna would rush up and bring down the day's booty, proud of how many marbles she had won from the boys. "Tomorrow," advised her father, "Only play with the marbles you won today! Don't risk your whole capital at one time. Save all you can!"

"That way my father taught me not only how to handle marbles, but how to handle my season's profits when I began making money on cattle years later," Anna explains. "Saving, conserving capital, risking only what you make from one profitable operation – those are the lessons I really learned from his teaching me to risk only the marbles from one day's winnings when the next day's game begins."

Imiola Church, founded by Makua Laiana, Waimea's beloved pioneer missionary Lorenzo Lyons, was often the site of bazaars and socials in which the William Lindseys were most active. The courthouse was another community center. Weekends, something was always going on at either place. Anna's favorite times were when the Daughters of Hawaii, to which her mother belonged (and which Anna herself joined when she grew up) held a function where they sold homemade ice cream and cake. She eagerly spent her pocket money on that although, heeding her father's advice, she usually kept a reserve handy in her special hiding place – an empty talcum powder tin.

For a while the talcum tin was full of gold pieces. This was because of her paternal grandfather, Tom Lindsey, who wanted to stop drinking, telling Anna: "Whenever you see me drunk, sister, I'll give you a five dollar gold piece!" It was an opportunity of which Anna took full advantage. She would watch for him to ride by, swaying on his horse, and then run to his place and quickly station herself in the barn. As he rode up, tipsy, she would confront him. "Grandpa! You're drunk again!" Sure enough, out of his pocket would come a five dollar gold piece for her. When William Lindsey found out what Anna was doing, he put a stop to it but while it lasted, Anna had a profitable enterprise. When, later, she left for boarding school, she took along the talcum tin which still held a number of gold pieces.

This exhilaration of playing baseball and shooting marbles with the boys, the independence of walking back and forth to school with her brothers, the long Hawaiian conversations with Puna in his saddle shop, the practical education of riding the range with her father, the busy community social life in which she and her whole family participated:- for Anna this was an idyllic childhood. Then, abruptly, everything changed. She was taken out of Waimea school and, because her parents wanted the very best for her, for a short while she continued her education at a small private school in the home of her friend Thelma Parker. Anna's classmates were the daughters of Sam Spencer, the bookkeeper at Parker Ranch who later became prominent in Big Island politics, and a Hawaiian girl from Kawaihae who was living with the Lindsey's as Anna's companion.

This little school did not last long. When it was disbanded, William and Mary Lindsey decided to send their daughter to Kohala Girls School as a boarding student. There in North Kohala Anna was no more than twenty miles from home but how she missed her parents and her brothers. How she missed Waimea! She was not yet nine years old.

Anna's homesickness was so acute that every night she would telephone her parents and cry, begging them to let her come back to the ranch. After two weeks they did, but her mother had made a firm decision. Kohala had been too close to home for Anna to adjust easily. Mary Lindsey made preparations to take her daughter to Honolulu, to enroll her in Sacred Hearts Academy, a boarding school run by Catholic sisters in Honolulu's Kaimuki area, where – as her brother Bill later would receive at Kamehameha and Charles at St. Louis High School, Anna would have the very best education.

Mary Lindsey's decision was not unusual. In those days island girls- and boys – from well-to-do families on the neighbor islands were sent at an early age to be educated in one of Oahu's several excellent boarding schools. At Sacred Hearts Academy, Mary Lindsey knew, Anna would not have the chance to call home every night. There too, she would experience the very different world of Honolulu, which had long been the capitol of the Hawaiian Kingdom and was now the bustling capitol of the Territory of Hawaii.

Keawewai

AT SACRED HEARTS Academy Anna was homesick at first too but somehow the distance from Oahu to the Big Island made the separation from her home and family more bearable. She grew up a notch at nine in realizing that at this time in her life, since this was her parents' wish for her, being away at school was something she had to quietly accept.

In those years the journey back and forth from Kawaihae to Honolulu was not an easy one. When Anna first went with her mother to be enrolled and left at the convent school, her father drove them down to Kawaihae in one of his handsome surreys. From the William Lindsey ranch it was a ride of nearly two hours to the wharf where interisland steamers hove to offshore, waiting while passengers and freight were lightered back and forth in large sturdy lapstrake-built rowboats. The old wharf was near the lighthouse. The area that is now Kawaihae's modern deepwater harbor was then a pleasant, palm-shaded Hawaiian village.

The interisland steamship trip from Kawaihae to Honolulu took twenty-four hours. En route, there was usually a stop or two on Maui. That first steamer trip to Honolulu was a big adventure for nine-year old Anna. And when she arrived, the city was a new and different world for her with its trolley cars, its traffic, its busy sounds and sights, its crowds and tall buildings like Kawaiahao Church and the elegance of Iolani Palace. Mary and William Lindsey had many friends and relatives in the capitol, all of whom invited Anna to come visit them on the one free Saturday a month she was allowed to leave Sacred Hearts campus.

There were also frequent holidays and vacations when she had the chance to go home. After that first trip over, she traveled by herself. When the steamer hove to off the Kawaihae lighthouse, and Anna transferred to a rowboat for the trip to the wharf where her parents awaited her, she often was carrying the fragile hand baggage of a bowl of goldfish or a songbird in a cage. Her initial homesickness had quickly vanished at Sacred Hearts Academy. She loved the convent, made innumerable friends among other boarders and day students, and loved the nuns who were the school's staff and faculty.

The spring she was ten years old, William Lindsey brought his daughter home so that she might be present on a very special occasion. It was special enough so that, thirty years later, the *Honolulu Advertiser* carried it as an item in 'History Thirty Years Ago', recollecting that "In 1910 George Washington Lincoln sells to William Miller Seymour Lindsey of Waimea his property at Keawewai including land, horses, cattle, swaine and poultry for $10,000."

Anna carried the ten thousand dollars in gold tied in gunny sacks on the back of her saddle as she rode ahead of her family the eight winding miles along the Mountain Road from their Waimea ranch to Keawewai. The South Kohala area of Keawewai was then, and is now, a choice property. Its three hundred acres are lush high pastures, rolling but not too steep, ideal for cattle. Most important of all in a lee district that is prone to intermittent periods of drought, Keawewai is possessed of an abundance of water. In the memory of the oldest of the numerous Hawaiians living there at the time of William Lindsey's purchase, even in the worst of droughts, when the stream at Keawewai is no longer running, the numerous deep pools – many with blue rock – hold a plentiful supply of water.

The purchase of Keawewai was one of William Lindsey's most far-sighted investments. Ten thousand dollars was a goodly sum to pay for three hundred acres of ranch land in 1910, but Grandpa

Tom Lindsey, by then a widower whose second wife was a much younger woman, had decided to give the money as an outright gift to his son. The gift was one which the new stepmother approved. Later, after Tom Lindsey's death, the rest of the family challenged this in court but the stepmother supported William Lindsey and he won the case.

For Anna, Keawewai became her favorite place. That first summer, she remembers staying there with Grandma Rose who was, at the time, still a vigorous and attractive woman. The following year, in 1911, Kanaina Rose died in Hilo. She was only 58.

Keawewai had been known to Anna from her having gone there earlier to visit a friend she called 'Grandma' Fannie Stevens. From those visits she clearly remembers Keawewai's previous owner, George Washington Lincoln, as "the tallest man I ever saw in my life!" Hawaii State Archives record that Lincoln was originally from Washington State. Before he came to the Big Island he had been a successful contractor in Honolulu. In July 1898, Lincoln was the top bidder and awarded the contract to construct a drain at the Government Nursery on the corner of King and Keeaumoku Streets in Honolulu. His price for the job was $209.

Just when George Washington Lincoln had moved from Oahu and acquired the prize 300 acres at Keawewai is not clear, but by 1910 he had been there long enough to stimulate a number of stories about him, stories ranging from his having reported hearing landshells singing in the trees at Keawewai at night, to his reputed miserliness when it came to taking care of his wives.

George Washington Lincoln's Hawaiian style household was just above a waterfall where the main stream of the property plunged into a deep pool. Today, in the pastures of Keawewai there stands an occasional wind-twisted gnarled tree, or the driftwood skeleton of one. These, and a few koai'e (*acacia Koaiia*) trees that Anna has protected in a preservation area just above the mountain road, are the only survivors of the dense forest that was once here. When Anna rode up to Keawewai the day her father bought the place, she remembers riding through forests of koai'e, na'io (false sandalwood), and ohia that flourished above and below the open pastures.

Below the stream, Grandma Fannie Stevens lived in a two-story stone house. Even before her father's purchase of Keawewai,

Anna had loved to ride over to visit Grandma Fannie, who would sit smoking her corncob pipe and telling Anna wonderful stories of the two Mrs. Lincolns. They were Hawaiian girls who were sisters and, according to what Anna remembers having been told, they had to scrounge to make the pin money which their husband refused to give them. Grandma Fannie told Anna how the two women had churned milk into butter, packed the butter into sections of hollow banana trunk to preserve it, and carried it the ten miles into North Kohala to sell. George Washington Lincoln had a brother who settled in North Kohala but who was nothing like him. It was this very quiet brother who founded the Lincoln family now living in this district.

Anna still has the gunpowder musket that belonged to George Washington Lincoln. He was rumoured to be so jealous of his two wives that at the approach of a stranger he would go out with his gun. Anna's earliest memories of Keawewai are of sleeping in the small bedroom that had once been his, and listening to the roar of the waterfall that seemed to be just outside the thin board walls. Though she strained to listen, she never heard the singing of the landshells that Lincoln claimed he heard there.

Anna had learned to swim in the pool behind her father's ranch in Waimea, but at Keawewai, swimming in the deep pool with the waterfall splashing into it became her particular delight. Through the remainder of her schooldays on Oahu, she looked forward to returning for however short a stay to Keawewai. Its three hundred acres encompassed all she loved best in her own big-sky world of horses, cattle, and the matchless natural beauty of the Kohala Mountain country.

"Father was a great one to make money," Anna recalls of those early days at Keawewai. To the stock he acquired from the purchase of the property, he added a flock of turkeys. Just before Thanksgiving and Christmas holidays, Anna would come home to help out. Herding turkeys was far more tricky than herding cattle. The big birds had to be led down along the government road the eight miles to Waimea, where they were put into a pen at the Lindsey ranch to rest for a few hours. The tricky part was the trip down along the road for if just one bird became startled, and took off in flight, the entire flock would follow. Getting them back together again took patience and immense amounts of time.

"When that happened, I was usually the one blamed!" Anna chuckles.

William Lindsey rested the flock in a pen at the ranch, and then had numerous helpers to load the birds into small crates for the trip to market. The crated turkeys were taken by truck from Waimea down to Kawaihae where they were transferred to an interisland steamer for the trip to Metropolitan Meat Company in Honolulu. "The turkey business was hard work, but it was great for making money!" says Anna.

It was during the first years of her father owning Keawewai that Anna remembers being taught how to judge cattle. "Now sister," her father would say. "If you were going to pick a heifer to take to bull, which one would you pick?"

"This – " Anna would choose.

"Why?" William Lindsey would want to know.

"Because it has a pretty face, father!"

"No! No, Sister!" he would laugh and then, in his painstaking, patient way, would teach her the breeding points – udders, withers, conformation. It was a totally different kind of education from the one she was acquiring from the nuns at Sacred Hearts Academy.

Companion to the Queen

THESE WERE SPECIAL girlhood years for Anna. She made many close friends at Sacred Hearts Academy. She was a good student, well liked by everyone. "I loved the nuns and they loved me. The nuns never tried to convert me," she remembers.

The Lindseys were protestants and whenever Anna was home in Waimea, she attended Imiola Congregational Church with her family. She was home on a school holiday when her friend, Thelma Parker Smart, died. The poignancy of Thelma's funeral was something Anna never forgot. As Anna and her family reached Puuopelu, where the services were held, there was a baby carriage down beside the stream. A nurse was wheeling Thelma's infant son, Richard Smart. At the funeral service, Thelma's mother asked Anna to come sit with the family because of the long intimate friendship between Anna and Thelma.

As she entered her teens, Anna began to think of her future and what the years ahead might hold for her. She often felt a strong wish – which she sometimes expressed – to become Catholic and herself become a nun. Yet, the sisters at Sacred Heart never urged her to do so. Much as she loved those dedicated nuns, Anna often gave them a bad time with her forthright approach to life. Taking a bath, convent style, was a primary

27

issue on which Anna confronted the school rules. Her position was eminently one of reason and logic as well as common sense – but she found even so she had to give in.

When she had come to Sacred Hearts Academy at nine, bathing in the full length long-sleeved high-collared Mother Hubbard garment required by school regulations had been fun. At first she thought it was hilarious to have the clumsy garment ballooning up around her in the tub but as time passed, and she grew older, her frustration grew. How could one get really clean bathing in such a way?

The day came when Anna made up her mind to rebel. She stripped off the Mother Hubbard, plunged into the tub and began enjoying a really good scrub when Sister Ladislas came in and shrieked at the sight of her bathing naked. " A me! A me!" moaned the good sister. She covered her eyes to hide the sight of Anna's nudity.

Anna didn't know what "A me!" meant, but she could tell by the sound of that exclamation that Sister Ladislas was thoroughly upset, in fact – shocked. "Sister," said Anna, "Look at it this way. Don't you think God can see you through all those clothes you have on?"

The question was one the good sister did not choose to answer and Anna's bathtub rebellion was the occasion for her first – and the convent's worst – punishment: not being allowed out on the free Saturday. Resourceful Anna turned the punishment into a picnic. None of the boarders left the campus that Saturday Anna was confined!

Hidden under her pillow was the talcum tin holding the remaining store of gold coins she had earned from all the times she had caught her Grandfather Tom Lindsey tipsy from too much drinking. This pocket money was Anna's salvation, and one she continued to use whenever her pranks got her in trouble. There was a Chinese store across the street from the convent. Anna would give one of her friends a gold coin, and instructions to bring back all the necessities for a picnic party from the store. This she would host out on the spacious lawns of the school. Even those who could leave on Saturday chose to stay back to enjoy the wonderful picnics Anna gave whenever she was punished by having her free Saturday cancelled.

Anna's dearest friend during these convent years was Lucy Searle, a Maui girl. It was through Lucy that Anna became a companion to Hawaii's beloved former monarch, Queen Liliuokalani, who had been deposed in a coup that ended the independent kingdom of Hawaii in 1893. Anna was perhaps twelve when she and Lucy began to be invited to spend weekends at the Queen's private home, Washington Place, a gracious two story colonial style mansion that is now the residence of Hawaii's governors. Sacred Hearts convent was in Kaimuki, quite a distance from the Beretania Street location of the Queen's home. On many a Saturday morning Liliuokalani would have her carriage, with its royal coat of arms, arrive at the convent to bring the two girls to spend the day, and often Sunday too with her.

Those were memorable weekends. The rituals of Hawaiian royalty were still carried out by Liliuokalani's attendants, who escorted the Queen with tall feather kahilis, the Hawaiian symbol of ruling chiefs and chiefesses. At mealtimes, they would come in chanting, *oli oli*. Anna would be seated at the right and Lucy Searle at the left of the Queen. Lunch was usually raw fish and poi, together with a variety of other foods. Whatever the Queen ate, the girls ate too. At night, the two teenagers slept in the bedroom next to the Queen's. Anna can still identify the room where she slept when she visits Hawaii's present day Governor's Mansion, the former residence of Queen Liliuokalani – Washington Place.

In private life, Liliuokalani was the widow of John Dominis, whose family had built Washington Place. At the time when Anna and Lucy Searle were spending those weekends with her, Liliuokalani was much enjoying the company of her grandchild, a tiny baby recently born to her son, John Dominis, Jr. and his wife, the former Sybil McInerny. Liliuokalani was beloved by her people not only as a gracious and valiant Queen, but as the composer of beautiful Hawaiian songs, the most famous of which is that well known classic, "Aloha Oe". Music was a large part of Anna's weekends at Washington Place. Sometimes, during the day, Anna and Lucy would accompany the Queen to her cottage on Kuhio Beach. Waikiki was a tranquil place then. Liliuokalani had a long pier extending out into the shallows. A bedroom built on that pier was the Queen's favorite place to relax, and to enjoy

Hawaiian music.. "Her nurse, Rose Traub would be there. Sometimes a girl named Josephine Hopkins would come too," is
Anna's recollection.

To Anna at fourteen, her close friendship with Lucy Searle,
the memorable weekends with Queen Liliuokalani, the warmth
and kindness of the nuns, made the convent as dear a part of
her life as was home, and her family, and Keawewai. She looked
forward to vacation time and a return to Waimea, but she was
quite as happy at vacation's end to return to the warmth of the
convent. Then, once again, all this was abruptly changed. One
day the principal, the Reverend Mother, came to Anna's classroom, surprising her by saying, "Anna, your mother is here."

Anna was overjoyed at this unexpected visit – until she
entered the school parlor, where her mother was waiting, and
was told, "We're taking you out of this school!"

Anna was devastated. She was doing well here. Wasn't her
name on the honor roll hanging in this very parlor? The reason
for the change was never made clear to Anna, but looking back,
years later, she wondered if perhaps it had been the inadver-
tent mention of her wish to become a nun which so disturbed
Mary Lindsey that she came to transfer her only daughter to
another fine private girls boarding school, the Anglican-run
St. Andrew's Priory.

"Those days," says Anna, "you didn't question your parents'
decisions for you. Whether you liked it or not, you did what they
wanted you to do. That was how it was then with girls, anyway."
Leaving the convent, she cried. The nuns cried. The girls cried.
Her first few days at the Priory, Anna cried so much she became
ill, and had to be put in the infirmary. Then, before long, the
new school began to be as familiar and beloved as had been the
old one. Anna settled happily into her new environment.

Her final poignant memory of Liliuokalani is of the funeral
of the seventy-nine year old Queen, who died on November
11, 1917. Anna was in the Hawaiian choir at the Priory. Her last
sight of the monarch with whom she had spent such unforgettable weekends was as she looked down from the choir loft of
Kawaiahao Church at the Queen's body. Liliuokalani was laid
out in state on a bier draped in white with the rich white material
garlanded with flowers. Women kahili bearers were a royal

guard around the bier.

When the funeral service ended, the Hawaiian choir of the Priory joined in the long, mournful funeral procession from Kawaiahao, the church of Hawaiian royalty, to the Royal Mausoleum far out Nuuanu Street. Those who lined the route to pay tribute to Hawaii's last Queen, and those who walked in the procession as did Anna, had faces streaked with tears. Liliuokalani was much loved by all her people. Like the others, Anna wept the entire way to the Royal Mausoleum. For her, as for so many there that day, it was as if the very spirit of Hawaii itself had passed on.

While she was at the Priory, Anna's parents requested that she be confirmed as an Episcopalian, which she was – by the Anglican Bishop. Not long after her confirmation, Anna suffered her first critical illness. She was stepping up onto a tram one weekend, on her way to visit her Aunt, when she doubled over with a sharp, almost unbearable pain. She continued on to her Aunt's home on Alakea Street and there, as the pain continued, Dr. Straub was called to the house. His diagnosis was a ruptured appendix.

Anna was immediately taken to Queen's Hospital where she lay in ice packs until her mother could reach Honolulu on the interisland steamer. Not until Mary Lindsey arrived and saw both her daughter and Dr. Straub was the operation performed. For weeks afterward Anna was watched over not only by her mother, but by a private nurse as well. At long last, when she was well enough to leave the hospital, Anna went to the home of her parents' friends, the Sam Kanakanui's, to convalesce.

Their son, young William Kanakanui, thought he knew just how to restore Anna to good health. He took her to Waikiki to surf! Anna was a good swimmer who loved the ocean. She took to surfing with zest, not at all bothered by the fact that usually she was the only girl out catching the waves. Her companions were William Kanakanui, Fred and William Beers, and Carl Farden from Lahaina. In those sun and spray-drenched days she became so tanned that her mother was provoked. "I was the first girl who stood on a surfboard at Waikiki!" is Anna's proud boast. Even though she was a beginner, Anna competed with the boys and, as usual, often won.

William Kanakanui had not intended her to plunge with such all-out energy into the rigorous sport, but Anna never did anything by halves. Neither she nor the Kanakanui's realized that her incision had not healed sufficiently to withstand the strains she was putting on it. When Anna returned to Dr. Straub for a checkup, back she had to go to Queen's Hospital for a second operation to repair the damage done by her strenuous surfing. Once again she missed weeks of school.

At fifteen Anna was a stunning young woman. Every evening, she and her classmates had to tie cloth veils over their heads and attend vespers in St. Andrew's Cathedral before dinner. Outside in Queen Emma Square the boys would sit and wait for the girls to file by. Somehow admirers found out Anna's name and much to her embarrassment, for she was shy at 15, bicycle messengers would next day bring her boxes of American Beauty roses. Another day, an admirer would send notes and boxes of candy. Anna went to the principal in tears after the first few gifts and notes of this kind. The principal was a wise woman who only shook her head and laughed, saying, "Anna, you should be happy to receive attention like this!"

But the attention Anna was used to receiving was that of her fellow boarders flocking around her, shrieking with appreciation as she described to them in vivid pantomime the buxom figures of the divas whom she saw and heard in the operas that came to Honolulu. Anna's parents had instructed the school to see that she attended. The tickets were charged to her father. A teacher always chaperoned her. "How did the singing sound?" the girls at the Priory would ask when Anna returned from a performance in the Opera House, which was located on the site of the present downtown Post Office. "They scream! They don't sing – they scream!" Anna would laugh, mimicking the high notes. That enforced attendance she grew to appreciate, for she developed a lifelong liking for opera and classical music.

At sixteen, she was still continuing the piano lessons that she had started at Sacred Hearts Academy. Along with her academic subjects, she was learning the practical domestic science arts like millinery, which she enjoyed, and dressmaking, which did not excite her creativity as did the designing and making of smart looking hats. By sixteen, Anna was no longer so dismayed at the attention the boys gave her. She was as popular back home in Waimea as she was in Honolulu. Whether she was in school at the Priory or vacationing at her parents' ranch, she was always being invited to parties and dances.

That sixteenth summer, she accompanied her mother on a visit to Hilo. One of Mary Lindsey's old friends was a Hawaiian-Irish woman who had become Mrs. Lai Hipp and raised a family of four daughters and three sons. Anna went with her mother to call on this old friend one afternoon, but since Mrs. Lai Hipp wasn't home, Mary Lindsey decided to call on one of the daughters, Matilda Lai Hipp Watson, who lived next door. It was during this afternoon visit that Matilda's brother, Henry Lai Hipp, stopped by. He was a handsome young man in his early twenties, home on vacation from St. Mary's College in Dayton, Ohio. One look at Anna Lindsey, and – he told his sister later that afternoon – he had fallen in love. "I'm going to marry that girl some day!" he vowed.

During Anna's stay with her Uncle Otto Rose in Hilo later that summer, Henry Lai Hipp was her escort on a round of parties and picnics. With a group of young people they took a picnic dinner to Kilauea Volcano. "Our fronts roasted and our backs froze!" Anna recollects. "We had an unforgettable spectacle sitting there on the ledge of Halemaumau with the lave lake boiling and churning, and fountains of lava shooting up into the sky!" At a gala dance in the Hilo Armory, Anna and Henry foxtrotted, waltzed, and then took a short walk out into the starry Hilo night. Those were the days of innocence. When Henry took her to his car and kissed her, Anna thought she too might be falling in love.

At summer's end she returned to the Priory and Henry went back to the Mainland for his senior year at college. He wrote to her frequently – ardent letters pledging his love. He kept telling her he was determined to make her his wife one day, but at sixteen Anna was not ready to consider marriage. For her, now, Henry was only one of her many admirers – though she considered him the best looking of them all, as well as the best dancer, the most charming and full of fun. She had as yet no idea that at nineteen she would decide to become Mrs. Henry Lai Hipp!

Anna was enjoying the wonderful years of being young and popular. These were happy times. During holidays when she returned to Waimea, Bill would be home from Kamehameha Schools. Her younger brother Charles was on holiday from St. Louis High School in Honolulu. William Lindsey was working hard to make money to provide the best possible education for his three children. In addition to running his ranch and serving as Deputy Sheriff, he was now the assistant to the manager of Parker Ranch.

Whenever Parker Ranch's manager A.W. Carter was away, it was William Lindsey who acted as the ranch manager. Another extra enterprise Anna's father pursued on weekends whenever he was free to do so, was catching wild goats to sell to the Filipino plantation laborers. Kohala, Honokaa, and Paauilo plantations all had new workers coming in from the Philippines. For these newcomers, goat was a favorite delicacy. Lindsey would take a truck and some helpers down to the coastal area that in modern times has become the luxurious resort coast of South Kohala. In the dry barren countryside that coast was then, wild goats were numerous. He and his helpers would trap the animals, load them into the truck, and head back the long dusty way to the plantations to sell their catch at a good cash profit.

Anna's father also made money selling and shipping polo ponies and fine race horses to Maui. Whenever they were home, her father depended on Anna and her brothers to help him in all these enterprises. Work was Anna's habit, something she really liked and she continued to treasure her frequent visits back to Waimea and Keawewai. At the ranch, there was usually an array of interesting visitors. Mary Lindsey's heart and her kitchen were both large. She set an excellent table, where there was always enough food for unexpected guests. Over the years, the ranch had become a favorite stopping place for friends and acquaintances making the long trip back and forth from Hilo to Kohala.

Among the many drop-in visitors who enjoyed Anna's mother's hospitable dining table was Doc Hill, who later became a Hilo millionaire, owner of the Big Island's electric power company and a political tycoon in the Territorial legislature. However, in the days when Doc Hill would stop in at the

Lindsey's for a free meal, he was merely a traveling salesman, going from plantation to plantation with a briefcase full of eyeglasses to sell to plantation laborers.

The last time he visited her parents' ranch, according to Anna, Doc Hill left behind his briefcase full of spectacles. Mary Lindsey kept it a long time, waiting for his next trip – but Doc Hill had finished peddling eyeglasses. He was staying in Hilo, making his first million in other ways. "So after awhile my mother just gave those eyeglasses away!" laughs Anna. "Anyone in Waimea needing reading glasses, or distance glasses, would come to her. She would have them try on one pair after another until they found one that felt right to them. They'd go home so happy with those free eyeglasses from Doc Hill's old briefcase!"

Another famous Hilo entrepeneur who enjoyed the William Lindsey's hospitality on trips from Kohala back to Hilo was Pete Beamer, founder of the Beamer clan whose contributions to Hawaii's music and hula have been so outstanding. Beamer was riding a bicycle in the days he was a frequent guest of Anna's parents. He too traveled from plantation to plantation selling odds and ends until he acquired the capital to start his Hilo hardware store.

The William Lindsey home was, ordinarily, harmonious as well as hospitable. The few times that her parents did disagree were, however, times of great embarrassment for young Anna–as late one afternoon when she was entertaining a group of friends in the living room. She was chagrined to hear resounding above the chit-chat of her friends the loud voices of her mother and father having an argument in the kitchen. Anna's chagrin escalated to overwhelming embarrassment as the voices grew louder and louder, more and more heated. Close to tears, she rushed to the kitchen to plead with her parents to be more quiet. They seemed not to hear her, continuing the argument with their voices louder and still more heated. Anna was so ashamed that she fainted dead away in front of them. That did it! When Anna came to, they were bending over her, all concern, the argument forgotten. She got up from the kitchen floor, and went back to join her friends in the parlor. To her immense relief, the rest of the afternoon passed without any sound coming from the kitchen.

Her parents' rare battle had, she found out, centered around William Lindsey's having returned from work that day to find Mary Lindsey had sawed a valuable highboy into two sections so that she could move it up the narrow stairway to a second floor bedroom. William Lindsey was furious. She would ruin that highboy – in fact he was sure she had already ruined it! But Mary Lindsey was as clever with hammer and saw as she was with embroidery needles and crochet hooks. "Mother put that highboy back together with not a mark to show where she had taken it apart!" Anna recalls.

Moving furniture, and rearranging the household was what Mary Lindsey loved to do – a venture in which William Lindsey refused to participate. This did not deter his wife. "There are still big scratches on this living room floor – gouges really," says Anna pointing to an area covered by one of her beautiful carpets. "They're from my mother moving the piano back and forth by herself."

The Jockey Who Bet On Herself

ANNA WAS NINETEEN when she decided to say 'yes' to Henry Lai Hipp's pleas that she become his bride. They had known each other for three years. Henry had been proposing to her all during this time. Anna's family were well acquainted with his. It seemed an ideal match.

Henry had graduated from college and was back on the Big Island, serving as District Court Practitioner in Olaa, a village in the Puna District, seven miles east of Hilo. In those days, law school graduates were in short supply in Hawaii. Those with a good college education, such as Henry Lai Hipp had received at St. Mary's in Dayton, Ohio, were encouraged to take the rigorous legal examination qualifying those who passed to be appointed to a special judgeship known as District Court Practitioner. On the bench at Olaa, Henry Lai Hipp presided over all except felony cases, divorce cases, and probate.

In 1919 when Anna finally said 'yes' to to becoming his wife, young Judge Lai Hipp was overjoyed. Because Henry was a Catholic, Anna converted to Catholicism before her wedding. "I was really married twice –" says Anna. "My father didn't understand about Catholicism. He and my mother wanted to give me a big Hawaiian style wedding at home. The priest in Waimea was so understanding. Henry and I quietly went to

37

the church in the morning, and he married us. Then at home later that day, the priest went through the ceremony again – and nobody knew it was already performed in the proper way in church!" Only Anna's brother Bill had been at the first ceremony, and he kept Anna's wedding at the church a secret as she had asked.

Anna was a beautiful bride and Henry the most handsome of grooms with his soft dark hair, the blend of Irish, Hawaiian and Chinese in his features, and his athlete's build. He had just finished having a 3-bedroom home constructed in the Waiakea section of Hilo for his bride. The young couple settled there immediately. Not until a year later, in 1920, did they take a delayed honeymoon trip to the mainland. It was Anna's first time away from the islands. She loved the five days aboard ship on the passage to California. They had a wonderful month in San Francisco. Henry gave her a superb introduction to the City by the Golden Gate. As did many islanders in those days, the Lai Hipps stayed in the Hotel Stewart. They did everything. They went everywhere. On board the ship returning to Hawai, when a masquerade ball was held, Anna borrowed a Spanish shawl, wound it around her, put a high comb and a rose in her hair and won first prize as a beautiful Spanish dancer.

Anna and Henry's social life in Hilo was not all that exciting, for they were seldom invited out in the evening. In Hilo's every-day business world Judge Henry Lai Hipp moved in the highest professional circles. One might assume the young couple would automatically be welcomed into Hilo's social life, but such was not the case.

It was Anna's mother who asked the critical question of her one day. "You get invited to all the teas, and you're asked to bridge parties and lunches, but why is it you and Henry aren't ever asked to the dinner parties?"

Anna had to admit that, for the first time in her life, she had encountered discrimination. For Hilo society, Henry's Chinese blood was a problem. They were willing to admit part-Hawaiian. But in that era, to be anything other than *haole* (Caucasian) or part-Hawaiian was a social obstacle. Once she saw this, Anna resolutely created their own social life.

With no problem whatsoever, she and Henry swam at the old Yacht Club. They played tennis, the great game of plantation

Hawaii, when matches were held every Sunday. In the '20's and '30's, plantation communities took turns hosting players to a match and then having a lavish brunch for all who came. Henry and Anna liked the game, but neither was keen to play competition tennis. In his college days, Henry had been a champion runner. He excelled at baseball and basketball, an all-star player in both those sports. He had a beautiful voice, and loved to sing and play the steel guitar. Anna's training as a hostess now stood her in good stead. She held such great parties of her own that her close friend Kate Koehnen told her, "No matter what's going on in Hilo, if I'm invited to one of your parties, Anna, I'll drop everything else and come!"

It wasn't easy, being a lavish hostess on Henry's modest income, but Anna's parents would send in a turkey or a suckling pig. Anna would transform her tiny kitchen into a buffet. Henry would make music. With his and Anna's effervescence the parties to which they weren't invited no longer really mattered.

As time went by, and the children Anna had hoped for never became a reality, she found the round of bridge and tennis, house-keeping and parties left her with much extra energy to spend. Then too, after the first idyllic months, the romantic dreams she had had of a perfect marriage began to fade. Henry was a charmer, but he was a philanderer. Women were always after him, and he found it hard to resist although he kept protesting to Anna that he loved only her. To be faithful was just not Henry Lai Hipp's nature.

In 1926, when her younger brother Charles suffered a terminal illness, Anna promised him she would always take care of his two little ones, a girl and a boy. Her parents also were eager to care for their grandchildren, but at first, Charles' young wife and the two children – Richard and Florence Lindsey – came to stay with Anna in Hilo. Charles' wife soon moved on but as her husband had asked she left Richard and Florence to be raised by their Auntie Anna and by William and Mary Lindsey, who had become their legal guardians. They were sometimes with Anna, sometimes in Waimea with their grandparents. Anna was fond of both, but Richard was closest to her all through his boyhood and, still today, he is as loving and caring as if Anna was his mother, not his aunt.

Anna and Henry soon moved from the Waiakea house to a home in Hilo's most elegant neighborhood – Puueo. Richard Lindsey cherishes his memories of all the good times with his Auntie Anna in those years. However, despite the frequent joy of caring for her nephew, the circumstances of Anna's first marriage were such that her heart was heavy. She said nothing to her mother and father about her troubles, yet it was they who came to her rescue by saying "Get busy! Do something!" Reflecting on what it was she most missed in her life in Hilo, Anna realized it was the chance to get out every day and ride horseback. How she looked forward to her frequent trips to Waimea, getting into the saddle and riding off across the green hills.

It was on one of her long solitary rides on a visit to Waimea that Anna's horse stumbled at a place where the ground had caved in. Dismounting to see what might cave in on an open pasture where cows were grazing all around, Anna was shocked to see it was a grave. A tumbled down tombstone revealed that this was the last resting place of Makua Laiana, Rev. Lorenzo Lyons, Waimea's beloved pioneer missionary. He had been buried here long years ago, on the far side of the stream from the old Lyons' homesite. As time passed, evidently the location of his grave had not only been neglected, but forgotten.

Anna no longer had close ties with Imiola, the Waimea mission church which Makua Laiana had founded. In Puueo one of Anna's neighbors, a woman she also knew from their both being members of the Hilo Women's Club, was a Mrs. Bond who was descended from one of the early missionary families. Anna turned to her for help, suggesting that the grave be moved to Imiola churchyard. Through the Mission Childrens' Society, Mrs. Bond was able to do just this. Imiola Church moved the remains and the tombstone of its founder to the churchyard, where it has since been well cared for. Few ever knew that this was because of Anna's concern.

Anna's father, realizing how keenly she missed riding, about this same time offered to bring a string of horses to Hilo for her use. It was an offer that led Anna to get the idea of setting up a riding stables. It was her first venture into the business world and she planned each step carefully ahead of time. First, with well drawn plans for what she wanted to do, she approached the county authorities, asking permission to use a tract of vacant land adjacent to Hoolulu Park and its race track. Her proposal was that she build a riding stables on this tract, with the agreement that the building and all improvements revert to the county at the end of her tenancy. A shrewd business plan for a girl in her twenties – and an audacious idea. But, with no hesitation, the county agreed. Anna's father came to Hilo to help her build a riding academy and stables.

She had no time now to feel lonely or yearn for the ranch life of Waimea. The riding stables, and the riding academy she conducted were not great moneymakers, but they were tremendous for her morale. Her zest for life was back, "I just managed to make ends meet!" says Anna, "But I had a very good time doing it." Caring for Richard, often having her niece Florence too, and operating this full time riding business kept her mind off her marital problems.

Her charge was one dollar per hour for lessons – a bargain price even then for instruction from one of Hawaii's best horsewomen. Some of her young pupils have since become well known statewide – Senator Richard Henderson for one, and community leader Maxine Carlsmith for another. Riding students, and those who came to rent horses or participate in her programs much enjoyed Anna's moonlight rides, and her long trips with picnic lunches. Often her beloved nephew Richard shared these.

One day, on a long trail ride taking her students through the forested outskirts of Hilo, Anna glimpsed a house out in the middle of nowhere. She was astonished to see pretty women in filmy chiffon dresses sitting on the verandah, and even more astonished to note the traffic of male visitors arriving at that remote place. When she returned home, she learned from Henry that she had stumbled upon the location of the brothel known as 'The Mango Tree'.

It was some time later that four of the prostitutes from 'The Mango Tree' came to Anna's stables asking to rent horses. Anna held no moral discrimination against prostitutes, but her intuition was that renting her horses to them might not be a wise business practice. Politely, she refused, apologetically telling them all her horses were taken for the day and she was just waiting for the riders to arrive. Her feeling was, and is, that these women and their profession provided a healthy safety valve for society. "Not the number of rapes in those days!" Anna says.

Renting out her horses could be risky. Anna absolutely refused to rent her horses to sailors or naval officers after one harrowing experience. This happened when a navy ship was in port in Hilo and men from the vessel came to patronize her stables. Luckily Anna had insisted she ride out with them, since they did not know the Hilo area. To her dismay, instead of their letting her be their guide, it was they who led her on a fast furious trip, galloping over the town's macadam roads to Kuhio Wharf and on to a wild circuit of Hilo. "Crazy!" she recollects. "And me following them! My horses were worn out by the end of that day. I never again rented a horse to a navy man!"

Anna's riding academy at Hoolulu Park was only one of the ways in which she put her skill in horsemanship to good use. For many years, even before her marriage to Henry, she had been asked by Eben Low, prominent Honoluluan and former Big Island rancher, to be a *pa'u* rider in the big parades with which Honolulu celebrates Kamehameha Day each June 11th. A popular feature of these parades are *pa'u* riders – girls and women dressed in the skirt known as *pa'u* – yards and yards of material wrapped and draped into a long, trailing divided skirt. The *pa'u* was the original riding costume of Hawaiiian royalty and is traditional for those chosen to ride in parades as the Queens and Princesses of each island. Their costumes, their leis, and the garlands draping their horses are the special colors and flowers of the island they represent. Eben Low was an expert horseman whom Anna much loved and respected for his knowledge of Hawaiiana, his expertise in riding, and his inimitable personality.

As Hawaii's Queen, Anna wore vivid red – the traditional color of the island of Hawaii. Her leis, and those worn by her horse, were of red ohia blossoms strung on garlands of fragrant green maile. Her *pa'u*, her velvet riding skirt, was fourteen yards long. Eben Low had known Anna's grandfather, knew her father well, and – according to Eben's son Brother Low – Eben Low thought Anna was "the best *pa'u* rider there was." He would either ship her own horses over for her to ride in the parade or arrange through someone like Alvah Scott, then at Aiea Plantation, to provide Anna with a good horse. "Eben Low always had Anna ride first in line. For him she was the Queen of all the pa'u riders!" was Brother Low's recollection.

Anna remembers her father's stories of 'Rawhide Ben' as Eben Low was called. Eben Low's mother was the only daughter in the original Parker family. Her husband was a descendant of France's famed Napoleon Bonaparte. Eben Low's paternal grandmother, Elizabeth Pamahoa Napoleon, was a high chiefess of Maui, granddaughter of a French woman who had once been a maid in Napoleon's household. As nonagenarian Brother Low told me his father's family history he described how "Napoleon climbed into the wrong bed one night". The girl became pregnant. Fearful that when her child was born Napoleon might take it away from her, she fled, leaving France on a sailing vessel, a pearler bound for the Pacific. Her child, a boy, was born when the pearler reached Honolulu. She disembarked there, and stayed on in Hawaii, giving her son his father's name as his surname. Also in Eben Low's background was an ancestor who had been Tahitian royalty.

Low was called Rawhide Ben because of his great skill at lassoing and roping. Unfortunately, when he was still quite young, a rawhide lasso that became knotted around his left arm resulted in such damage that his hand had to be amputated. This was done at his mother's home, the old Parker Ranch house at Mana. Eben Low's hand was buried under one corner of that long koa house which – years later – A.W. Carter had torn down.

One of the tragedies of the Parker family was the enmity resulting from the one daughter being denied a fair share of her inheritance. According to Anna's father, Eben Low was so bitter about this he once tried to put dynamite under the Parker Ranch office to blow the place up. After that unsuccessful attempt, he was forbidden ever again to set foot on any Parker Ranch land. He worked first at Maliu Ranch near Mahukona and later at Puuwaawaa, the Kona ranch owned by his relatives, the Hind's.

Rawhide Ben did well enough in his career so that in 1908 he paid the way for three Waimea cowboys – his brother Jack Low, his half brother Archie Kaaua, and Ikua Purdy to accompany him to the mainland and enter the great rodeo competition at Cheyenne, Wyoming. With his one hand, Eben Low was still an expert at lassoing. He came out with first place honors in the roping competition at Cheyenne. Ikua Purdy was judged the grand champion, top cowboy in the world. Hawaii's *paniolos* had proved themselves second to none!

From the time of Anna's childhood, Eben Low had been an admirer of her beauty and of her skill in the saddle. Anna was thrilled to ride in a parade where he was Grand Marshal. "Not like today, with those long, long leis draped on the horses!" she protests. "Eben knew the right way to dress horses and riders. It was something! Ridiculous where they put leis on the horses now – even on their tails!"

Perhaps the most exciting use to which Anna put her horse-manship during these Hilo years of the '20's and '30's was racing. She was a woman jockey, riding in races herself. She also trained jockeys and exercised race horses – her own and those owned by Parker Ranch. Training and selling Parker Ranch horses added another dimension to Anna's riding business, and considerably more profit from the commission earned when she would sell one of their winning horses right off the track.

A.W. Carter, whom everyone referred to as 'A.W.' was the longtime Parker Ranch manager and trustee, an unimpeachably honest man who made Parker Ranch what it is today. He was not an easy man to work for or with. William Lindsey, who for several years was Carter's assistant, was even tempered, always fair with those who worked with and for him. Unfortunately, A.W. was inclined to be brusque and difficult. There came a day when Carter's arrogant unpleasantness was directed to William Lindsey just one time too many. As Mary Rosenberg Lindsey had long been urging her patient husband, he quit as Carter's assistant. It was a matter which did not involve Anna. She continued to deal with the gruff, outspoken, and shrewd A.W. in handling race horses.

William Lindsey had more than enough to keep him busy with his ranch, the slaughterhouse at Ahualoa, and serving as a local judge in the old Waimea courthouse. He also was in the business of shipping horses to Lahaina where he sold them at a good profit. Like his daughter, he was adept at doing a variety of different things and doing them all well.

Like his daughter, too, William Lindsey had always been a racing enthusiast. Although the fourth of July was traditionally the big horse race day on the Big Island, the sport was a favorite year-round activity in most communities. Hilo, the county seat and largest town on the island, was the center for the biggest and best races. Betting was part of the excitement. Anna bet with the best of them – shrewdly, on herself!

In those years, the Hilo Race Track was at Hoolulu Park, close to Anna's stables. In her red and white racing silks and jockey cap, she made as stunning a figure as a jockey with regulation crop, spurs, and thin, light racing saddle on the back of a fine horse as she did on a dance floor in one of her beautiful ballgowns. Her diminutive size was in her favor. Even more so was her daring in riding and handling the most spirited horses. Her renown as a jockey was such that one year, Maui County used her as an attraction to bring out the crowds to the famous Maui County Fair.

Newspapers in Wailuku, Maui's county seat, ran big ads urging people to come see 'the woman jockey'. Unfortunately, the Maui horse they were training for Anna suffered a split hoof just one day before the fair was to open – one day before the big opening race in which she was scheduled to be the star attraction. No time to ship a horse in from the Big Island. Ordinary horses were available to her, but Anna was determined to find a really fast racehorse.

Hearing that her father's old friend, a Mr. MacPhee, owned one of the fastest horses on Maui, Anna started to track the man down. She finally found him, getting a haircut in a barber shop. With no qualms she went inside and introduced herself. "I'm William Lindsey's daughter and I want to borrow your fast horse to race tomorrow at the Fair. The one they were training for me has a split hoof."

Anna's father was well known and well liked on Maui. For years he had been sending fine horses by barge to Lahaina where he swam them ashore and sold them. It was through this that William Lindsey had become so well acquainted with MacPhee. While Anna hoped that this friendship might prove her salvation in finding the fast horse on which she could win the race tomorrow, she was somewhat taken aback by MacPhee's strange reply. It was a 'yes' – but with qualifications that puzzled her.

"If you can sit your ass on its saddle, you can use the horse!" he told her. Anna left the barbership confused but at the same time much pleased. Now she would not disappoint the fairgoers who expected to see her perform tomorrow. She knew the Fair Committee was using her to draw a crowd. For weeks, the Maui papers had been carrying articles and pictures about her skill as a woman jockey.

That afternoon she mounted MacPhee's fast horse, so she could accustom herself to him – and him to her. Only then did she discover that MacPhee's blunt statement about keeping her 'ass' on its saddle had conveyed a kindly honesty she had not quite understood. All went well at first. Anna rode the horse around the track to exercise him. But as she started out through the gate, a group of Boy Scouts came marching by, practising for the Fair. At the sound of their band, MacPhee's fast horses reared up. Anna stuck to the saddle, but this was no ordinary rear and prance of a nervous horse. MacPhee's horse fell over on its back. Anna managed to roll away quickly enough so that the weight of the horse did not crush her. She staggered to her feet. She was staying with a doctor and his wife in Wailuku and when she returned, she showed the wife a six inch bruise the fall had left on her back. Next morning, Anna was black and blue all over. "You're not going to race on that horse!" her hostess protested.

"I am!" said Anna with determination. "I promised! They've drawn a big crowd to the Fair to see me race. I can't disappoint them."

By now, airplanes were flying between the islands. Henry had flown to Maui to be there for her races on the opening day of the Fair. Special reserved seats in the grandstand had been marked for them. Anna was dressed in her racing silks – white breeches, red and white shirt, red and white cap, regulation boots. She didn't tell Henry about the horse rearing or her bruises but as they went through the gate to the Fairgrounds, Anna saw an ambulance parked outside the racetrack. "I surely hope I won't need that today!" she thought.

She sat with Henry for a few minutes, still saying nothing about MacPhee's rearing horse, and then went down to get ready for the race. There was nothing to do now but grit her teeth and pray, both of which she did. With the bands playing and the noise of the crowd in the stands, she could see her horse was getting nervous, but she kept calm. She was the only one in the race with a racing saddle – a small, light saddle she describes as 'like a pancake'. The other jockeys, all women, were using western saddles. At the starting gun, Anna's horse reared up – but this time Anna knew just what to do. Fast as lightning she slid down off that horse's back, landing on her two feet, the dust of the track flying up to coat her white breeches. She was out of his way as the horse fell over backward, and the crowd roared applause at her bravado.

"If I could have gotten down there to stop her, I would have!" Henry later told Anna's father. But no one could stop Anna and her determination to show the fair crowd a good race. A young handler came running. The horse was up by now and Anna said to the boy, "Hoist me up!' She vaulted into the saddle and hit the horse on his head with her crop as he prepared to rear again. "He took off!" says Anna. Late a start as she'd made, she passed by several of the other horses in the race. No chance to win with that bad start, but MacPhee's fast horse – once he started racing – didn't want to stop.

Around and around the track went that fast horse, with Anna firmly in the saddle on his back. He was racing now all by himself and no one on Maui had ever seen a woman – or a man – race a horse at that speed before. Finally, after several times around the track, Anna managed to bring the horse to a halt and negotiate him out through the gate. The crowd in the grandstand had gone wild! The band struck up a fast number in tribute. Anna had given the fairgoers all the excitement those ads and articles about her had promised!

Unlike other women jockeys, who used a handler to start off their horses for them, and a handler grabbing the reins to lead the horse off the track at race's end, Anna held her own reins to start and stop the horse. "I wouldn't look like a trained monkey!" she said, expressing her opinion of how other women raced. It was her own handling of the reins, and her own handling of MacPhee's fast, rearing horse that won her the cheers of the Maui County fair crowd that day. Afterwards, when she joined Henry in the stands, Mr. Baldwin himself, Wailuku's most prominent citizen, came over to congratulate her on her spunk.

At races she entered in Hilo, Anna had been plagued by starting guns that seemed to go off before her horse was in place at the gate. It was almost as if those in charge of the races were determined she would not be able to win. However, each time she managed to come in nose to nose with the winner. Her dream was to find a horse so fast that regardless of starting difficulties she could come in a clear winner. There was keen competition at the Hoolulu track in the Ladies' Races which Anna herself had initiated and which she hoped to see upgraded so that regulation racing saddles and gear and thoroughbred horses would be the rule. A thoroughbred race horse was, therefore, her next – but secret – acquisition.

Her father had heard that on Maui there was a fast thoroughbred named the Maui Parrot that was capturing first place in every race he entered. He told Anna about the horse and together they went to Maui to see the Maui Parrot run. William Lindsey and his daughter sat in the grandstand, Anna with stopwatch in hand, clocking the Maui Parrot. "I never saw a faster race horse!" was Anna's exclamation when the race ended with, of course, Maui Parrot finishing in first place. She and her father nodded to each other. This was a horse they had to buy!

At the track, William Lindsey inquired, "Who owns the Maui Parrot?"

"Your friend MacPhee," was the answer.

So, once again, Anna – and her father this time – went to look for Mr. MacPhee. After some negotiations about the sale of his horse to them, Mr. MacPhee said to William Lindsey, "I tell you what! You send me one of your good polo ponies and I'll ship you the Maui Parrot!"

Anna was elated. She and her father decided to say nothing about their transaction, but to smuggle the Maui Parrot into Kawaihae under the alias of Kaala, the name of one of the mountains behind the Lindsey pasture at Puukapu. Kaala was a handsome horse. "He stood seventeen hands!" says Anna. She loved to ride him, and came often from Hilo to Waimea to exercise Kaala out on the plain. "Could he ever run!" She is still

Courtesy Kahua Ranch.

Grass house at Keawewai, circa 1880.

Lyman House Museum.

Waimea village – 1916.

Akona Store, Waimea, 1916.

Lyman House Museum.

Standing, rear – Queen Liliuokalani's nurse, Rose Traub, Lucy Searle, Josephine Hopkins. Seated – Anna and the Queen's grandchildren. Taken at Liliuokalani's Kuhio Beach retreat, circa 1912.

Photo by Wendell Carlsmith.

Fourteen year old Anna as *pa'u* rider, Hilo parade.

Courtesy Richard Lindsey.

Anna and brother Charles lead Buster Brown's riders in Honolulu parade, 1913.

Anna riding in front of Akona Store, Waimea, circa 1920.

Richard Lindsey on Kaala at Anna's Hoolulu Stables.

exultant at remembering that horse's speed.

When she felt the time had come, Anna trucked Kaala into Hilo to begin training him on the Hoolulu Track. A race horse is always trained with another horse along. To keep the speed of Kaala a secret, Anna and her jockey assistant worked Kaala and a second horse in the pre-dawn hours, wearing white shirts so they could see each other.

At least the day of the big race came. Kaala was ready. No one knew who the horse really was. Anna intended not only to win on the track, but to pick up side money on the betting. She was a jockey who always bet on herself! Before the race, she walked Kaala around the ring. The Filipinos who were Hawaii's newest group of plantation immigrants loved to bet and soon, several of them came to look at Anna's horse.

"This horse can run?" they asked, looking up at Kaala's size.

"Well," said Anna evasively, because she was never one who found it possible to lie, "he's used to working on my father's ranch in Waimea."

"For plow?" asked one of the Filipinos.

Anna shrugged. It could have been yes. It could have meant no. "You like bet he no can run good? You like bet one hundred dollars?' she asked.

Two men came forward with hundred dollar bets. A third had only fifty dollars, but Anna agreed to that smaller bet too. A neutral party was found to hold the money and Anna took Kaala around to the starting gate. Hilo is a wet place. The Hoolulu track was apt to be muddy and so, as a park commissioner – an office to which she was appointed in 1933 – she had had a fresh load of cinders put down to dress the track for this race.

Being a thoroughbred, Kaala was a highstrung, nervous horse. When she mounted him, he was already trembling from the sound of the band playing, and so nervous that he was running with sweat. The reins were wet in Anna's hands. A policeman, noticing this, came over, took out his handkerchief and wiped her reins dry.

Once again, there were several false starts – a tactic which made Kaala even more nervous. Finally Anna went way back, behind the others. "Drop the flag!" she yelled.

The astonished starter did just that. The horses ahead of Anna were off, rushing out over the fresh cinders. Anna held Kaala back until the others had all the loose cinders, then she let her horse go. Quickly he overtook the other horses. There was a sweet taste of victory for Anna as she passed the lead horse in the race, and Kaala's flying hooves sprayed cinders in that rider's face.

To her great disappointment, that was the only victory Kaala was allowed to win. The horse's identity as the famous Maui Parrot was now clear. Doc Hill, as president of the Hilo Jockey Club, made the strange decision that because the Maui Parrot, alias Kaala, was a registered thoroughbred he would not be allowed ever to race again in Hilo!

Anna challenged his decision. "Don't you want to encourage better races by having thoroughbred horses? With a horse like Kaala in the competition, other riders will want to bring in thoroughbreds and your races will really be upgraded!"

Doc Hill evidently did not agree with her. The Maui Parrot was forever barred from entering the Hilo races. So, for a long time Anna kept this beautiful fast race horse in her Hoolulu Stables, allowing no one but herself and her nephew Richard to ride him. To her and to Hawaii's racing enthusiasts,- Doc Hill's decision was a considerable disappointment but in those days in Hilo, what Doc Hill decided was how things had to be.

A Lei for Amelia Earhart

IN 1935, WHEN Henry Lai Hipp ran for a seat in the Territorial Legislature. Anna threw all her energy into campaigning for him. Things had not eased in their marriage. Henry constantly promised her he would change his ways. But as always, during the time that he served in the Territorial House of Representatives, it was Anna who changed her life for Henry.

She interrupted all the activities that ordinarily filled her busy life in Hilo to accompany him to Honolulu for the legislative session. There she patiently sat waiting for the interminable political meetings to end and Henry to come home. She did not wait idly, however. The embroidery, cutwork and crocheting her mother had taught her were pastimes Anna much enjoyed. During the sessions of Henry's legislative term, Anna crocheted several intricate bedspreads. She went to Liberty House for instructions in how to knit. Always a fast learner she was soon knitting socks and sweaters by the dozen. In no time she was designing and knitting handsome suits and dresses for herself.

It was, all Hilo agreed, Anna's popularity that had helped Henry Lai Hipp win his seat in the legislature. As early as 1932 her standing in Hilo had been recognized in a promotional contest in which she won first prize. Emma Saiki, daughter of

51

a Hilo banker, was the second prizewinner. Together she and Anna enjoyed their prizes: a trip to the World's Fair in Chicago and then on to Washington, D.C. "Emma Saiki was a great companion. A good sport! A fine girl to travel with!" Anna remembers.

This second mainland trip sharpened Anna's appetite for travel. She and Emma crossed the country by pullman train and Anna loved every minute of it. In Washington, D.C. she was reminded of home, and of George Washington Lincoln, the previous owner of Keawewai when she and Emma visited the Lincoln Memorial and the Washington Monument. Looking at them Anna realized how aptly George Washington Lincoln had been named. She remembered him as tall, gaunt, rangy in build just as Abraham Lincoln was portrayed in his statue in the capital. And, she remembered also, what somber features George Washington Lincoln had – exactly like those in the capital's portraits of George Washington.

Since 1933 Anna had been a parks commissioner for Hawaii County, a task she carried out so well that when the parks superintendent took his vacation, they appointed Anna to act as superintendent in his absence. In this unpaid position as parks commissioner, as in all of her community activities such as chairing the Outdoor Circle of the Hilo Women's Club, Anna put as much time, enthusiasm and commitment as she did into caring for her nephew Richard, her riding academy business and Hoolulu Park stables. For eight years she served as chairman of the Hilo Women's Club Outdoor Circle, a group that under Anna's leadership contributed much to the beautification of Hilo and its nearby parks.

Shortly before Anna took office as a park commissioner in 1933, the great baseball hero, Babe Ruth, had been a Hilo visitor. The park commission invited the baseball star to plant a banyan tree near Hilo's only bayfront hotel at that time – the gracious old Naniloa. As a park commissioner, and with the assistance of her good friend, Territorial Forester L.W. 'Bill' Bryan, Anna expanded the tree-plantings that honored famous visitors to Hilo into the project whose result is today's magnificent Banyan Drive which winds past the golf course and hotel strip that now grace this section of Hilo Bay.

Anna's friendship with Bill Bryan and his wife Irma began soon after her arrival in Hilo as a bride. The Bryans, although several years older than Anna, were also newlyweds – marrying in Hilo in 1923. Anna and Irma Bryan saw a great deal of each other at the Hilo Women's Club and were both active in the Outdoor Circle. Irma Bryan, years later, remembered watching Anna and Henry at Yacht Club dances. "They were the most beautiful couple on the dance floor!"

Anna's friendship with Bill Bryan was further cemented by Bill Bryan's close friendship with her father, and by the fact that Bill had been very fond of Anna's brother Charles, who had worked for him. Each month when he made an inspection trip to North Kohala, Bryan always stopped in to see William and Mary Lindsey. Anna looks back on him as a very special person whose contributions to the Big Island environment – and to that of the entire state – have never been adequately recognized. Bryan was a New Englander, a veteran of World War I who had stayed overseas in 1919 to help reforest France's devastated battlefields. In 1921, having itchy feet after a year in California, he came to Hawaii "to see the islands". The Hawaii Sugar Planters Association was looking for a trained forester. His first day in Honolulu Bill Bryan saw their advertisement, applied for the job, was hired, and immediately went to the Big Island to plan and oversee the reforestation of watershed areas. These had been damaged first by the Hawaiian chiefs' decimation of the sandalwood forests in the early days of the nineteenth century, and then by overgrazing and the depredation of the wild longhorns.

The great passion in Bill Bryan's life was trees. Anna likes to remind people that in his sixty years of reforestation activities Bill Bryan saw to the planting of more than 100,000 trees and introduced 14,000 new species of plants and trees into Hawaii. When Anna became chairman of the Outdoor circle, and all during the eight years she continued as chairman of that very active group, she worked closely with Bill Bryan on the beautification of Hilo and such nearby parks as Akaka Falls, which Bryan had carved out of the territorial forest reserve back in 1923.

It was Anna who spearheaded the project of planting the wide variety of torch ginger and other exotic gingers along the park's trails. Today, Akaka Falls is one of the most scenic Big Island parks. And it was Anna who created the idea of living Christmas trees for Hilo. She got the trees and the help in planting them from

Bill Bryan. She raised the money to light the trees every Christmas from Hilo merchants. Every December the town was graced with living, lighted, outdoor Christmas trees – one at Hilo Iron Works, one in Kalakaua Park – across from the old Hilo Hotel, one near the Armory, just above the store owned by the family of Anna's dearest friend, Kate Koehnen. A fourth tree was planted at the junction of Waianuenue Avenue and Kaumana Drive.

No longer in existence is the handsome hibiscus hedge with which Anna lined the road to Kuhio Wharf. Every time Walter Todd would see Anna coming, he'd say, "I know, Anna! You want me to give another load of dirt for your hibiscus!" Regrettably, after Anna's tenure, the hibiscus were neglected. Today, no remnant of the once handsome borders remain.

One very special tree planting project which Anna planned, and at which she and Irma Bryan did the lei-giving honors, took place behind the Hilo Post Office. Irma Bryan personally made the jacaranda lei for the ceremony, and it was Anna who asked Bill Bryan to plant the jacaranda tree. Bill invited the Superintendent of Hawaii Volcanoes National Park to do the honors. It was, Bryan and Anna both recollected, "quite a day". A big crowd was on hand for the ceremony since, as usual, with whatever Anna spearheaded in the community, the event was well publicized and the public invited.

It was the Banyan Drive project that was both Anna's and Bill Bryan's favorite. Bill would furnish a banyan and the knowledge of where to place it for best future advantage while Anna planned the ceremony, contacted the honoree, and made sure a wooden plaque was ready to mark the name of the honored visitor and the date of the ceremony. She also was the one who presented the honorees of each occasion with a lei. Particularly prominent in her memory is the time when novelist Fannie Hurst planted her banyan in Hilo. Most poignant for Anna is her remembrance of the day when she put a lei around the shoulders of Amelia Earhart, several months before the famous aviatrix disappeared on a flight across the Pacific.

All during this period, neither Anna's parents nor her closest Hilo friends knew how difficult her life had become. Her nephew Richard, who attended school in Waimea, came to Hilo on weekends and holidays to be with his Auntie Anna. For him those memories are of nothing but the happy times she gave him. He remembers Anna and Henry taking him to Mass Sunday mornings. After church, Henry would stop at Sun Sun Lau, Hilo's famous Chinese restaurant, and bring home orders of fancy Chinese-style delicacies for a sumptuous brunch.

Richard never guessed at the reality of Anna's life with Henry Lai Hipp. Valiantly, Anna had continued to be supportive of her charming and quite undependable husband. The truth was that had she not become a devout Catholic when she married him, Anna would long since have filed for a divorce. To her, however, marriage was the sacred bond her church considered it. Although to live with Henry brought her increasing anguish year by year, as did many in those far more restrictive days Anna regarded 'for better or worse' as a vow she would never break.

By 1937 'worse' with Henry had become almost unendurable. Loyally Anna campaigned for his try at re-election to the Territorial Legislature. At the onset of the campaign, Henry suffered a severe attack of appendicitis. Surgery and weeks of recuperation immobilized him. It was Anna who went out and successfully gathered the votes that made it possible for him to win.

Once again she accompanied her husband to Honolulu for the session. These were held in Iolani Palace where the Governor and Lieutenant Governor had their offices on the second floor, in what had once been the bedrooms of Hawaii's kings and queens. A patchwork of ramshackle plywood additions to the palace ground floor and basement area distorted the historic building. Legislative sessions were held in the former throne room and dining room on the ground floor with spectators watching proceedings through the open windows and doors of the palace lanais.

In Honolulu as she had in Hilo, Anna put on her usual brave front but inside, the heartache was becoming more than even her phenomenal strength could bear. In 1938, when her father fell from a horse and broke his leg, Anna made this the excuse to return to her parents' ranch. Ostensibly, she was there to help care for her father. In reality, she was separating from Henry

Lai Hipp, who was soon in trouble with the law. After years of judicial service on the bench, he had been charged with subornation of perjury by Hawaii County Attorney Martin Pence. Pence, a genial Kansan who years later became Hawaii's senior Federal Court Judge, recollects that the case stemmed from Lai Hipp's having illegally obtained marriage licenses for two Filipino clients who wanted to marry girls under the age of legal consent.

Henry hired his brother-in-law, William Heen, one of the top lawyers in the territory, to represent him. When Bill Heen came over from Honolulu for the trial, and found Anna was in Waimea, separated from Henry, he called her on the telephone. "You've got to come support Henry this one last time!" Heen pleaded. "Without you here it's like a cart without a horse for him!"

Many women would have said, "serves him right!" – but not Anna. She came to Hilo and remained at Henry's side throughout his trial. She was in the courtroom every day, playing the part of the devoted wife who could not conceive of her husband doing anything wrong. The jury selected was all male, most of them part-Hawaiians. Each day of the trial Anna appeared – "looking gorgeous!" Martin Pence remembers. She sat in the front row of the courtroom, in full view of the jury. Pence noticed that frequently Henry would go over and sit beside Anna. For all the jury knew, from the way Henry and Anna looked at each other and from their actions, they were the closest of couples.

"I had the evidence that Henry Lai Hipp was guilty," Pence recollects. "Bill Heen, his attorney, was afraid I was going to get a conviction."

Finally, one mid-afternoon, the jury was ready to begin its deliberations. At eleven o'clock that evening they returned to the courtroom with a verdict that dismayed Martin Pence. "Not guilty!"

Pence knew one of the jurors very well and later, he asked the man, "How come that verdict?"

The former juror shrugged. "Oh, we knew Lai Hipp was guilty. But we were sorry for dear Anna. She's such a sweet, pretty woman – we couldn't do anything to hurt her!"

Immediately after the trial, Anna returned to Waimea.

William Lindsey's condition had steadily grown worse. He had never in his life suffered illness and when he fell from his horse, he refused to go to the hospital to have his broken leg set. Neither would he have a doctor come to the house to put his leg in a cast. Instead, he placed his faith in the ancient Hawaiian method of curing fractures by a type of massage known as *lomi lomi*. Regrettably, in his case, this did not work. For months he remained bedridden, weaker and sicker by the day. While Anna helped her mother nurse him she never let her father guess that she was there not only because of his condition but because she had decided to leave Henry.

Anna and her mother devoted all their energy to try to help William Lindsey regain his health. Trustingly, they left the business of the ranch and slaughterhouse in charge of a person that both they and William Lindsey regarded as reliable. After months of illness, in 1939 William Lindsey died. As was Mary Lindsey's wish, he was buried in the garden fronting the ranch house.

It was now that Anna forced herself to take an honest look at the truth of her marital problems. After all, William Lindsey had raised her to be a woman capable of coping and surviving in a world that still does not accept women as having that full potential. After her father's death, coping and surving were what Anna knew she must do. With courage, she faced the reality of Henry's inability to ever change his ways as he kept promising her. Separation had not made a difference. He was still his old philandering self. In 1939, she made the decision to divorce him, a decision that in many ways had been making itself over the long difficult years of her marriage.

When she went to her priest in Hilo to tell him she had filed for divorce from her husband, Anna was surprised to hear that he already knew and had, in fact, just returned from Honolulu where he had consulted with Bishop Liebert about her case. Before he went to the Bishop, the priest asked a number of Hiloans about Henry and Anna's relationship. Without exception, they told him Anna should have left Henry many years ago, that she had been a model and faithful wife in every way. Anna was overwhelmed to hear that the Bishop had said, "Tell Anna she may continue in the church and furthermore, that she may continue to receive communion."

That fall of 1939 Henry was again a candidate for re-election to the territorial legislature. Anna refused to campaign for him, and this time he lost. Anna was now openly in the process of moving from Hilo. No longer would she be a park commissioner or active in the Outdoor Circle. The exciting days of being a jockey, a horse trainer and trader, a riding instructor and owner of Hoolulu Stables were behind her. Taking only her clothes and the Buick Henry had bought for her (but for which she had had to make payments out of her own earnings), Anna prepared to go home to Waimea for good. "My mother needs me there," she told her Hilo friends who urged her to stay in touch.

That Christmas eve, Anna went to attend mass at St. Joseph's in Hilo. "They all looked at me as I walked to the rail to receive communion that night," she recollects. "And after the service, there was such a commotion about my being a divorced woman, and having taken communion that when I got home, I had a phone call from Brother John, a Hilo boy who had become a lay brother. 'You really stopped traffic at the church tonight, Anna,' he said. 'But didn't you get special permission from the Bishop to receive communion?' "

"I didn't ask that permission, but it was given to me," confirmed Anna.

"I thought so!" said Brother John. "And that's what I told all of them."

That was Anna's farewell to her married life in Hilo. She was now once again Anna Leialoha Lindsey, a single person, living in Waimea with her mother, caring for her mother and involved in new problems, new crises that left her no time to even think about having ever been Mrs. Henry Lai Hipp. Once again home for Anna was the white ranch house where she had grown up. Henry continued to try to see her and continued to telephone, but she was adamant. From now on she would be an independent, free, and determined woman – on her own.

One Sunday Henry called for the last time. He had received Anna's summons for a divorce. Mary Lindsey answered the phone. She talked to Henry for a long time. Then, her face anxious, she turned to Anna. "Will you talk to Henry?"

No!" said Anna.

Mary Lindsey repeated her daughter's refusal, listened to Henry's reply, and with even more anxiety turned to Anna. "He says if you don't speak to him he'll take his pistol out in the back yard and shoot himself!"

"Tell him to go ahead!" Anna retorted. "That will save me the trouble of going to court."

Becoming the Boss

GRIEF WAS A luxury in which Anna and her mother were not allowed to indulge for very long. Bill Lindsey, as the only surviving son, insisted he should administer his father's estate, and have charge of the ranch. It was clear that he thought considerable assets were involved, and he felt he should have control of them. After all, he was a man. How could two women manage the place, even if they were his mother and sister! He told them he was going to see that he was the one the court appointed.

At the time, Bill Lindsey was a police captain in Laupahoehoe, on the Hamakua Coast. He had always disliked working on his father's ranch. He knew little about raising cattle. But, he reminded his mother and sister even before the funeral, he was after all the eldest son. He turned a deaf ear to his mother's protests that Anna was more capable at knowing what to do on the ranch. Anna was home now, she knew cattle, she liked ranching and she was a worker. Nothing would dissuade Bill Lindsey. Immediately after the funeral, he hired Martin Pence to take his case to court.

To represent her mother and herself Anna hired Bill Heen from Honolulu. The case was to be heard by West Hawaii Circuit Court Judge J. Wesley Thompson whose reputation was that of a fondness for the ladies. Soon Anna heard that her brother Bill was telling people his mother and Judge Thompson were 'close'. The insinuation was that this being so, it was unfair for Thompson to decide who should administer William Lindsey's estate.

Anna knew her mother well enough to know this was not so. A trip the two of them had to take to Judge Thompson's office in Kona proved to her how unfounded her brother's allegation was. Only the mountain road existed between Waimea and Kona. It was a rough thirty-five miles that wound past Puuwaawaa Ranch, past the small cowboy community of Puuanahulu, through stands of eucalyptus, silveroak and jacarandas that Bill Bryan's Civilian Conservation Corps had planted during the worst of the Great Depression, several years earlier. Here and there stunted groves of ohia covered the rocky, dry pastureland.

It was a long trip that, luckily, Anna made without tire trouble in her Buick. She and her mother both remembered that Bill Bryan told them to count on at least one flat tire when you drove this road! As they descended at last towards the seaside village of Kailua-Kona, coffee farms were on either side where, today, rows of suburban homes in developments like Kona Palisades sprawl down the hot, dry, lava-dappled slopes.

Kailua in 1939 was a small quiet village. The wharf and freight shed came alive only on days when interisland steamers like the 'Mauna Kea' and the 'Hualalai' arrived to pick up passengers, mail, and freight. Where the King Kamehameha Hotel now stands there was 'Lumberyard' beach and a large, open-sided lanai-type county gym. There, every evening, local kids practiced basketball while older people sat on the gym steps strumming ukuleles and guitars or just enjoying the balmy night air. On the oceanfront site where Hale Halawai is located was a coconut grove surrounding a picturesque two-story brick courthouse. It was undoubtedly one of the most beautiful places in Hawaii-nei.

Anna parked the Buick in front of the seaside courthouse and helped her mother up the courthouse steps. Mary Rosenberg Lindsey suffered from arthritis. She walked with difficulty. Her eyesight was no longer dependable. She was nervous at the prospect of these court procedures, totally distraught at her only surviving son's hostile attitude towards her and his sister. As she helped her mother up the steps, Anna kept thinking about her brother's allegation that Judge Thompson should be barred from handling this case because Thompson was too 'close' a friend to Mary Lindsey.

Judge Thompson's office was on the second floor of the building. While they were still on the first floor of the courthouse, Anna and her mother met Roy Wall, a clerk, who greeted them.

"Is that Judge Thompson?" Mary Lindsey asked, peering at him. It was obvious to Anna that her mother had never seen Judge J. Wesley Thompson, and that her brother's allegation was totally without grounds.

When the case was heard, it was in the Waimea courthouse. The courtroom was filled with Lindseys, most of whom believed that Bill Lindsey, as the surviving son, should be administrator of his father's estate. It was in this same courtroom that William Lindsey's flowing Spencerian script filled the records from his tenure as deputy sheriff. Alone in the front row sat Anna and her mother. "Anna looked as pretty as ever!" reminisces Martin Pence. "I knew I was on the losing side as Bill Lindsey's lawyer and I knew that Anna should rightly win. She had the skill, the drive, the interest to take care of the ranch and the estate which everyone then thought was worth a lot of money – money I knew Anna and her mother needed to support Charles' two children, whom they were raising." This, Pence realized, was something Bill Lindsey had not taken into consideration – but the Judge well might. Anna, her mother, and Charles's two youngsters, now in their teens, were a majority of William Lindsey's heirs.

Pence was relieved when, at noon, Judge Thompson took a recess and asked the two lawyers to go to lunch with him. When they returned that afternoon to court, the Judge called Anna into his chambers. Both Martin Pence and Bill Heen were present and told her they were in full agreement with the decision the Judge was about to give her.

"I am going to name you Administratrix of your father's estate, and manager of the ranch," said Judge Thompson.

"No. Please use mother as Administratrix," protested Anna. "I don't want my brother to think he has ousted mother from any part of handling father's affairs!"

"You are right. We hadn't considered that," said the Judge, and with the concurrence of both lawyers, the Judge returned to the courtroom to announce his decision, the one Anna had requested.

That same afternoon, Martin Pence insisted to Bill Lindsey that he go to his mother's home and make peace with her and with his sister. It was an angry Bill Lindsey who accompanied Pence to the ranch house. Anna, seeing her brother's hostility, went out to sit on the porch. Bill Heen came and pleaded with her to come in. Then Martin Pence came and pleaded with her. Anna went in the living room to find her brother shaking his fist at her father's portrait which hung on the wall and raving against his own father. Mary Lindsey was heartbroken. She could not understand the antagonism of her eldest son who through all this and from then on refused to speak to her. Whenever Bill had been down and out and in trouble, Mary and William Lindsey had taken their son in and cared for him and his family until he was able to find another job. As a police officer in Waimea he had been transferred at the request of Parker Ranch after he harassed Hartwell Carter at an intersection where although there was no stop sign, Bill Lindsey had decided there ought to be one. He had even gone so far as to harass his own mother about not stopping at that intersection.

Neither Bill Lindsey nor anyone else suspected the sorry reality of William Lindsey's affairs. As soon as her mother was appointed administratrix, and herself ranch manager, Anna discovered that during her father's long illness the ranch had plummeted from prosperity to the verge of bankruptcy. Cattle had been purchased and not paid for. They had been slaughtered, the beef sold, and the income siphoned off by the helper Mr. Lindsey had trusted to carry on the business while he was ill. Taxes had not been paid. Most alarming of all was that a once substantial bank account in Honolulu's Bishop Bank revealed a current balance of only $150. "That's all there was – to pay bills, pay the taxes, and feed the six of us!" Anna remembers.

Alarmed, she called Judge Heen in Honolulu. "You must retire those debts immediately or the ranch may have to be forfeited!" he warned. The amount, in 1939 dollars, was staggering. Quickly, Anna reviewed her options. Riding out to check on her father's herds, she found that only a few scrub cattle remained in the ranch's rich pastures. She did not let her mother, or her niece and nephew guess how desparate conditions were. How could she pay up all the back taxes, pay off thousands of dollars of debts, restock the ranch with cattle, and feed six people for the next few months on just $150?

Immediately Anna realized that what she needed was a loan. Parker Ranch Manager A.W. Carter gave her advice which, in good faith – and because there seemed no other alternative – Anna accepted. "Don't go to the bank for your money!" he told her. "Parker Ranch will give you a loan." As security, he asked her to put up the entire ranch, the ranch house, and its contents. It was a hard bargain, and a risky one – that Anna well knew.

Looking back at those hard times Anna remembers that "My mother always kept saying – isn't Mr. Carter kind to let us have that money." Anna shakes her head. "There was nothing kind about it. A.W. Carter expected me to fail – and to get our ranch and everything on it for a few thousand dollars!"

Interest and payments on this loan had to be met each month. Anna knew she must never fall behind. With the loan money she had paid off the back taxes and retired some of the debts, but a large amount of outstanding bills remained. Her attorney, Judge Heen, warned Anna that creditors were threatening to put a lien on the estate properties if they were not paid right away. She did some quick calculations. The only option that remained was for her to sell off some of those lands before any creditor action could be taken. She dared not wait for the usual slow process of real estate sales and escrow. To auction off the property was what she decided must be done. But how? She could not afford to hire an auctioneer–.

To help solve her problems, Anna went to Hilo to see her old friend, Judge Osorio. She told him her intention of auctioning off four parcels of land in Waimea and six houselots on Piopio Street in Hilo. "How do I go about doing this?" she asked.

"Put a sign on each parcel, telling when and where it will be auctioned off – be sure to put the exact time and date," said Osorio.

"That I can do," said Anna. "But I can't afford an auctioneer. I've got to do it myself. Can you tell me how to do that?"

Judge Osorio could and did, giving her an instant one-hour

course in how to auction off property. Thanking him, Anna left his office, went to a sign shop in Hilo and had the signs made, herself put the signs on each of the six Piopio St. houselots, then drove back to Waimea and put signs on each of the four parcels there.

The morning of the auction, she had set an early time at the Waimea courthouse. A crowd was already there when she arrived. Bidding went fast. In less than an hour she had sold the large lot where the Edelweiss Restaurant is now located, and a back lot with a small cottage; the property where the Great Wall restaurant and a cluster of small shops now stands; the tract on which Moon Sameshima later built a small hotel; and a hillside lot just above the location where – years later– Governor John A. Burns built his home. Mr. Iwamasa of Puuwaawaa Ranch was the successful bidder for this last lot.

With the buyer's checks in hand, Anna immediately climbed into her Buick and drove to Hilo. Before noon she was pacing the verandah of the old Hilo Police Station, stopping traffic with her auctioning off of the six Piopio Street houselots. Her old Hilo friend, Mr. Wung, helped her get good prices by sending some of his friends to up the bidding. In less than an hour, with these checks added to the ones in her purse, Anna was at Hilo airport, boarding a plane to Honolulu.

"You did it!" congratulated Judge Heen when she reached his downtown office and handed him the checks. "You've beat the deadline on those creditors!" he rejoiced.

"And I'll have a little left over to feed the six of us on the ranch for the next few months," said Anna. She wasted no time at Heen's office, caught the next plane back to Hilo, and that same evening drove home to Waimea. "When you're poor, you can do the impossible. You have to!" she comments. "I worked for no salary as ranch manager that first year. Finally I paid myself $40.00 a month! Until then, I didn't even have my own toothpaste. I had to borrow my mother's!"

With determination, Anna went to work to bring the ranch out of the red. Her first act was to fire Kazu, the man who had not been the trustworthy assistant that her father had believed. No help meant that Anna must do everything on the ranch by herself– and she did. Not long after she fired Kazu, he was arrested for stealing cattle in Waimea. He escaped from the Waimea jail, hid out in the forests and made his way to North Kohala where the police caught up with him. They locked him in a jail cell in Kapaau that night. Next morning, when they came to take him to breakfast across the street at Nambu Hotel, they found Kazu dead. Somewhere, somehow, he had hidden enough poison so that during the night he had been able to commit suicide.

With no experienced ranch helper anymore, Anna was really on her own! Her responsibilities were far more than just that of running a nearly bankrupt ranch. Her mother, a gentle and giving woman, had taken in two Hawaiian girls from Kona who were wards of the court. Richard and Florence were still being cared for in the household. With no cash reserve, no income, and few cattle, with a Parker Ranch loan to pay off and all those mouths to feed, Anna had no time to brood over her divorce from Henry, no time to mourn her father, no time to worry about what to do with her life. Her faith in herself, in all the training her father had given her, in the productivity and potential of the lands he had acquired, and in her ability to somehow put the ranch back in shape never wavered.

She felt it urgent to put up the best possible front. Never once did she share her troubles, complain, or talk about how poor they had become. Mornings, before she saddled up, she would wash and polish her Buick. Mid-afternoon she would ride in from the range, or clean up from the slaughterhouse work she did with the local butcher-specialist, a man everybody called 'Killdabeef'. After a good bath, she would dress in her very best, put on a hat and gloves, freshen her lipstick, climb into the Buick, and by four o'clock would be driving leisurely through Waimea. Everyone seeing her thought, "She's really well off! A lady of leisure! Such a happy girl!"

Anna's gutsiness paid off when she went to the bank to ask her father's old friend, bank manager Frank Fraser for a loan of $4000. "do I need a co-signer?" she asked. Fraser said no, and without further ceremony handed her the money.

With this six months loan, Anna bought steers from Kahua, a ranch along the mountain road to North Kohala. Kahua was owned by Atherton Richards and Ronald Kamehameha

VonHolt, descendants of two *kamaaina* families. Ronald VonHolt, known as the last child to be born under the Hawaiian flag, he was Kahua's manager, and a firm friend of Anna's. In his bachelor days, Ronald VonHolt was one of Anna's ardent admirers.

Anna put the steers she bought from him on her best grasslands. Before the six months of her loan period ended, she had slaughtered enough of those fattened steers, and sold enough meat to her father's long-time good customers in Hilo to be ready to pay off the bank loan. In addition, she managed to continue making small regular payments on the $19,000 Parker Ranch note.

"Don't pay off this six months loan in advance of its due date, Anna," advised Frank Fraser when she came to him, ready to do so. "Let me show you how to use money to make money —" he offered. Anna listened intently. From then on, she borrowed successfully, three times, at six month intervals. With this money she made money, buying dairy cows and slaughtering them. "They didn't eat any grass! They really made me money!" Anna laughs. She also bought and slaughtered the cattle tethered along the roadside in Kohala by enterprising Puerto Rican families. From each check she received by selling the beef to Hilo Meat Company, Hilo Hotel, and Volcano House – her primary, dependable customers – she paid what she could to Parker Ranch. From her own one third interest she managed to set aside enough to buy out the interest of her brother Bill. "It was Leslie Wishard, the manager of Honokaa plantation who arranged that for me," says Anna. "The ranch was worth little then but even so that price to Bill was hard for me to raise. Les Wishard told Bill it was my mother buying him out. Otherwise Bill would never have sold to me!"

This first year of Anna's becoming 'boss lady', Mary Lindsey was enormously proud of her daughter. 1940 was a year in which the mother and daughter, always close, grew even closer. Anna worried about her mother's frail health, for heart trouble was now added to Mary Lindsey's other problems. In her turn, Mary Lindsey worried about being bedridden and burdening Anna with her care. "When I go, I want to go quickly. Just die!" she often told her daughter.

One morning Anna sat with her mother at breakfast before she rode out for the day's work on the ranch. It struck Anna how well her mother looked this morning. "How clear your complexion is today. And how beautiful you are!" said Anna. "You must feel really well today!"

In answer, Mary Lindsey just said, "Thank you, dear," and smiled.

In the middle of that morning, while Anna was on the way to her pastures at Puukapu, she saw her helper driving up in Mary Lindsey's Packard.

"Your mother is very sick! You drive home – I'll bring your horse back!" The helper tossed Anna the car keys. She jumped behind the wheel and raced home but she was too late. Mary Lindsey had suffered a fatal heart attack. She had gone quickly – just as she had told Anna she hoped she would die.

As Mary Rosenberg Lindsey had wished, Anna buried her mother in the garden plot beside William Lindsey. Again, Anna's life abruptly changed. Florence Lindsey's mother came to the funeral and took Florence home with her to live. Anna returned the two court wards to Kona. Her childhood friend Thelma Parker Smart had put in her will a provision that the children of Parker Ranch employees be given scholarships to fund their education. Since Charles had worked summers as a cowboy for Parker Ranch during the years he attended St. Louis High School, Anna went to A.W. Carter with a request. "My nephew Richard will qualify for one of the scholarships that Thelma's will provides, won't he? Remember, Charles worked for Parker Ranch!"

To her relief, Carter approved the scholarship and Anna was able to send Richard to Lahahinaluna, a boarding school on Maui, for his high school education.

Anna was alone on the ranch now. She keenly missed her parents, she missed her nephew, but she had no time to feel lonely with all there was to be done each day. Her resolve was to prove her parents' confidence and trust in her, and that of the court, by making the ranch a success. Faith was her sustenance – faith in God, faith in herself, faith that everything would come out all right.

Anna had already begun to study everything she could find on cattle breeding and new grazing techniques. The last year of her mother's life, the first year of Anna again being Anna Lindsey, a single woman, she had spent evenings pouring over cattleman's journals, absorbing the latest information coming in from the mainland and abroad on the arts of cattle ranching and new techniques in animal husbandry. That was the beginning of years of intense study and openness to new ideas. Few ranchers in Hawaii knew more about the horizons and potential for their industry than did Anna Lindsey.

The more that her study and each day's experience added to the basic skills her father had taught her, the more Anna appreciated William Lindsey's foresight in purchasing and leasing the finest of grazing lands in the Waimea area. Not only were they good pastures, rich grasslands, but they were lands supplied with ample water. On an island where too much rain can be followed by years of extreme drought, dependable water supplies such as she had in the deep pools at Keawewai were invaluable.

Throughout 1940 and 1941, while the wars in Europe and the Far East continued their insidious spread from country to country, Anna worked harder than ever. She was never late with her payments on the Parker Ranch note. In addition she was accumulating enough of a personal reserve to buy out the remaining one-third interest in the ranch– that of Charles' two children.

She was puzzled one day about this time when A.W. Carter sent one of his men to bring her in to his office. Anna was working in one of her pastures. It was not convenient to leave what she was doing, but, "Boss wants to see you about something. Important!" urged Carter's messenger.

Anna knew that the bluff, aggressive manager of Parker Ranch was used to getting his own way in everything with just about everybody. She was loathe to jump to his command, but she was curious as to what could be so important for him to need to see her in the middle of a working day. It could not be about the money she owed the ranch. That she knew, for her payments were up to date.

When she arrived at Parker Ranch headquarters, Mr. Carter

ushered her into his office – the polite gentleman as always whenever he talked to her. Yet, today, there was something in his manner, something about his smile and his condescending tone of voice that aroused Anna's suspicions.

"What's a pretty little thing like you doing trying to run a ranch?" he asked. "I know three wealthy men who want to give you $32,000 for it right today! Why not sell it, Anna. Take your money and have yourself a good time. $32,000! That's a lot!"

"The ranch is worth more than that to me!" said Anna. She could tell that her sharp reply angered Carter for he shifted his cigar from one side of his mouth to the other, a habit of his when anything was upsetting him. "Mr. Carter," she continued calmly, "I cannot be worse off than I am now. If I sink, the ranch will sink with me. If I make it, it will be a feather in my cap." She made it clear, with this, that there was nothing more to be said. "Now, if you would, Mr. Carter, have your man drive me back to my pasture. I must get on with my work!"

Nothing could have done more to spur Anna's resolve to succeed. She walked out of Carter's office with her head high and her eyes flashing, her boot heels clicking a determined staccato on the wooden office floor. From that day on she worked even harder, taking charge not only of her ranch and its finances but keeping the house in as immaculate order as if she expected important guests. Her heirloom koa furniture and fine silver were kept polished. The rooms were fragrant with fresh flowers from the garden.

"When you're poor, you can do anything!" says Anna – and she did. She had one young boy to help with the heavy chores around the yard and the sheer manual labor that had to be done each day on the ranch. When she needed extra hands to help brand or move cattle, she hired Parker Ranch cowboys for a few hours. Otherwise, Anna did everything herself, quietly and well. Among all the many other things she saw to it that there were always fresh flowers on the graves of her mother and father, and that the lawns and garden around the graves were kept mowed, weeded and trimmed.

Anna had already talked to Mr. Anderson at Bishop Trust, where she had placed the affairs of Charles' two children, about buying their interest in the ranch. Now that she was ready

Mr. Anderson was negative but Richard and Florence were so loyal to their Auntie Anna, they agreed to sell their share in the ranch to her.

As soon as Anna became the ranch's sole owner, she put up a sign at the road, where her driveway interrupted the stonewall boundary between the front lawn of the ranch house and the increasingly busy traffic on the Government Road. It was a sign whose letters were drawn to look like the rope of the cowboy lasso at which Anna was so adept. That sign read – and still reads – "Anna Ranch".

"I've never called myself a cowgirl," Anna emphasizes. "I'm a cowboy – doing a man's work on the ranch, riding and lassoing and doing all of the things a man does." This pattern which she set for herself after her father's death in 1939 was one she never abandoned. With the exception of cattle buying trips and rare vacations or even rarer periods of illness, Anna continued this as her daily routine. Her ordinary life, six days a week, was doing a man's work as a man would do it, in all kinds of weather. Not only was that work the regular riding of the range checking cattle, moving cattle, checking and mending fences, branding, selecting cattle for slaughter and buying steers from Kahua or small independent ranchers in Kohala. Anna also helped 'Killdabeef' in the slaughterhouse, leaving only when he bled the animal, since at first the sight of all that blood really bothered her. After her helper loaded the carcasses in the truck – Anna was the one who drove the rickety old truck to take the beef to market. The trip into Hilo was never an easy one – around the winding curves of the old Belt Road, through the Hilo Coast Plantations and past picturesque Onomea Arch. At best, in 1939 and 1940, taking her beef to market at Hilo Meat Company and the Hilo Hotel was a five hour trip each way.

All work and no play was not, however, Anna's obsession. She never stopped enjoying her life no matter how hard she had worked during the week. What refreshed her was dressing up, going to a party, having a good time. She was seldom without the chance to do this. She was asked everywhere in Waimea, invited to parties at Kahua Ranch where Ronald and Dorothy Von Holt were genial hosts. There were plantation parties in Honokaa and Kohala. Whenever she was in Hilo, her dear friend

Kate Koehnen would cajole her to stay in and enjoy one of the functions at the Hilo Yacht Club or Hilo Women's Club. Anna had kept up her membership in both.

There had been a period after her father's death, and her divorce, when Anna refused every invitation – including that of Eben Low to ride as Hawaii's Queen in Honolulu's Kamehameha Day parade. But at last she began to go out again. She would wear one of the outfits she had had in Hilo, drive to the party in her Buick and walk in – the elegant, well groomed, affluent-looking lady. No one could guess that she had been out as a working cowboy all day. And certainly no one suspected that she was still poor.

Fatigue was never a luxury which Anna allowed herself. Evenings at home she spent pouring over accounts, doing the book work, studying the latest information on cattle breeding and raising. As she did so, she made up her mind to pursue a new avenue of ranch business. The first chance she had, she was going to go to the Mainland and buy quality bulls to upgrade her herd. She was eager to experiment with crossing Herefords and other varieties to produce a steer that would yield more and better flavored beef. She was planning to do just this when World War II temporarily changed her life – and the lives of just about everyone in the Territory of Hawaii.

The Damn-You Girl

ON DECEMBER 6, 1941, Anna slept up at Keawewai. During the night she had such a vivid dream that she woke remembering every detail. In the dream she saw hordes of soldiers coming down the hill from the ridge above her ranch house. There were so many soldiers – and they kept coming, thousands of them. Strange thing to dream she thought as she woke on the morning of December 7th. She had no radio at Keawewai, and no telephone of course. She was all alone there, enjoying the peacefulness and beauty, and taking time for once to relax. She did not ride home until afternoon.

To Anna's surprise, back at her ranch she found one of the Parker Ranch cowboys lying on the grass beside his horse, waiting for her. The moment he saw Anna approach, he sprang to his feet. "Mr. Hartwell Carter sent me to tell you the news," he said. "The Japanese attacked Pearl Harbor this morning. Mr. Carter says things look bad. He says turn your radio on and stay by it, Miss Anna!"

Hartwell Carter, son of Parker Ranch Manager A.W. Carter, had long been one of Anna's friends and admirers. He had known she was up at Keawewai for the night. That morning, when he himself first heard the news on his radio, he was concerned that she find out what was happening as soon as possible. Having no idea just when she might leave Keawewai, Hartwell had decided the best thing to do was to send a cowboy to Anna Ranch to stay there and wait for her. Anna did as Hartwell had suggested – spent the rest of the day and evening beside her radio. Like everyone else in the islands she found it hard to believe that Hawaii had been attacked and that invasion might be imminent.

In the weeks that followed, her dream of December 6th became more and more eerily prophetic as the military swiftly moved to convert each island into defense bastions. Barbed wire barricades were laid along such remote coastlines as that between Kawaihae and the North Kohala sugar shipping port of Mahukona. Civilians in North Kohala, and in each district of the Big Island, were pressed into duty as coast watchers. The need for surveillance was urgent, for on December 30th, two small Japanese submarines surfaced along the Kohala coast and continued on around past Pololu, Waipio Valley, and the Hamakua Coast, to shell Hilo.

At Pohakuloa, on the high interior saddle between Mauna Loa and Mauna Kea, a military camp sprang up and a small airfield was bulldozed. Soldiers and supplies poured into the island, landing at either Hilo or Kawaihae. Coastal airstrips like Upolu Point in North Kohala were developed and in South Kohala quonset huts were erected along with vast tent cities. By spring, 1942, the quiet green hillsides of Waimea were transformed with military activity. Thirty thousand G.I.'s were eventually stationed on and around the pleasant upland plain that Lord Vancouver had so admired one hundred and fifty years earlier. In the village of Waimea, on the roads leading in and out of it, in the pastures, down along the coast, and on Anna Ranch – soldiers were everywhere.

One afternoon Anna came home and, looking up at the hillside above her ranch house, was startled by the sight of a group of naked soldiers around the pond under the waterfall where, long ago, her father had taught her and her two brothers how to swim. "They looked for all the world like a bunch of white leghorns running around up there!" she laughed. What happened the next day was not that funny. Anna rode into her yard, startled to find naked G.I.'s lounging around the stream right behind the ranch house. At this she called the Colonel who saw to it from then on that Anna Ranch and its pools were off limits to his men.

In the first hectic weeks following the Pearl Harbor attack, a number of men in the Japanese American community of Waimea were picked up, taken to Kilauea Military Camp at the Volcano, and questioned as to their activities. Some were released. Others were sent to mainland internment camps and kept behind barbed wire for the duration of the war. Anna was appalled at the hysteria of some in Waimea. She was relieved when the majority of Waimea's Americans of Japanese ancestry, including her friend and fellow cattleman, Yutaka Kimura, remained in the village.

Waimea was bulging under the impact of so many G.I.'s. Business was good for the community's vegetable farmers, and those who had bus or taxi services. Ranchers like Anna could now market every pound of their beef but the problem was that meat prices were controlled by the military government. Profits were hard to come by, especially when Anna faced rising costs. 'Killdabeef' wanted so much for his butchering services that in desperation Anna decided to take on that job herself. When she told him what she had decided 'Killdabeef' said, "Miss Anna, you can't do it!" He reminded her how she always had to hide when he bled an animal.

"If I can't pay you I have to do it!" said Anna. To receive a butcher's license from the Board of Health was no easy process, and a most unusual one for a woman to pursue. Anna did it! Her butcher's license remains her pride. "I was one of the first lady butchers in the islands!" From then on, every other week, her young helper Bruce Beerman would stun the steers with a blow to the forehead, after which Anna did every step of the slaughtering herself. 'Killdabeef' had been slitting her hides. Anna took care to handle the carcasses so that the hides were in perfect condition. The blood ceased to bother her. With as much equanimity as she handled a lasso on the range, a race horse on the track, or a delicate piece of cutwork or embroidery, Anna degutted the animal, skinned it, and got the carcass ready for Bruce to either hang or load in the truck for her trip to Hilo.

Because she didn't like a slaughterhouse to look like one, Anna had the exterior of that building whitewashed, bordered with plants, and kept as immaculately clean as she kept the ranch house. She had no problem marketing her beef. Some she sent to a Honolulu company who sold to the military, but Hilo Meat Company – which had stood by her in the difficult days after her father's death – was her primary customer.

One day Dick Devine, who was manager of Herbert Shipman's Hilo Meat Company, called Anna on the telephone. "We just have to have some beef, Anna," he begged. "We're down to no supply. Can you help us?"

Anna did. It took much adroit maneuvering of steers, and consignment of beef to Hilo Meat Company rather than to the Honolulu firm that expected her shipment – but she herself made the run to Hilo with a truckload of carcasses for Hilo Meat Company. She saved our business that time!" Dick Devine recollects. "Anna is something when it comes to being loyal to her friends!"

With the influx of GI's, the social life of Hilo, Waimea, Kohala and many other Big Island communities changed. The nightly blackout made evening parties impossible. Tea dances in the late afternoon were the great thing. Anna was invited to afternoon parties at the old Kohala Social Club where officers had their tea dances as well as to similar dances held at the Honokaa Club and at Hilo Yacht Club. Waimea's Kahilu Theatre was the site of the USO where servicemen were entertained with dances, movies, coffee and refreshments, and were able to make friends with volunteers from the community. Anna was active in Red Cross at the time too.

She was reluctant to let it be known that she was single, a divorcee, and living alone at the ranch. From the beginning, as the military moved into the region, she encountered all kinds of attempts from soldiers trying to get acquainted with her. She would be riding along the government road, herding cattle, when a jeep would stop and call out to her such strange questions as "Which way is Waimea?" – when she knew they had just driven up from the village. Often, G.I.'s would meet her up on the range, and ask questions like, "Where is the dump?"

"Dump?" Anna laughs. "They knew and I knew that they were just asking any old question to start a conversation. But I never let on that I knew what they were up to!"

As in her schoolgirl days at the Priory, when she was the focus of so many would-be swains, once again Anna was the recipient of boxes of candy, notes, and flowers delivered to the ranch. Officers whom she met at the tea dances kept telephoning her. "If you will go out with me, just once, they'll think you are my date and they won't pester you!" promised the Colonel, an older man whom Anna knew she could trust. And as he had told her, once she was seen being escorted by him, the junior officers ceased to telephone her.

Although she tried to be generous with her time as a Red Cross volunteer and other wartime community activities, Anna concentrated on getting and keeping her ranch on the profit side of the ledger. She personally chose the steers she bought from Kahua with her bank loans. Kahua's cowboys, watching how and what she chose to buy, kept exclaiming, *"Ma kau kau! Ma kau kau!"* – "She really knows what she's doing!"

Gone was Anna's childhood concern for a steer with a 'pretty face'. She had learned the importance of conformation from her father, and it was with a shrewd cattleman's eye that she judged which steers would have top potential for future marketing. Each of these transactions put her closer to financial solvency. It had taken her just two years to pay off all her debts and begin to build up her herd. Her first priority – keeping up the payments due on her note to Parker Ranch – had been met, always on time. Sakuichi Sakai, a North Kohala accountant and businessman who was the only American of Japanese ancestry to hold political office (as Hawaii County supervisor) during the war years, was Anna's friend and trusted advisor. He confirmed her intuition that the one person who would not make life any easier for her was A.W. Carter. "He would prefer you weren't able to keep up your payments on his note," Sakuichi agreed.

Carter made just one more try to harass Anna. This happened one day when she was bringing a bunch of steers she had purchased from Kahua to put in one of her Waimea pastures. She and her helper were driving the cattle along the stream behind the village when four Parker Ranch cowboys rode up and accosted her. "Where you been getting these steers?" they wanted to know.

The way they asked, and the very fact that they asked,

aroused Anna's indignation. The cowboy who accosted her was her father's cousin Albert Lindsey. Anna suspected who had sent them!

The question they asked was not one she would answer without personally confronting their big boss, A.W. Carter.

Immediately, Anna and her helper put the steers into a nearby paddock. She left her man with the cattle and rode off into the village. She had her spurs on, and when she dismounted and tied her horse to the hitching post at Parker Ranch headquarters, she did not bother to remove those spurs from her boots. Frank Murray, head bookkeeper in the Parker Ranch Office at the time, remarked, "When I heard those spurs, I could hear William Lindsey coming!"

In his office, Anna angrily faced A.W. Carter. "Did you send four cowboys to see whose cattle I was herding?" she demanded.

He countered with the question his cowboys had asked. "Whose cattle are they, Anna?"

The insinuation in his voice and manner made Anna still more furious. "Send somebody to see whose brand is on them!" she answered.

"No. You tell me!" Mr. Carter's voice was less strident with this demand.

"No!" countered Anna. "You send somebody!"

He stared at her. Anna stared right back at him.

"I'll send Joe Pacheco," he agreed.

"That's right. Send an enemy!" Anna countered, for Joe Pacheco's wife was one of the many Lindseys who had supported Bill Lindsey's case against Anna and her mother after her father's death.

When he rode up to the paddock, Joe Pacheco took a long time studying the brand on each steer, so long that Anna finally said, "What are trying to do – put a 'P' on that 'K'?"

The big white Parker Ranch manager's home was along the Government road, the next place towards the village from Anna's spacious ranch house. Anna was well aware of her neighbor's habits. By now, he would have gone home from the office. She rode there, galloping far ahead of Joe Pacheco. At A.W.'s house, she rang the doorbell. Then, without waiting for an answer, she opened the door and strode inside. Booted and spurred, she tracked across Carter's fine lauhala mats. "Mr. Carter!" she announced. "They are Kahua cattle I'm moving, cattle I've just bought from Kahua Ranch and am putting in one of my pastures. Your man is on his way to tell you so – but he took a long time looking, trying to find some way to put a 'P' on that 'K'!" She stalked out of the house, spurs jingling, mounted her horse and rode back to finish moving her cattle out of the paddock and into her pasture before sundown. It was the last time A.W. Carter ever chose to take on Anna Lindsey.

During the first two years of the war, Anna put every spare dollar into war bonds. This was not only patriotic, it was prudent good business. By 1943 the value of her bonds reached exactly the amount she needed to pay off the balance of the Parker Ranch note. With enormous relief, Anna cashed the bonds and brought her check to Parker Ranch office where she received the cancelled note and receipt of payment. At once she flew to Honolulu to tell A.W. Carter what she had done. He was no longer well, seldom in Waimea any more. From Honolulu airport, Anna went directly to his downtown office. She was, as usual, dressed for the occasion, stylishly turned out in a smart white dress, red shoes and handbag, white gloves and a pert red hat.

Mr. Carter's longtime secretary, Lucille Brundage, ushered Anna into his private office. There Anna took the receipt and cancelled note from her purse to show him. "I wanted to tell you in person, Mr. Carter. There's a feather in my cap now! I have just paid off the nineteen thousand dollar note. Parker Ranch no longer has any claim on my place!"

For a moment A.W. Carter was speechless. Then he pounded the desk with his fists. "How did you manage to do that?"

"Hard work and determination. And faith!" Anna replied. She knew she looked cool and collected, but inside she was trembling with the awesome relief of having been able to pay off this debt. The ranch was indeed now hers – and she had staved off such a formidable opponent as this man!

A.W. tried one last time to get at her. "You still owe us for back taxes on your grandfather's place – the T.W. Lindsey estate!"

"No I don't!" said Anna. "I've always paid my share of those taxes and I have proof of my payments." She was grateful to

Sakuichi Sakai, who had also been her father's tax accountant, for keeping her aware of that necessity.

A.W. shifted his cigar from one side of his mouth to the other. He looked both baffled and angry. "How did you do it!" he repeated.

Without deigning to answer him Anna simply smiled, nodded goodbye, and left his office. Outside, Lucille Brundage led her down the hall into a private room. She closed the door. "Good for you, Anna!" said the secretary. "No one has ever stood up to A.W. Carter like you have. No one has ever talked to him like you have. You have spunk!" Miss Brundage took out a handkerchief and handed it to Anna. "Now, cry!" she said. "It's okay now!"

And cry Anna did, letting out all the tensions of those years of knowing A.W. Carter was so eager to take over her ranch and the great relief of knowing she would never have to live with that worry again.

It was an elated Anna who flew back home to Waimea where, for one Army officer, she was not only a beautiful escort and a fantastic horsewoman – she was the 'damn-you girl'.

With military traffic heavy on the government road, and the military making new dirt roads all over the Kohala slopes and coastline, herding cattle from Keawewai to other areas of her ranch was sometimes difficult for Anna. Usually the military vehicles would pull off the side when they saw cattle being herded down over a narrow place in the winding mountain road. But one day, as Anna and a helper were driving cattle down the road, a convoy of jeeps and trucks just kept coming. The frightened steers were ready to stampede. If they did, Anna knew it would take an extra day to round them up again.

She rode up to the officer in the lead jeep and yelled at him. "Get off the road!"

He didn't even slow down.

"Damn you!" shouted Anna. "Get off the road!"

The officer looked at her in astonishment. A woman swearing at him? But it worked! He stopped the jeep, motioned the convoy to pull over while Anna herded her cattle on by.

The next afternoon Anna happened to be invited to attend a tea dance at the Hilo Yacht Club. She came in from her ranch

Irma Bryan and Anna with jacaranda lei for Hilo tree planting ceremony, 1920's.

FIRST PRIZE PA-U RIDERS

June 11, 1930 – July 4, 1930

MAMALAHOA LODGE   ORDER OF KAMEHAMEHA

Anna wins first prize as *pa'u* rider in Hilo, 1930.

Newlyweds Irma and Bill Bryan, 1923.

Anna riding the famous Maui Parrot, a.k.a. Kaala.

The jockey who bet on herself– Anna and racing trophies.

Anna on Parker Ranch thoroughbred she trained for racing. Hilo, 1920's.

Trophy Room, Anna Ranch. Souvenirs of Anna's many triumphs.

Unknown woman, Emma Saiki, and Anna with movie star Buster Crabbe on mainland prize trip, 1932.

Anna as a young matron, active in Hilo Women's Club.

Lyman and Anna on their wedding day, September 1943.

work early, bathed, dressed in one of her loveliest afternoon frocks, put on a stylish hat, and drove in to enjoy the dance. Her tiny feet and shapely ankles were set off by the latest fashion in high-heeled shoes. When she arrived at the Hilo Yacht Club, to her dismay she saw the very same officer whom she had had to swear at before he would pull over to let her drive her cattle on by. "He'll never recognize me!" she thought.

It was not long before the officer came up and asked her to dance. He kept staring at her as they whirled around the dance floor. "I never forget a beautiful woman like you!" he told her. "I know I've seen you before. Weren't you the one who swore at me up on the mountain road in Kohala yesterday?"

Anna looked him straight in the eye and with an impish smile told him "Oh, that must have been my sister. She's a wild one. She uses terrible language sometimes!"

"Hmmmmm," said the officer. Anna could see that he didn't know whether to believe her or not. He kept coming back to dance with her, and each time he kept gazing at her in a quizzical way. Finally, at the end of the afternoon he said, "Anna! You *are* the 'damn you' girl! I know you are!"

That was the beginning of a long friendship for Anna. Captain Davis was an ardent horseman himself. Each time he had a free day he came over to go riding with her. He also went to church with Anna. When he was transferred to the Volcano District's Kilauea Military Camp, Captain Davis still made the long drive by jeep on his day off to go riding with Anna for even one short hour.

The colonel who had originally helped Anna stave off the onslaught of military admirers had also become her close friend. He knew she had a regular schedule for trucking the beef she slaughtered into Hilo. On one of these scheduled days, with Dick Devine of Hilo Meat Company depending on her prompt delivery of beef to him, Anna found out that the belt road to Hilo was closed because of a terrible rainstorm at Laupahoehoe. Runoff flooding down the steep hillsides above that portion of the highway made it impassable. Anna was determined to get her shipment of beef to Hilo by taking it the long way around the island, from Waimea to Kona, over the long lonely route around South Point and Ka'u, and through Volcano down into Hilo.

Via that route to get to Hilo for a late morning delivery, she would have to leave Waimea in the middle of the night. This meant several hours of extremely dangerous travel in blackout conditions. Somehow her friend the colonel heard of Anna's plans. Late that afternoon he telephoned her to say, "I'm assigning a soldier to escort you to Hilo. It's no trip for you to take alone!"

Sure enough, that night as Anna prepared to leave, a soldier arrived. He sat in the front seat of the truck at first, but when they reached the Kona road he had Anna stop. He got out and crouched on the front fender of the truck, calling out which way she should steer to stay on the road until the first dim gray pre-dawn light made it possible to begin to see the turns and twists that lay ahead.

At noon, after she had delivered her carcasses to Hilo Meat Company, Anna took the soldier to lunch at the Hilo Hotel. Everyone there kept telling her that the weather was bad between Hilo and Laupahoehoe. Continuing heavy rains. The road was still under water. After lunch Anna stopped at the police station to check these rumours. If possible, she didn't want to make the long drive back through Ka'u and Kona to get home.

"The road is open at Laupahoehoe, but it's really bad," the police told her. "Water is still running across the road, so you have to drive across the worst place on planks."

Anna decided to risk it. At Laupahoehoe she found the police had been correct in calling the situation 'really bad'. At one of the deepest gulches near Laupahoehoe, where mudslides and torrents of run-off often accompany bad storms, the water still rushed hub-cap deep across the road. County workers were trying to clear the way of boulders that kept rattling down with the runoff. As the police had warned, the risky way through was across a flimsy set of planks that had been put down to try to bridge the flooded area.

"We can make it!" Anna reassured her soldier escort. Without hesitation, she drove the truck on over those tricky planks, mud and water flying up in all directions. As she reached the far side of the stream, she heard a county worker yell in disbelief to his friend. "That's a *wahine* – a woman – drove the truck through there!"

Lyman

PERRY-FISKE IS an unusual name – one of a kind in Hawaii and elsewhere. Lyman Perry-Fiske, the man who became Anna's second husband was himself a unique person with whom Anna spent thirty-four years. He was older than Anna, a handsome, vigorous man, a keen horseman who loved the outdoors, but who also had a quiet, bookish and sometimes moody side. For much of his life, he suffered increasingly severe asthma attacks. He had a temper that could ignite for no apparent reason at all, but he also had a charm that made him most personable. "Lyman always liked to dress like a cowboy!" Brother Low reminisced many years later.

Like Anna, Lyman loved the Kohala Mountain country. He had been born and raised in one of the most beautiful, and inaccessible plateaus on the windward side of North Kohala at Awini, where his parents established the Awini Land and Coffee Company. Lyman had left Kohala by the time he was twenty. At fifty, he told Anna he was ready to retire from his position as engineer with the City and County of Honolulu and return to the Big Island to live – with her.

Lyman was just one of the many suitors making proposals to Anna at this time in her life. She made it clear in refusing each of them that she was not going to consider marrying again until her goals of financial independence and success on her ranch were achieved. This did not dissuade Lyman Perry-Fiske. He kept proposing – in person, and by mail.

Anna's cousin Edwin Lindsey, principal of Waimea School, was Lyman's close friend. It was he who first brought Lyman to call on Anna and her mother. There was a twenty-five year difference in Lyman's and Anna's recollection of when that first visit occurred. Lyman always insisted he came to the house with Edwin Lindsey when Anna was only sixteen. He said he remembered Anna as a young girl sitting in the parlor embroidering something for her hope chest – as was the custom in that era. "If he did call on us then, I don't remember it at all!" says Anna.

It was during the year following her father's death that Anna remembers Lyman's first visit having taken place. Lyman often flew over to stay with Edwin Lindsey that year, but after the initial call, when Edwin introduced him to Anna, Lyman came to the ranch house by himself. Anna's mother liked him. "Lyman is from a fine family!" she told Anna.

At one time North Kohala was called the English Coast because so many Englishmen had settled there. One of them was Lyman Perry's father, who in partnership with Walter Rodenhurst – a transplanted Welshman – operated the Awini Land and Coffee Company on a high plateau above the third valley towards Waipio from Pololu. The only way in – or out – for people and supplies, or for produce, was on the foot and mule path now known as the Kohala Ditch Trail. At the turn of the century it was a government trail, in essence a public highway. From the end of the government road in Niulii, the trail, which went on past Awini to even more remote valleys, began as a series of narrow steep switchbacks down into Pololu Valley where, until about 1910, Chinese farmers were growing rice. At the far side of Pololu, even steeper and more precipitous switchbacks climbed up the ridge above the next valley, Honokane-iki, and finally on to Awini and the Perry's acreage.

Lyman's mother, who was a Hawaiian from Makapala, sometimes took her eight children there to stay during the heavy rains that made the trail from Awini impassable. Otherwise, Lyman and his three brothers and four sisters walked the four miles from Awini to the government school at Niulii. The Perry's had a spacious home on their remote plateau. "It was," recalls Walter Rodenhurst's son Tommy, "a grand place!"

Water is the great treasure of the Kohala Mountains. Honokane stream is a headwater spilling the summits' five hundred inches of annual rainfall down into the sea in spectacular waterfalls and subsidiary run-off streams, giving ample moisture to the rich soil of Awini plateau. The Perry's found their location and climate ideal for growing citrus fruit. Walter Rodenhurst, their partner who was roadmaster for the Hawaiian Railroad Company's line from Niulii to the sugar shipping port of Mahukona, planted the coffee orchards at Awini. Together, Rodenhurst and Perry planted the cypress trees that today are the only marker of the site where the house in which Lyman was raised once stood.

Lyman was, essentially, a self-made man. In 1905, Hawi plantation owner John Hind, Waimea's Sam Parker and J.T. McCrosson obtained water rights to Honokane stream, Awini, and adjacent areas. They formed the Kohala Ditch Company to take irrigation water to Kohala's five sugar plantations. Mr. Perry was hired as manager of Kohala Ditch Company. Lyman, then only 13, left school to become supervisor of a group of the Japanese laborers who were doing the dangerous and difficult job of building 20 miles of irrigation tunnels and ditches. By June 1906 this system was carrying 20 million gallons of fresh water a day to cane fields that had previously suffered from Kohala's erratic rainfall.

Lyman's brother Richard (who died young) and his brother Al Kealoha Perry, who became a well known island musician, both were sent to Punahou to complete their education but Lyman's formal education ended when he went to work for the Ditch Company. He was determined however, to continue his education on his own. Studying every night by kerosene lamp, Lyman diligently made his way through all the courses he would need to fulfill his ambition of becoming an engineer. At 16 he was hired as a *luna*, a plantation supervisor, by George Watt, manager of Kohala Sugar Company. In his new job Lyman rode horseback through the fields, supervising Japanese women *hoe hana* laborers whose job was to hand cultivate the young cane.

Lyman would work a ten or twelve hour day and then study all evening. Despite his asthma he had energy and determination in abundance in those early years. Since he was a bright as well as a self-directed young man, he achieved his goal. He took and passed the territorial licensing exams for civil engineering. When his certificate arrived, it was a red letter day in his life. Lyman moved to Honolulu to start his new career.

A strange coincidence which Mary Lindsey recalled when Lyman came to the ranch with Edwin Lindsey was that when Anna had been a patient at Queen's Hospital in Honolulu during her school days at the Priory, a Mr. Perry from North Kohala was the patient in the room across the hall from hers. That happened to have been Lyman's father. What Mary Lindsey did not tell Lyman, but reminded Anna after Lyman and Edwin left that day was that in those longago days at Queen's Hospital she had seen Lyman pass by and pointed him out to Anna as a very handsome young man. She remembered teasing her daughter by saying, "Look! There's a good boyfriend for you, Sister!" At her mother's recollection, Anna shook her head and laughed. Neither she nor Mary Lindsey ever dreamed that Lyman Perry would one day be part of Anna's life.

During the months before Mary Lindsey died, Lyman made a number of visits to the ranch. Each time he came to call on them he enthralled Anna and her mother with his tales of adventures he'd had on his early engineering jobs in the Far East. Through Judge Heen Lyman had had a chance to go to China to work. From China, he had gone on into Tibet where the Buddhism he encountered much attracted him. Lyman entered a Tibetan monastery, and began studying under a lama. He would, he often told Anna later, have probably stayed on for years but, after six months, the Abbot called him in. "Lyman, you must leave for Hawaii at once!"

"But I wish to continue my studies here. Am I not doing well?" Lyman protested.

It was, the Abbot informed him, not a question of how he was progressing in his studies. "Your father is ill," Lyman was told. "If you leave Tibet now, you will reach Hawaii in time to see him before he dies."

Because Lyman respected the extraordinary powers of perception he had seen demonstrated by the Tibetan monks, he never questioned as to how – in far away Tibet – the Abbot could know what conditions were in Hawaii. Without further protest he prepared to leave the lamasery and start the long journey home. It was several months before he could reach Hawaii. Two weeks later, across the hall from the room at Queen's Hospital where Anna lay convalescing from her appendectomy, Lyman's father died.

It was then that Lyman Perry became an engineer for the City and County of Honolulu, but it was not long before circumstances led him to change his name to Lyman Perry-Fiske. His nephew, James Lyman Perry, had the unfortunate habit of signing 'Lyman Perry' on bad checks. Each time this happened, Lyman had to go to police headquarters to prove he was not *that* Lyman Perry. Then, one day a policeman came to Lyman's desk in the engineering department at City Hall. "You're Lyman Perry?"

Lyman nodded, wearily expecting trouble over another of his nephew's bad checks. But this time was different – and this time, for Lyman, was the last straw. To his surprise the policeman did not take Lyman to headquarters, but to the maternity ward of a hospital. In one of the beds was a young Hawaiian girl who had just given birth to a child.

"Well," the policeman said to her. "Here's your Lyman Perry that you said was the father of your baby!"

"That's not *my* Lyman Perry!" the girl replied.

Knowing that it was his nephew who had again used his name when he got the girl in trouble, Lyman decided he must put a stop to such incidents. His paternal grandmother's maiden name had been Fiske and so, legally, he changed his name to Lyman Perry-Fiske – the name he carried when he came to call on Anna and her mother in 1939.

Anna was pleased when, on one of Lyman's visits that year, he asked if he might ride up to Keawewai with her. They had a grand time, for Lyman could be utterly charming. When Mary Lindsey died, Lyman flew over to attend the funeral. Anna was much touched by this, and by his concern that she was working too hard. Aware that she was carrying the heavy burden of ranch work by herself, Lyman offered to help by sending over his young nephew, Bruce Beerman, the step-son of Lyman's sister Violet. Bruce was 16 years old, a big strong boy but, when he arrived, totally ignorant of the chores to be done on a ranch.

Anna soon trained him to do everything she needed a helper to do – including to ride a horse!

Bruce was a pleasant boy who always called his Uncle Lyman's friend 'Miss Anna'. From her, he learned how to stun steers with a blow to their forehead as the first step in the slaughtering process. Anna much appreciated having Bruce on the ranch. About the same time, she accepted as her charge a Hawaiian boy who was a ward of the court. As had her mother, who was always helping Hawaiian girls who had been made wards of the court, Anna had a full measure of Hawaiian compassion. She even displayed this towards her brother Bill, who had given her such a bad time over their father's estate.

When Bill fell on hard times, Anna bought lumber from the Army and built a house on the ranch where he and his family lived rent-free. Bill Lindsey had unsuccessfully applied for Hawaiian Homes land but was refused, since he was only one-eighth Hawaiian. Bill Lindsey looked more British and German with his light hair, fair complexion and blue eyes.

Having help with the heavy physical work on the ranch did not alter Anna's pattern of continuing to work hard herself. With little or no payroll to meet, she was able to keep her overhead at a minimum and profits a maximum. The cost of this success strategy was her own strength and health. In the summer of 1943 her doctor insisted Anna needed a vacation – at least a month away from the ranch and her saddle. Just before this, Anna had consented to become engaged to Lyman. She was, however, loathe as yet to set a wedding date.

When Lyman heard what the doctor had told her, he offered to come and look after the ranch while she took a vacation. It was an offer she accepted with gratitude and relief for she too knew that she needed to get away. She spent a relaxing month in one of the lovely seaside cottages of the old Halekulani Hotel in Waikiki. It was her first vacation in years. Every day she would call Lyman, check on the ranch and tell him what needed to be attended to. At the end of the month she told him she was ready to come home – that he could leave now.

"No, I'm going to stay right here!" Lyman announced. "I'm not leaving. I'm retired now, remember?"

Anna did not know what to say. How could she move back

into her ranch house with Lyman there? The fact that they were by now engaged made no difference to her. She had an impeccable reputation and Lyman knew it. What a way to try to force her into marrying him! Distraught, not knowing quite what to do, Anna flew from Honolulu into Hilo. From the airport she called her dear friend Kate Koehnen, seeking advice – and perhaps wanting more than anything else to hear what her heart would direct her to do. She was near tears as she told Kate of Lyman's announcing he did not intend to leave the ranch.

"It's his way of having you set a wedding date!" guessed Kate Koehnen.

"I don't think I'm ready to–" said Anna.

"You've always said you would wait to marry until you were financially independent and had made a go of the ranch. Well, you have done that, haven't you, Anna? And you did decide to become engaged–" Kate reminded her.

Anna realized Kate was right. Her decision had already been made – and she herself had made it! "You're right, Kate!" she exclaimed. Then she burst out with a statement she hadn't realized she was ready to make. "That's why I'm thinking of going ahead and marrying Lyman now!"

"Where will you have the wedding?" Kate asked.

This had not been anything Anna had as yet thought through. "I suppose we'll just go to Rev. Desha and have him do it. I can't have a Catholic wedding since I'm divorced."

"Let me have the wedding here!" urged Kate. "We'll make it a beautiful one, Anna. I'm coming down to the airport and pick you up. You are staying with us until your wedding!"

So, in Hilo, Anna stayed with her friends, shopped for a pretty wedding dress and hat, and made plans with Lyman via telephone. He kept assuring her they would be pleasant companions in life, that he wanted to be someone she could lean on when she needed. Lyman was now fifty-one, ready – he told her – to just enjoy life with her. Over the years he had acquired several good properties, among them the drydock at Keauhou Bay in Kona. Managing his own affairs would keep him busy enough.

From all this it seemed to Anna that Lyman understood her need for space and independence, that he appreciated her determination to continue to be a self-reliant, self-directed business woman, cattle breeder, ranch manager and cowboy. She in turn was resolved to create a pleasant home life for him. Both anticipated enjoying the parties and entertaining that were a large part of Anna's relaxation.

The date set for the wedding was September 25, 1943. Hartwell Carter, one of the few guests invited, sent in a carload of roses to decorate the Koehnen's beautiful home in Hilo. Lyman's brother Al Kealoha Perry (of the famous oldtime radio program 'Hawaii Calls') and Al's wife, Kathleen McGuire Perry, flew to Hilo to stand up with Anna and Lyman as their witnesses. A Protestant clergyman, the Rev. Stephen L. Desha of Hilo, performed the ceremony. Afterward, Anna and Lyman drove to the Volcano House for a two day honeymoon.

From now on Anna had a new, and even busier routine. She was up well before daybreak every morning, put the house in order, and cooked Lyman an ample breakfast which she served – as she did every meal – on her finest china. Afterwards, unless his asthma was bothering him, she and Lyman would ride out together to do whatever Anna decided needed to be done on the ranch that day. Sometimes it was herding cattle from one pasture to another. Sometimes the job to be done was mending fences or setting new fence posts. Often it was to check water supplies and salt licks and to observe how frisky and interested her bulls seemed in the cows with whom Anna had them pastured.

In the evening they would return home in time to bathe and change. Anna would cook dinner. She was always hoping Lyman would notice the way in which she set a formal table just for the two of them. Some nights she would use her Canton china. Other nights the table would be set with one of her services of fine English chinaware. They used her best silver for every meal, and linen or damask napkins. "Lyman never seemed to notice these niceties!" Anna sighs.

Evenings, while she worked on the ranch books or studied her cattleman's journals, Lyman would read. He loved books. He also kept up a voluminous correspondence. Weekends were times for socializing. The Perry-Fiskes were invited everywhere, as Anna had always been invited to parties and dinners in

Waimea, Kohala, Hilo and Honokaa. In turn, Anna continued her mother's tradition as a frequent hostess whose table setting was always exquisite and hospitality unfailingly generous. This second marriage had made Anna legally Mrs. Perry-Fiske, but essentially she was still Anna Lindsey, now taking care of Lyman as well as of herself and her ranch, managing her affairs as an independent, energetic, untiring boss.

There was one lack both she and Lyman felt in their lives. Like Anna, in his first marriage – which had also ended in divorce – Lyman had been childless. The Hawaiian custom of *hanai* – adopting a child – appealed to both of them. Early in their marriage, through the tragic death of Anna's niece Vivian Lindsey, that chance came. They were, however, to wait several years before their *hanai* son Weston came home to live with them.

Cattle Buyer and Candidate

NO ONE APPRECIATED Anna's ability as a buyer, breeder and raiser of fine cattle more than her longtime friend and fellow Waimean, Yutaka Kimura. A Hawaii-born *nisei* (second generation descendant of immigrants from Japan), Yutaka Kimura is a jovial, handsome Parker Ranch retiree with an international reputation as a cattle-raising consultant. He is widely known in Japan as the 'King' of Kagoshima because of his expert cattleman's advice to lessees ranching government acreage there. He is also recognized as an expert in cattle breeding and cattle raising in Australia, where he has frequently been called as a consultant by prospective ranch buyers. Like Anna, Yutaka grew up on the back of a horse, riding the green hills of Waimea and learning the cattle business at a very young age. Also like Anna, who insisted it be told here, Yutaka Kimura's life story is vintage Hawaiiana, and insight into the background and contributions of the large Japanese American community of Waimea.

The mainstream of Japanese immigration to Hawaii began in 1885, but not until 1898 did Yutaka Kimura's father leave Hiroshima to come to Hawaii as a contract laborer. He first worked in the cane fields on John Hind's Hoea Plantation in North Kohala. With the completion of that three year period, he worked for a time as John Hind's buggy driver. Early in the new century he shifted to Kona's Puuwaawaa Ranch to work at pasture clearing for Robert Hind. It was while he was at Puuwaawaa Ranch that Mr. Kimura wed a girl who had come as a picture bride from a village near his own in Hiroshima. Unhappy with her initial husband in Hawaii, the girl left him to marry Mr. Kimura. Their first son was born at Puuwaawaa in 1903. Two years later, in 1905, their second son, Yutaka, was born on that same ranch – a pleasant upper elevation area midway between Waimea and the Kona village of Kailua.

When Yutaka was four years old the family moved to Waimea so that his big brother could go to school. Yutaka's father was considered a rich man at that time, for he had saved what was then the large sum of $700. With some of this capital, the family leased farmland. They had high hopes of succeeding as independent farmers, a dream later immigrants did achieve. Unfortunately the acreage in which they had invested proved too small to be profitable. Mr. Kimura used the remainder of his savings to lease another, larger farm – a decision which resulted in hard times for the family. Within a few years they were deeply in debt. They owed $900 to I. Oda store for the necessities they could not raise or make themselves. No amount of hard work altered their desperate situation. Year by year the amount of their indebtedness grew beyond their ability to pay. The result was that Yutaka was able to complete only the sixth grade before he went to work to help out his family.

A.W. Carter had had his eye on Yutaka Kimura as a bright, dependable young boy. In those days, school leaving age was legally set at 15. However, when Yutaka was just 13, Carter gave an ultimatum to Miss Taylor, the school superintendent in charge of Waimea school. "You let this boy out of school or else!" Carter demanded. "I am hiring him!" And so it was that at 13 Yutaka Kimura went to work up in the mountains for Parker Ranch.

He saved his money and over the next three years managed to pay off $600 of the $900 which his father owed I. Oda store. With two thirds of the debt now paid off, Yutaka begged Mr. Carter to allow him to go back and finish school. He was sixteen, and more than anything else at the time he yearned to be able to continue his studies. "You'll get a better education working for me!" Carter told him. That refusal ended the matter, Yutaka knew. He did not ask again, though he yearned for years to have been able to complete his elementary school education and go on to Hilo, to the Big Island's only high school. In the Japanese immigrant family tradition, it was his older brother who was having that chance. There was no resentment in Yutaka about this. It was how things were, and he was grateful that at least his brother had the opportunity to finish school.

When his brother was about to graduate from Hilo High, Yutaka went to Mr. Carter to try to borrow $50 to buy a suit for his brother to wear at graduation. "How come you need to borrow? You've been working a long time now. What are you doing with your wages?" Carter asked. When Yutaka told him, this gruff Parker Ranch manager made a kindly suggestion. Why didn't the Kimuras sell their farm leases and – since Yutaka's father was an experienced ranch hand – Carter would hire him as a ranch foreman. The job would entitle the family to a free Parker Ranch house, along with wages and such perquisites as free beef, milk, and poi.

This arrangement brought Yutaka's family out of debt at last, for the amount from the sale of their lease was enough to complete repayment of their indebtedness to I. Oda Store. The improvement in the family's finances was too late for Yutaka to change his career. However, true to his word, A.W. Carter was giving him a very special kind of education. Yutaka's job was to replace the cattle on Parker Ranch with purebreds through a systematic program of breeding. By the 1930's, thanks largely to Yutaka Kimura's expertise, Parker Ranch had the largest number of purebred Herefords in the world.

During the years that William Lindsey was assistant manager of Parker Ranch, Yutaka Kimura worked closely with Anna's father. "In those days," Yutaka likes to reminisce, "horse racing was a big thing in Waimea. The government road was the race track – a quarter-mile length ending at the old Fukushima Store. That was before Richard Smart built a race track out near the airport. And in the old days, there was always lots of betting at Waimea horse races. The police would come around to try to stop it, but they had no luck. For a girl to race then was really unusual. All the boys and girls in Waimea rode horses but of all the girls, Anna was the only one who raced. She was always on a fast horse. And she usually won! She's a terrific rider. No matter how wild the horse is, Anna can handle it!"

In the 1950's Yutaka Kimura was one of the rare people who supported Anna against the many critics who scoffed at her having bought prize bulls from the Mainland to upgrade her herd. "She knows what she's doing! She's way ahead of you people!" Yutaka always said when other ranchers criticized Anna's crossbreeding that she began once the war was over and she had accumulated the necessary cash to buy the very best bulls. Her years of studying cattleman's journals, reading up on all the exciting new options in the cattle raising industry, had long since convinced Anna she should try out her own unique ideas. She kept her plans to herself, waiting until she had begun her experiments in cross breeding before she let Yutaka or anyone else know what she was doing. It took her a while, but Anna was patient when she had to be. In business she knew that both patience and keeping her plans to herself would pay off.

By 1946, with the war over, shipping between Hawaii and west coast Mainland ports was again open to civilian use. It was that year, 1946, when Anna became a cattle-buyer – another new business activity for her, a most unusual one for a woman, and one at which Anna made money. She knew that the kind of champion bulls she wanted would cost a great deal more than she had available in ready cash. She could have easily borrowed the money, but a better, no-cost way occurred to her.

She became a cattle buyer for the Oahu dairymen who had not been able to replenish their herds since the start of the war. Through her old friend, Honolulu realtor Tom McCormack, Anna got in touch with Alfred Vierra, head of one of Honolulu's Savings and Loan Associations. Vierra was Anna's contact with the dairymen who had neither the time nor the expertise to go to Seattle and pick out the best milking cows to import. With her knowledge of cattle, Anna knew she could do well for them as a cattle buyer. And with the money she made on this venture, she would have enough after a few such trips to buy a prize bull. For the short while she would be gone, she could depend on Lyman to look after the ranch. On her first cattle buying trip in 1946 Anna began her practise of taking along two Waimea cowboys who could tend the cattle for her on the freighter trip back to Hawaii. From Seattle, Matson had no freighter run where passengers could be accommodated and until she began buying bulls in the Los Angeles area around Blythe and Holtville, she was not permitted to ride on the same vessel with the cattle she was shipping.

On each of her three trips to Seattle to buy dairy cattle from Carnation Farms, Anna hired two different cowboys so that as many as possible from Waimea were able, through her, to have their first experience of the mainland. She paid their plane fare to the coast, put them up in a hotel and took them sightseeing. For herself, Anna preferred the relaxation of going over by ship. In Honolulu, waiting for boat day and discussing final arrangements with Vierra and the dairymen, she stayed in a suite at the Alexander Young Hotel which once stood where the handsome new Pauahi Tower thrusts into the sky in downtown Honolulu. The Young Hotel was headquarters for neighbor island executives when they came to 'town'. The suites which Anna occupied when she was in Honolulu were beautifully furnished and decorated. Sitting in the lobby of the Alexander Young, looking beautiful and vivacious in one of her designer suits with a modish hat and matching gloves and accessories, she did not in the least resemble a cattle-buyer. No one would have guessed that Anna Perry-Fiske ever did anything more strenuous than play bridge or have a manicure. When she sailed on the 'Lurline', her favorite ship, she spent the five days enjoying shipboard life. She was always seated at the captain's table, and always dressed in a different formal gown each evening.

On the return trips out of Seattle, her cowboys had a most difficult job to do. One of the freighter regulations was that any calf born during the voyage must be thrown overboard as soon as it was delivered. This was difficult for tender-hearted Anna to think about, and difficult for her cowboys to have to do. They hated having to toss newborn calves into the sea. "It was something that had to be done," explains Anna. "The stalls on the freighter were so narrow that if the calf wasn't taken away at once, the mother would soon trample on it and kill it anyway."

Once she had delivered the cows to the dairymen in Honolulu, and banked the payment she received, Anna would fly home to Waimea where Lyman had been taking care of the ranch in her absence. Sometimes she would be home for only two weeks before she flew back to Honolulu to get ready for the next cattle buying trip.

June of 1947 was Anna's third and last trip to Seattle to buy cattle to sell to Oahu's dairymen. By then she was ready to buy her first champion bull. She invested several thousand dollars of her cattle-buying profits in a bull that the Honolulu papers described with enthusiasm as "one of the nation's finest pedigreed Holstein-Friesian show bulls". His name was Vernway Imperial Fayne. He had an impeccably blue blood ancestry, having been sired by a bull named Carnation Imperial Madcap Lad, son of the three times All-American show bull, Carnation Governor Imperial.

On the freighter leaving Seattle for Honolulu, Anna also shipped sixty-four Holstein and Guernsey milking cows destined to be sold to the dairymen on Oahu. It was her most profitable trip so far as the milking cows were concerned. Her purchase of the bull was quite another matter, for she lost every dollar she had paid for him. The news headline, "High Pedigree Bull Coming from Seattle to Improve Big Isle Herd" was accurate in conveying Anna's intent. The news photo of her new champion bull was impressive. Vernway Imperial Fayne did well on the freighter trip, and on the Young Brothers barge trip from Honolulu to Kawaihae. Anna trucked him proudly up to her ranch where she put him in a separate paddock to rest and become used to the change from Seattle's damp cool climate to the more tropical environment of Anna Ranch.

Alas! Three weeks later, for no apparent reason, the very expensive, champion Holstein Friesian show bull died. As usual with all her hard times and difficulties, Anna took this blow with equanimity. "What has happened, has happened. Don't cry about it. Just have the faith and strength to go on!" was and is her philosophy.

Other ranchers were beginning to experiment with artificial insemination of cattle but such a technique did not interest Anna. Her conviction was that healthy young bulls, allowed to graze freely with heifers, keep a steady supply of strong, healthy calves replenishing the herd. "When a bull loses interest, I put him off in a pasture by himself for a while." says Anna. "Then when he begins eyeing heifers again, back into their pasture he goes. It's a system that builds me a strong, good quality herd."

In 1947 cattle ranching was the number three income producer in the agricultural economy of the islands. One-third of all the land in the Territory was devoted to ranches that ranged in size from Parker Ranch, now owned by Richard Smart, son of Anna's childhood friend Thelma Parker Smart, to small spreads with no more than 20 head of cattle. Island beef had become a far more profitable item since 1853 when domesticated longhorns, slaughtered, brought $2.50 a carcass. By 1947 the price of beef could bring a rancher three hundred dollars or more a slaughtered carcass, depending on the dressed weight of the animal.

Anna's ambition was to develop a new crossbreed with such superior quality, texture, and flavor that her beef would command the market's top prices and of such a size that by weight alone she would come out with a wide profit margin. The competition she knew she faced in marketing her beef only sharpened her determination to go ahead with her cross breeding experiments. Her old steady customers, Hilo Meat Company, Hilo Hotel and Volcano House and Tom Okuyama's Suresave supermarket chain would, she was sure, stick with her quality beef. Now that she had the capital to do it, Anna began researching mainland ranches that might have the kind of bulls she needed to carry out her development of a new, superior breed of cattle. Another new dimension came into Anna's life around this same time, when she and Lyman adopted the son who was to give Anna years of great joy but, eventually, the deepest hurt and anguish. The boy was the grandson of her brother Bill, with whose children Anna had maintained a close and affectionate relationship. Family had always been important to her, and she treasured her ohana ties, taking good care of the youngsters of both of her brothers, emotionally and financially.

Bill's daughter Vivian had his coloring – fair haired with blue eyes. She was a girl of whom Anna was very fond. As a teenager, Vivian was often taken on trips to Honolulu with her Aunt Anna. In 1942 Vivian married John Silva, a young police officer in Kona. Anna was delighted when the couple had a son whom they named Weston, after the Lindseys' famous British ancestor, Thomas Weston Lindsey. One afternoon when her baby was about a year old, Vivian drove to Waimea, left little Weston at her mother's home, and came to call on her Aunt Anna. There was no special reason for her visit. She just enjoyed coming to call and talking over all kinds of things, enjoying the quiet of her Aunt's spacious home.

When Vivian left that day, Anna had a sudden premonition. She knew Vivian was about to drive to Kona to pick up her husband from work – something she often did. Today, however, Anna felt uneasy about her niece's departure. "Be careful!" she urged.

From Anna Ranch, Vivian drove directly to the police station in Kona, picked up her husband, and began to drive home. On the way the two began to argue. Vivian, an impetuous and quick-tempered girl, became so angry that she stopped paying attention to the road. The car swerved, careening off the pavement and slamming into an embankment on the driver's side. John Silva was able to walk out of the car with only minor injuries to hail a passing car for help. Vivian, badly crushed, was taken by ambulance to the Kona hospital.

It was from the hospital that John Silva called Anna to tell her what had happened. Vivian, he said, was asking to see her Aunt Anna. "I'll be right there!" Anna assured him. The road from Waimea to Kona was then paved only in one lane. The hospital was far beyond the village of Kailua, up in the mauka area of Kealakekua. From Anna Ranch this would ordinarily have been a good hour and a half drive. That evening Anna made it in less than forty-five minutes. At the hospital she was shocked to see her beautiful niece – head swathed in bandages, jaw and face wired together. "Get me an eggnog!" Vivian pleaded. Anna did, and held the straw to Vivian's lips so she could drink.

"If I don't make it, Aunt Anna, will you look after my baby?" Vivian asked.

Anna wept as she made that promise. "But you'll be all right, dear!" she insisted. To Anna's sorrow, such was not to be. Next morning, at four, she received a phone call from the hospital. Vivian had just died.

At first, despite Vivian's dying wish, Weston was cared for by his grandmother, Lillian Lindsey. When Anna told the family of her promise to Vivian, and her wish to adopt the boy, John Silva agreed. "Please do!" he urged. "You'll give him more than

we would ever be able to." But for the next few years Lillian
Lindsey was loathe to give up the care of her grandson.
Compassionately, Anna understood. John Silva kept urging
Anna to go ahead with the adoption. Lyman agreed that to adopt
the child was a fine idea. To be able to raise a son much appealed
to both of them. Richard Lindsey was grown now and Anna
looked back with nostalgia on his boyhood days with her.

When Weston was five, Anna and Lyman went to court and
got adoption papers. From then on, they supported Weston,
who took their name – Weston Perry-Fiske. His grandmother
still was reluctant to give him up so Anna waited patiently for
the time when she could take her *hanai* son home. In the meantime she continued her research into crossbreeding, carried out
her usual schedule of ranch work and kept her household in
immaculate order, entertaining and enjoying the busy Big Island
social life.

In 1948 Anna was talked into running for election to the
territorial legislature. Her initiation into politics was one of those
totally unexpected opportunities that for the moment sweep
aside any other plans or ambition one has. It was late summer
that year when, at a dinner party in North Kohala, Republican
legislator Kenneth Bond told Anna he did not intend to run for
re-election as West Hawaii's representative. The district he served
in the legislature extended from North Kohala, through South
Kohala, North and South Kona and included Ka'u, southermost
point in the United States.

"Anna," said Kenneth Bond. "Why don't you run for my
seat? You'd be terrific!"

His suggestion appealed to Anna. Others at the party urged
her to follow through on Kenneth's idea for both they and she
assumed from what he said that he did not intend to run for
re-election. Anna was no stranger to politics or to the territorial
legislature. In Hilo, ten years earlier, she had enjoyed campaigning for her first husband. It was she who had won elections for
Henry Lai Hipp. Now why not for herself?

Losing and Winning

LYMAN WAS NON-COMMITTAL about Anna's decision to run for the legislature. He was not enthused but, at the same time, he did not try to discourage her.

Early in the fall she announced her candidacy, assuming her only opponent in this 1948 election campaign would be the Democratic candidate, Akoni Pule, a former Kohala Sugar Company employee. Pule had the backing of the ILWU, the International Longshoremen and Warehouseworker's Union. The Republican party, however, had been the dominant party in Hawaii since the beginning of the Territory nearly fifty years earlier. Anna was quite justified in 1948 in believing that, as a Republican, her chances of winning were excellent.

The problem was, she turned out not to be the sole Republican candidate for the West Hawaii seat! To Anna's consternation, on the final day for filing nomination papers, Kenneth Bond announced he was running for re-election. Anna was stunned by the news. How could he have encouraged her to run, told her he was not running again, and then do just the opposite. Kenneth Bond, grandson of the pioneer missionary who had founded Kohala Girls School, drew his support from the same people on whom Anna had counted. This was, she realized, a new and different ballgame from what she had been led to believe.

Undaunted, Anna put all her energy, time, and considerable money into her campaign. She made speeches in Hawaiian in those areas where many West Hawaii people still used the language. Day after day she stayed on the road to cover the sprawling district. She campaigned hard in places like Ka'u's Naalehu and Pahala, all of North and South Kona, her home base of Waimea, and the plantation precincts of North Kohala.

At first, Anna thought she might be doing all right. Her initial misgivings came when, on a trip to Pahala – a plantation town in Ka'u – she found the brochures she had trusted her man there to pass out for her were scattered along the side of the road. "Since the ILWU is not backing you, we can't help you," her Ka'u people informed her. Anna did some quick mental arithmetic on the impact that ILWU voters would have in Ka'u and North Kohala, areas where plantation labor was beginning to follow the union direction to vote only for Democrats or union-endorsed Republicans. Their vote, she knew, would be solid for Akoni Pule. Kenneth would have the Republican strongholds in Kona and South Kohala. In the past, that had been the majority vote, and the incumbent was usually at the advantage.

On election night, the Waimea farmers gathered at Anna's home. As voters were tallied, results came to her on the phone. When the outcome became clear, Anna phoned Kenneth Bond, who was at an election night 'victory' party at the home of Kohala's plantation manager. She was elated at the chance to get even with him for deceiving her about his candidacy.

"Kenneth! Congratulations!" said Anna.

"Oh! Thanks!" he answered, evidently thinking he deserved congratulating. In the background Anna could hear the joyous sound of everyone celebrating what they had been sure would be his re-election.

"But Kenneth," said Anna, "Haven't you heard? Akoni Pule has won this election!"

The ILWU precincts had come through with more solid support for their candidate than Kenneth Bond had expected. Anna had siphoned off too many of his solidly Republican votes. Bond, who had not been honest in running against a candidate he had urged to try for his seat, stayed home from then on. It was Akoni Pule who became West Hawaii's representative in the territorial, and later in the state legislature.

Anna learned enough in this one short campaign to make up her mind it would be her last venture into running for elected office. Her being a woman, and women being rare in politics then, had nothing whatsoever to do with it. Instead of people offering to help out with her campaign expenses, they had expected her to help *them* in return for their support. "People would come asking me for a carcass of beef like it was a leghorn chicken!" she said wryly. In addition, her eyes had been opened to the kinds of compromises one had to make as a politician. "Things you never do or stand for, you have to do because you're in politics? Not me! I don't want to have to live like that!" With an honest sense of relief at having lost the election, Anna returned to full-time concentration on her ranch – and to her ambition of developing new cross-breeds that would give her a top quality herd.

Size, she felt at first, was important. Yutaka Kimura encouraged her in this ambition as did state veterinarian Dr. Wally Nagao. No longer was Anna's herd at all like the lean slab-sided cattle her father had raised. When she first began riding the range with her father, there were still plenty of wild cattle on the mountain. Like her friend Yutaka Kimura, Anna remembered these wild cattle as fierce animals with small bodies, big heads and big horns. Hair covered their eyes. They were fast-moving, but so small that a horse could easily handle them. Not until the 1930's were the last one hundred or so of the wild cattle left on Mauna Kea destroyed by territorial forest rangers. "They shot the last of the wild horses then, too," Yutaka Kimura reminisces.

Anna remembers how, in the early days, Yutaka himself owned a wild horse. A colt and its mother had come through the Parker Ranch fence. Yutaka discovered them, and led the colt to Waimea – the mare following. At his home, Yutaka fed the colt milk and grain and gradually trained it to become a fine cattle horse. "That horse was so great for roping and cutting that Hartwell Carter offered to trade Yutaka two purbred horses for that wild one," says Anna.

In 1949, as a result of having lost the election, Anna was free to accept an appointment to the Board of Governors of Hawaii Preparatory Academy, a private boy's school opened that year in

Waimea under the sponsorship of the Episcopal Diocese. The school offered grades 7-12. It was first housed in a series of old Army buildings which remained on the grounds of St. James Episcopal church in the heart of the village. Anna was most enthused about the new school, which aimed to provide a rigorous academic education for boarding the day students.

During the same year that HPA took its first students, Anna was ready to try again with importing a purebred bull to upgrade her herd. She contacted the Chamber of Commerce to help her find out where the most reliable mainland ranches raising champion bulls were located. They recommended the Wayne H. Fisher ranch in Blythe, California as best producer in the west of the big champion Brahma bulls in which Anna was interested. Her instincts were that Brahma bulls had two qualities she wanted to upgrade her herd. They were huge animals with plenty of meat, and they had a natural capacity to thrive in Waimea's weather.

"Brahmas? And you intend to cross them with your Herefords? That's crazy. It will never work," many of her Waimea colleagues told her. Anna, as usual, turned a deaf ear to such negativism. "She's way ahead of you people in trying new crossbreeds!" Dr. Wally Nagao, Waimea's state veterinarian, defended Anna's plans.

Anna packed her designer suits and elegant formal gowns for the five day trip on the 'Lurline' to Los Angeles. There she checked into the Biltmore Hotel where she had already made arrangements to meet Wayne H. Fisher. As soon as she arrived, she telephoned him to confirm the time he had said he would meet her in the Biltmore lobby.

"How am I going to know you?" she asked him.

"How am I going to know you?" was the reply, to which Anna gave an immediate, impulsive response. "Oh, you'll recognize me! I'm a cattle rancher!"

The Fishers had invited Anna to go to lunch with them so that they could get acquainted and talk business before taking her to Blythe as they planned to do on the following day. They were to pick her up in the lobby at noon this first day. Anna was down in the lobby exactly at twelve. She was wearing a black suit and dashing hat which she had had custom made for her by a designer in San Francisco. As she sat there waiting for Mr. Fisher, whom she envisioned as a rugged, tanned cattleman in broad-brimmed hat and western style boots, she knew she was going to confuse him for she looked more like a socialite or a movie star than a cattle rancher. Anna was always one to enjoy a good joke. She laughed to herself as she sat there anticipating that Mr. Fisher would be looking for a big, rough-looking woman.

Ten minutes passed. Then fifteen. Still no cattleman in sight. A tall slender business man kept walking around the lobby obviously looking for someone but he was so different from her mental picture of him that it never occurred to Anna he might be Mr. Fisher. And it never occurred to him that the beautiful woman in the elegant black suit and hat would be his bull-buying customer. They kept looking past each other in the lobby and waiting for their mental pictures of each other to make an appearance. At last Mr. Fisher had Anna paged.

He was stunned when she rose to answer it. "You're my client? You're a rancher? he exclaimed, astonished.

Outside the hotel, Mrs. Fisher was waiting in their car. She took one incredulous look at Anna and shook her head. "We sure had you pictured all wrong!"

"I had *him* pictured all wrong!" laughed Anna.

This first meeting, Anna knew she had come to the right place for her bulls. The Fishers were her kind of people– shrewd, honest, and knowledgeable. The following day when they took Anna to Blythe and their ranch, the Fisher's respect and admiration of her zoomed as she unerringly selected and bought their finest bull.

Mr. Fisher wanted to take a picture of Anna. At the ranch she was wearing a smart riding shirt, western style riding breeches, boots, broad brimmed western style hat and riding gloves– all of the very best quality and superb fit. In the saddle or out of it, Anna was a totally fashionable woman. She liked to look her best whether she was polishing silver in her kitchen, dressing a carcass in her slaughterhouse, riding the range on her ranch, or sitting at the Captain's table on one of her many trips on a Matson liner.

"I'll bet you wouldn't dare get up on that Brahma bull so I

can take your picture," challenged Mr. Fisher.

Anna was never one to turn aside from a dare. "I'll bet I would get up on him!" she retorted.

"Go ahead. I'll have the camera ready!" said Mr. Fisher.

Heart pounding, inwardly quaking with fear, Anna strode into the corral. A cowboy lifted her up on the enormous back of the bull. There she sat, terrified but flashing a big smile and waiting for the camera shutter to click. The second it did, she jumped down and retreated to a safe place outside the corral fence. The photograph, a testament to her gutsiness, is a reminder of how and when she began bringing in the big bulls for which she became famous.

"You look so at ease– so nonchalant astride that huge Brahma bull!" everyone comments.

Anna never dissembles. "I do, don't I," she laughs. "But was I scared inside!"

As luck would have it, a shipping strike began before Anna could send her new prize bull home. When he heard about the strike, Wayne Fisher called Anna at her hotel. "What will you do?" he wanted to know.

"Oh, I'm using the time to take a ten day trip to Mexico City. I've always wanted to see a bull fight. I'm all booked to fly out tomorrow."

"By yourself?" Fisher asked.

"Of course. I'm here alone. I'll go to Mexico alone," Anna had already phoned Lyman to tell him of her plans.

"Do you know Spanish?" asked Fisher.

"Not one word. But there will be Mexicans who speak English – if not, I'm good at talking with my hands."

"But what about pesos – do you understand Mexican money?"

"I'll learn!" said Anna, and with her usual confidence she flew off to Mexico City the following day.

She was amused as were her fellow passengers by the Mexican mis-pronunciation of her name. First they called her "Mrs. Fiskee". Another time it was "Mrs. Perrywinkle". Anna took this with good humour. At the airport in Mexico City she quickly discouraged an ardent would-be escort and self-styled guide. He squeezed into the taxi with her, but she said a firm good by when she reached her hotel. She had arranged for a special tour each day – and first was a boat tour of the floating gardens of Xochimilco. "They were so beautiful!" she remembers. On the tour she met two teachers from New York City, whom she suggested accompany her to a bull fight.

Anna's seat was in the best area of the ring. "Mexican ladies really dress to the hilt to go to a bull fight!" she was told. So Anna went in her best, too. She wore a purple dress that had been designed for her in the long-skirted style fashionable that year. Her hat was the same deep purple decorated with a bright yellow bird whose tail feathers were hanging down the back of the hat. Purple maline trimmed and softened the hat's brim, framing her face. "I really looked gorgeous!" she recollects. "Everyone was admiring me!"

The bull fight was not quite what Anna had anticipated. "Nothing like the one Richard and I saw years later in Spain!" she says.

First, the Mexican bulls got loose. Everyone except Anna fled the stands.

When they returned, a man behind her tapped Anna on the shoulder. "Weren't you afraid?" he asked.

"No. The bulls can't get up here. I know, because I'm a rancher. I just bought a big beautiful Brahma bull in California to ship home to Hawaii."

The bullfight was about to resume when suddenly it began to thunder. Lightning crackled across the sky. Heavy rain poured down. Everyone hurried to get to cover. Anna ran with them this time. She was drenched before she reached the narrow, tunnel-like corridor leading from the stands out to the street. People were jammed tight. Anna had the straps of her purple handbag wrapped twice around her wrist. She had been warned that purse-snatchers were common in Mexico City. As the crowd jostled around her, she felt a tug on her handbag. She looked down to see a dark brown hand yanking at the straps. Anna yanked back. He tugged away, but at last she discouraged him. No one helped her – no one paid any attention to what was going on but that would-be robber found that Anna Perry-Fiske was not about to have her purse snatched!

Anna finally made her way to the street to look for the

two girls from New York whom she knew had also come to the bullfight. As she stood outside, she saw that everyone would stare at her, head to toe, and then laugh as they passed by. Anna looked down at herself and for the first time noticed that her purple dress had shrunk to her knees. A good foot or more of slip was dragging below the sodden hem of the dress. Then she examined her hat. The maline was drooping, the yellow feathers bedraggled and the bird's once-gorgeous bright tail falling down to one side of her face.

"What a sight I was!" says Anna.

Just then the two New York teachers appeared. "Go ahead. Laugh!" said Anna. "I know how funny I look. Shrunk and sodden, that's me today!"

"What a good sport you are!" admired the girls. They rode with her in a taxi to the hotel. There Anna was relieved to have a bellman escort her from the curb to a side-entrance where no one could see her, and then a private way to the elevators. "I gave that fellow a good generous tip," says Anna. "I would have been mortified if I had to go through the hotel lobby the way I looked!"

The only drawback of this ten days in Mexico City was that Anna lost a pound a day. The problem came from her not understanding about pesos. On the menu, each item was in pesos, but with a dollar sign beside the number. Her first day there, Anna read the hotel menu. "Fifty dollars for a bowl of soup!" she exclaimed to herself. "One hundred and fifty dollars for an entree! Heavens, I can't afford that!" So, for breakfast each day she had tea and one slice of toast. For dinner each night, the same thing again. Lunch was on tour, and since it was local food she dared not eat it. Only on the ninth day of her trip did a man from New York explain to her the prices on the menu were in pesos not dollars – but by then Anna was ten pounds lighter and so hungry she could have eaten the table cloth!

"One good thing though," she remembers, "just eating tea and toast I never got the stomach problems so many tourists get in Mexico."

The ten days south of the border was Anna's first trip out of the U.S.A.

Back home, when the shipping strike ended, and as soon as her Brahma bull was acclimated to Waimea, Anna put him in the pasture where Hereford heifers were grazing. "He got busy right away!" she was delighted to note. With excitement, Anna waited for the months of gestation to pass and the first calves to be dropped. Taking a chance on guessing when that would happen, she sent out invitations to a 'baby luau'. Her guests assumed that the party was to celebrate Anna's having adopted another child. To fuel their speculation when they arrived at the luau was the sight of a baby buggy which – few knew – held Helie Rohner's youngest child.

Anna's old friend Martin Pence remembers her having told him that she wanted him to come out to see her new fur coats. "I never suspected that Anna was talking about fur coats on the hoof! I should have known that these calves would mean more to Anna than any mink coat that money could buy."

The 'baby luau' was a great success. "You should have seen their faces when Les Wishard brought two big beautiful crossbred calves down from the corral for me," Anna reminisces. "They were such gentle calves – only two days old! I had been just right in timing my baby luau!"

Everyone at this outdoor party could see by these big calves that Anna's innovative crossbreeding was a success. She was more confident than ever that the crossbreeds would become beef animals of outstanding size and quality.

Anna had long since developed her own technique with cattle. "My cattle are not nervous or scared. That's because I don't chase the calves – I bring the herd back to them." She used this successful technique with her new crossbreeds. Although many of her fellow ranchers used dogs to herd their cattle, Anna never did. "If you have a good horse and it's yours only," she says, "You and the horse are a 'couple' who know instinctively how and where the cattle can be herded to your and their best advantage!"

When Anna's Brahma-Hereford crossbred calves became full grown steers they dressed out at some 120 lbs. heavier than the average beef carcass. Anna was jubilant. In July 1951 she made another trip to the Wayne H. Fisher ranch in Blythe, California, this time purchasing three more Brahma bulls. The picture of one, a prize 2300 pound Brahma bull named Dave, was published in the Honolulu Star-Bulletin of August 16, 1951. "Dave," reported the news article, "was now at home on Anna

Ranch. He and the other two Brahma bulls had been brought to Hawaii in July on the ship 'Hawaiian Wholesaler'. On that voyage, marveled the reporter, "Mrs. Perry-Fiske acted as cattle tender."

"Dave," concluded the article, "will leave his mark in the Waimea ranch by siring heavier hybrid cattle and make Hawaii a little more self-sufficient in meat." So it would and, most important to Anna, her cross-bred steers were making her a great deal of money.

It was in the 1950's that Anna hired a returned GI veteran, Bull Awaa, as a full-time ranch hand. Bull was an immensely strong Hawaiian who could do the heavy physical jobs as she directed. He could single-handedly pick up a heavy fence post and run up a hill with it. With only his two powerful hands, he was easily able to pull a fence post out of the ground! From the very first day he came to work for her, Bull Awaa called Anna 'Boss'. His loyalty to her, and his understanding of what she expected of him, he expresses in a few succinct words. "When Boss says something she doesn't go back on her word. And when she says *that* calf, she means that calf and you know she means that one." Over the years Anna has built a small house for Bull, which is his to use for as long as he lives. He keeps her lawn mowed, and follows her explicit directions in tending the garden, keeping the cars cleaned and polished, going to the post office, and in general being her dependable, only, full-time ranch hand.

When she needed extra help of an expert nature, Anna hired Willy Andrade. "Together we work like six cowboys!" she compliments him. Anna had a mental blueprint of every drive – every step planned in her head before she and Andrade rode out in the morning. "In half a day, with good planning, you can get a full day's work done. Give my father credit for teaching me that!" says Anna. For big jobs, Anna hired several Parker Ranch cowboys. She would use the same men year after year. Her ability to judge a cowboy's skill is such that today those same men are head men at Parker Ranch. One such is Walter Stevens and his brother Charlie, "They're among the best!" says Anna. "And faithful!" Also invaluable over the years has been Anna's nephew, Richard Lindsey, who has always been like a son to her.

Martin Pence' affectionate description of Anna is "She's a charmer!" He chuckles as he tells how Anna could sell cattle to men who really didn't need any but could not resist her personal magnetism. "Because she's a woman, and a positive one, men are afraid to argue with her," says Pence. "Sometimes Anna gets away with murder!"

As Anna increased the size of her herd, she needed more pastures. A choice 300-acre parcel of the government-owned 10,000 acre leasehold tract known as Kawaihae One adjoined her boundary, and was ideal for her purposes. In 1952, not anticipating any problem in her desire to sublease this 300 acres from Kahua, Anna went to Ronald Von Holt, Kahua's part owner and manager. To her dismay, when she told him she wanted to sublet the top 300 acres of Kawaihae One, from the forest line down, Von Holt flatly refused. Not only did he refuse, he would not even discuss the offer with her.

Later that year, the territorial lease of Kawaihae One came up for renewal. Anna knew she could not handle a winning bid on her own but a fellow rancher, a Mr. Choy, told her he would go in with her. At one time Parker Ranch had been the lessee of Kawaihae One, but was outbid by Kahua. The 10,000 acres of grazing lands provided Kahua with much of its pastureage. As the day of the bidding for a new lease approached, with bidding to be held in the old Armory building in Hilo, Ronald Von Holt was determined not to let Anna get the lease away from him.

She almost did! Each time she raised the bid over Ronald's figure, Da Von Holt, Ronald's wife, who was in the bleachers would shout to Anna, "Stop it! Stop it!"

Also across the room was Mr. Choy who sat looking more and more anxious as Anna bid higher and higher. Von Holt finally reached an amount at which Anna let him have the lease. She had made her point. He had to pay twice as much for leasing Kawaihae One as he had paid before.

With this single exception, relations between Anna and her Kahua neighbor continued to be most cooperative – crossing each other's pastures, sharing locks on gates. After Ronald Von Holt died in 1953, Atheton Richards' nephew Monty became Kahua's manager. The same relationship with Anna continued, and remained a close friendship when Ronald's son Pono became co-manager of the ranch with Monty Richards.

The Parties No One Forgets

NO MATTER HOW exciting these years were for Anna in her cattle business, her life seemed to her empty whenever she saw or thought of her *hanai* son, Weston. His grandmother still insisted on keeping him although Anna and Lyman yearned to bring Weston home. In the meantime, Anna saw to it that he had the best of everything. When he was very young, she arranged for him to be given special tutoring lessons by Mrs. Daley, an outstanding teacher who had formerly had a private school in Hilo. Mrs. Daley, whom Anna knew well from her Hilo days, was now at Hawaii Preparatory Academy's Little School, a coeducational program for grades one through six. As a result of Mrs. Daley's work with him, Weston entered first grade at an age when most children are just beginning kindergarden.

Weston was eleven when finally Anna had the full joy of mothering him. Concerned about his health, for he seemed always to have a deep cough, Anna finally put her foot down. She went to her sister-in-law's home one day and told her, "Lily, I'm taking Weston home with me. Now."

When Anna took Weston to Dr. Brown in Hilo for a check-up he told her she had acted none too soon. Weston had a small spot on one lung. According to Dr. Brown, the boy was on

Anna and Lyman relaxing at Keawewai– 1940's.

Anna roping calves for branding at Hartman's corral, Waimea, 1950's.

Photo by Sakata Art Studio.

Anna and Lyman dining in Monarch Room, Royal Hawaiian Hotel, 1950's.

Anna leaves on the Lurline to buy bulls on the Mainland.

Anna and Lyman at holoku ball celebrating the 125th anniversary of Parker Ranch, January 1962.

Courtesy Parker Ranch

Anna's *hanai* son Weston.

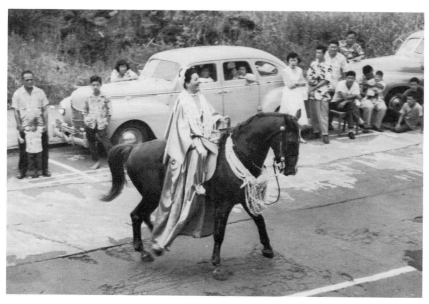

Anna as *pa'u* queen in Hilo, 1940's.

Bull Awaa.

Anna's nephew Richard Lindsey, circa 1940's.

Lyman (3rd from left) on his way from China to Tibet.

the verge of tuberculosis. Under Anna's loving care, he soon became healthy. Although Weston remained much attached to his grandmother he flourished with the change in his life, a change for which he was most eager. He was an exceptionally bright boy, and a very handsome one – always at the head of his class. Anna and Lyman thoroughly enjoyed having this adopted son with them.

Weston was a good student but the academic load at Hawaii Preparatory Academy was heavy. As early as the seventh and eighth grades, teacher expectations of students were inordinately high. Often, as he studied evenings, Weston would fall asleep over his books. To encourage him, Anna sat up with him, knitting while he did his long hours of homework.

"It's hard for you because at the end of the day you're too tired to concentrate," Anna advised. She helped Weston experiment with various study routines, finally suggesting that he try going to bed early and getting up, as she did, at 4:00 A.M. Then his mind would be fresh. The schedule at HPA began with the first class at 8:00 A.M. After the last class of the day, every boy turned out for a strenuous three or four hours of sports activities. As a result, not only Weston's mind but his body was always fatigued by evening. Anna's suggestion to him of early to bed and getting up at 4:00 A.M. with her to do his homework was the key to his continuing to receive honor grades.

"Mother, you're right!" he said after a few days on this schedule made his homework seem far less arduous.

These years of the fifties were when Anna began her practice of giving and of stimulating others to give to the causes that she felt most worthwhile. First, for her, was the Heart Association. Since her mother's fatal heart attack, Anna had wanted to help the Heart Fund. Once the note on her ranch was paid off, the war ended, and her cattle buying ventures for the dairymen completed, she put her mind to what she could do to help raise more money for the Heart Association and its research programs. Her first fund-raising activity for this purpose was an annual coffee-fest, held in her big ranch house. As many as 200 or more invited guests would attend the 3:00 to 6:00 p.m. affair. Anna would be up at 2:00 a.m. on the day of the party, making dainty tea sandwiches, arranging fresh flowers throughout the house, and setting out her finest china and silver on tables covered with her best damask, linen, and lace cloths.

Each year Anna planned entertainment for her guests. Sometimes it was Hawaiian music and hulas. Once it was a fashion parade of Japanese wedding kimonos, with Anna herself welcoming her guests in a stunning traditional kimono. Lyman grumbled about these coffee fests. With the money Anna spent flying in pastries from the Alexander Young's German bakery, hiring servers for the afternoon, and often paying for entertainment, her outlay was usually more than the generous amount put in the Heart Fund calabash by her and her guests.

These first years of her marriage Anna learned to ignore many of Lyman's complaints. She understood, as many did not, that frustration over his frequent difficulty in breathing made him irascible. For her the emphasis was on making the relationship work. Patiently she encouraged his futile search for a cure, but meanwhile she kept on living life to its fullest in the way she best liked to do. Had she not, Lyman might well have given in to becoming an invalid.

One of Anna's favorite charitable activities was the Easter Seal benefit spring fashion show and luncheon held at the Royal Hawaiian Hotel each year. Like her service on Hawaii Preparatory Academy's Board of Governors, Anna felt the Easter Seal Association, which funded programs of research, support and therapy for crippled children, was another way in which she could express her deep interest in helping young people. It was she who suggested to the Association that the luncheon add an Easter hat contest to its program. This was an enormous success, for the woman in the audience whom the judges felt had the most beautiful and unique hat, then donated it to be auctioned off. Hats were one of Anna's passions. Her custom-made millinery was always a prizewinner. Once, early in the 1950's, her prize winning hat brought $1100 into the Easter Seal treasury. Another year her hat was auctioned for $800.

It was towards the end of this decade that Anna's old friend Eben Low died. His daughter, Annabel Ruddle, contacted Anna asking if she would be willing to ride Eben's ashes up to the summit of Mauna Kea. His two last wishes had been: to see Anna again, and to see the top of Mauna Kea. His family felt that

Anna accompanying Eben's ashes to Mauna Kea's summit would be answering both requests.

It was hard for Anna to realize that the man who had been the great horseman and rancher of her youth, the vigorous older man who had ridden as Grand Marshal of the big parades to which he had invited her as Hawaii's *pa'u* queen, was gone. Sadly she prepared for the trip to escort his ashes up the mountain. She first had to have her horses specially shod for the trip. Parker Ranch refused to do this so Anna went to the manager of Kohala Plantation who arranged for this to be done by a Kohalan who was expert in shoeing horses.

Eben Low's family had asked the minister of Kawaiahao Church in Honolulu, the Reverend Abraham Akaka, to fly to the Big Island to conduct the memorial service over Eben's ashes. When the appointed day came, Anna drove the truck loaded with saddles from her ranch to Humuula sheep station. Bull Awaa drove the truck with the horses – which Anna was supplying. Her cousin Thomas Weston Lindsey, who worked for Herbert Shipman, also brought some horses.

It was a cold rainy day as the small party of riders saddled up and mounted their horses at Humuula Sheep station to set out on the steep switchbacks of the trail to Hale Pohaku. Bill Bryan, Anna's Hilo forester friend, had developed a stone rest house at the ten thousand foot level of the mountain and thus the name for this point in the ascent – *Hale* being the Hawaiian word for house, and *pohaku* the word for stone. From Hale Pohaku, the trail became even more steep. Each rider wore a long rain slicker to shield them from the wind and the rain. It was not one of Mauna Kea's bright blue clear days but for Anna, the chill drizzle, and a sky draped in dark clouds was much more in keeping with how she and everyone else felt at the loss of such a man as Eben Low.

At Lake Waiau Tom Lindsey and a helper used concrete to embed a memorial plaque to Eben beside the alpine lake. One of Anna's regrets is that in later years, vandals removed the plaque from its site. From Lake Waiau William Kaniho, who was their guide, led the riders to the 13,694 foot summit. It was here, at the top of the Hawaiian world that Eben Low had so loved, surrounded by those who had much loved and respected him,

that Rev. Akaka performed the brief service of farewell. Rev.
Akaka opened the urn and scattered Eben's ashes as he had
wished. The wind took them. The rain soaked them. In
moments, Eben Low had become one with the mountain that
had been his favorite place.

When the riders returned to Humuula, Annabel Ruddle had
a hot lunch ready for everyone. There were reminiscences about
Eben – the kind of 'talking story' that islanders do in loving
tribute to those near and dear to them at the conclusion of
memorial or funeral services. It was that day on the mountain
when Anna decided that when her turn came, she too wished
to have her ashes scattered on the place she loved best. For her,
this was the summit of the Kohala mountains just behind and
above her ranch. She made no mention to Weston or Lyman of
this decision, nor to her beloved nephew Richard Lindsey. For
now, life was to be lived and savored and enjoyed whenever and
with whomever she happened to be.

As had her mother, Anna loved entertaining – whether for
a good cause like the Heart Association or for the simple joy of
giving her friends a good time. "Anna always gave the parties
of the year," remembers Hilo society editor Maxine Hughes.
"They were out of this world," reminisces Dick Frazier, now
retired and living in a peaceful, hilltop house in mauka Kona.
Frazier chuckles as he says, "Invariably when you walked into
one of Anna's formal parties, there was an overwhelming
fragrance of essence of mothballs. In this climate, with all the
insect pests, everybody kept their formal clothes well protected
between wearings."

When Anna entertained at formal dinners there was always
dancing afterwards. One evening Dick Frazier was dancing with
Carolyn Koehnen when he tripped on a porcelain horse in
Anna's living room. To his horror, the valuable art object crashed
to the floor before he could rescue it. He was trying to think of
how he might apologize, or when he might replace it, when
Anna came up looking completely unperturbed. She calmly
bent over, picked up the pieces and said, "Please don't stop
dancing, Dick! I just love to see people having a good time!"

On other occasions Anna entertained at informal luncheons
up at Keawewai. After the war she had refurbished George

Washington Lincoln's charming old house. With its cool mountain air, its waterfall and swimming pool, Keawewai was an ideal spot to relax. The files of the Hilo and Honolulu newspapers are full of descriptions and photographs from many of Anna's outstanding parties, both there and at Anna Ranch.

These were busy years as well as happy ones. Anna pursued her cross-breeding activities. She ran the ranch and its business as she always had, but she was adamant about finding time to do whatever Weston wanted or needed. She was, if anything, almost too indulgent a mother. How proud she and Lyman were when Weston graduated from HPA at the very young age of sixteen, the youngest in his class and one of the top students. His Senior year, just before graduation in May, 1958, Anna invited 200 guests to her annual coffee-fest. The affair was featured in a two-column story in the Hilo paper. A photograph shows Anna, beaming and beautiful in a black silk dress, wearing strands of white pikake caught at one shoulder with a white cattleya orchid corsage. Two of the Big Island's most prominent men are chatting with her – Judge Luman Nevels and Hawaii Preparatory Academy's Headmaster, James Taylor. As usual for her parties, Anna had decorated the ranch house with lavish arrangements of fresh flowers. She had polished her silver tea and coffee services until they shone like mirrors. Her best china was set out for her guests. Also as usual much of the array of pastries on her koa dining tables had been flown in from the Alexander Young's famous specialty bakery in Honolulu. Other pastries had been trucked over from the equally famous Robert's Bakery in Hilo.

At this 1958 coffee-fest Anna honored Weston and five of his classmates, all seniors about to graduate from Hawaii Preparatory Academy. At the beginning of the afternoon program she presented her son and his friends, –Robert Barwick, William Feliciano, Roger Giles, and Clifford Miller– with handsome Vanda orchid leis. Rose de Mercer of Kohala and her talented grandchildren entertained the guests with hulas. Hawaiian songs were sung by Mr. and Mrs. John Auna of Honokaa, by John Rickard of Waimea, and by Bill Sproat of Kohala. A special song, "Ciribiribin" was sung by Mrs. Winston Clark, wife of the minister of Kalahikiola Church in Kohala, which Anna then attended with Lyman. Thomas Toguchi of Ka'u did a Japanese number. Weston and his classmates climaxed the afternoon by giving a rendition of rock and roll tunes followed by their HPA theme song, 'Maikai Ka Makani O Waimea' and 'Pua Carnation'. To finish the occasion, Clifford Miller and Roger Giles did slack key solos for the guests. Even Lyman enjoyed this coffee-fest.

The following autumn Weston enrolled in the University of Hawaii. Anna again was immensely proud of her son as he made the Dean's list at the University that first semester in December of 1958. He continued to do well in the new year, 1959 – the unforgettable year when Hawaii, after sixty years of being promised statehood, was finally admitted as a full and equal partner in the union. No longer were the islands in the quasi-colonial status of being a territory. Hawaii's citizens, like any other Americans in the Mainland United States, now had the privilege of voting for their own governor and the advantage of their own senators and congressmen in Washington, D.C. Along with statehood came an influx of outside capital. As South Kohala became part of the statehood boom, Waimea began to change with new investments, new people, new lifestyles.

Earlier during this decade of the fifties Anna began to stay in a suite at the Royal Hawaiian Hotel. She stored a steamer trunk full of her fine designer outfits there, and on her frequent visits to Honolulu she often had designer Pauline Lake fashion her a unique evening gown or an unusual holoku, a formal, fitted Hawaiian style gown with train. Anna would frequently fly over to Honolulu for a few days just to be near Weston. She was always in Honolulu for Easter week, and the Easter Seal fashion luncheon and hat contest. Christmas was another favorite time when she and Lyman stayed at the Royal Hawaiian. "Royal Hawaiian Holidays" was the headline with which the *Hilo Tribune-Herald* reported in December 1959 that Mr. and Mrs. Lyman Perry-Fiske of Waimea were "back in Honolulu at their suite at the Royal Hawaiian Hotel, where they annually participate in Christmas and New Year festivities at their home-away-from-home." Weston, added the reporter, was always there with his parents.

Anna often had Weston come home to Waimea for special

parties. One such occasion was the surprise birthday party she gave for Richard Smart's friend and business associate, Robert Young, in September 1960. Anna held this up at her mountain retreat, Keawewai. She had asked her guests to come in costume and now, looking back, she realizes Weston was trying to give her a clue as to his preferred sexual identity when he came dressed as a girl. "He was so handsome!" Anna sighs. "And he had such beautiful hands!" The costume luncheon was covered with a half page spread by Society Editor Maxine Hughes in the Hilo Tribune-Herald. She began her account with a vivid description: "Take a setting high on the grassy slopes of the Kohala Mountains, add a group of fifty or more islanders, sprinkle liberally with good food and fellowship, spark with a generous amount of Hawaiian music and hospitality, and you have the makings of a gala Hawaiian party."

That it was, and a complete surprise to the man Anna was honoring. Robert Young thought he was being taken to look at some land at Keawewai, for his expertise was land development. At the time he was deeply involved with lease transactions for one of the most beautiful beach areas in South Kohala. Once known as Parker Ranch Employees' beach, it was about to become the site of Laurence Rockefeller's fabulous luxury resort – Mauna Kea Beach Hotel. Anna's old friend Richard Penhallow, who had once worked for Alvah Scott at Aiea Plantation had a major role in these negotiations. In March of this same year, Anna had surprised Richard and Olive Penhallow with an *Aloha Pa'ina* in celebration of Penhallow having been named manager of Parker Ranch. That party had been held at Anna's Waimea home. The Penhallows were among Anna's guests at her surprise party for Robert Young at Keawewai.

Before Young's planned ten a.m. arrival, the guests were transported up to Keawewai by jeep. Robert Young's first intimation that his 'business trip was not at all that was Anna's greeting him at the Keawewai ranch house gate. Instead of one of her usual elegant outfits, she was wearing a two peice palaka cloth dress of the material once used by plantation laborers. A wildly crazy hat was on her head. Grotesque sunglasses covered half of her face. Weird looking silver teeth were fastened over her own. Behind her were Robert Young's Big Island acquaintances and friends – all in costume– some as gay nineties bathing beauties. As Young stood there dumbfounded, the whole group broke into a rendition of Happy Birthday and then led him up to the house for what everyone still agrees was a party that no one – especially Dick Frazier and Richard Lindsey – will ever forget.

They were the only two guests not out to greet Young. Frazier, the genial manager of Honokaa plantation, and Anna's nephew Richard had been at Keawewai since early morning helping Anna set up the tables and get everything ready. Just before the guests were to start arriving, Anna encouraged the two men to cool off with a swim and then change to party clothes. She had no idea that Lyman intended to add to their relaxation on his own. He went down and seated himself on a flat rock beside the pool, a bottle of bourbon in one hand and a shot glass in the other. Each time the two Richards swam by him, Lyman gave them a shot glass of whiskey. Since the pool was not very large, they swam by often. When they finally staggered out of the water, Richard Lindsey made it as far as the grass in front of the Keawewai house, and then lay down and went to sleep.

Anna, looking out of the house, saw him there and hurried down with a quilt to put over him. At this, Richard Frazier decided he too needed a rest break and he lay down beside Richard, pulling part of the quilt over himself. Anna was angry with Lyman for breaking one of her party rules. Her bartender Lee Ueda had strict instructions to pour very small drinks for each round. Anna's parties were too much fun for anyone to miss enjoying them by getting drunk. So, while Richards Frazier and Lindsey slept off Lyman's bourbon, the rest of the guests enjoyed cocktails, hulas, and Hawaiian music – and then feasted on a sumptuous buffet lunch of gourmet salads, roast pork, corned beef, and – of course – an enormous birthday cake. It was, Anna's cousin Nancy Kerr remembers, a great party at which she distinguished herself by jumping into the pool in her muumuu. On her head was a lauhala hat with a lei of fresh roses for a hatband. When Nancy surfaced from her jump, the hat was still firmly on her head, every rose in place in the lei, and the muumuu floating up gently all around her in the water.

Pioneering Charolais

WITH HER USUAL tenacity Anna continued producing her big Brahma cross-bred steers although they were becoming increasingly difficult to market. "Best beef I ever tasted," complimented Dick Divine of Hilo Meat Company, "But Anna, those big cuts are sure hard to sell!"

Tom Okuyama of Suresave Supermarkets kept trying to tell Anna the same thing. Finally, in 1961, Okuyama had Anna come into his market and look at the problem for herself. The steaks from her Brahma cross-bred steers were so huge that they flopped out over the edges of the standard, steak-sized containers in which supermarkets display their meat. "They just don't look appetizing that big!" gasped Anna. "I never realized!"

Seeing was believing for her. She wasted no time making a change. Hilo Hotel and Volcano House had enjoyed her huge roasts but customers such as they were few and far between on the Big Island. Laurence Rockefeller had not yet built Mauna Kea Beach Hotel. Kona Inn and Hilo's gracious old Naniloa were, in addition to the Lycurgus' family's Hilo Hotel and Volcano House, the only major hotels of any size on the island. "What mattered was that if Tom Okuyama couldn't easily package and market my steers, then no matter how superior their flavor and texture was, I was in trouble."

121

Fond as she was of her Brahma bulls, and justifiably proud of the big new crossbreed she had developed, Anna recognized that a change was crucial to the continued success of her ranch. Once again she went to the Chamber of Commerce for advice on the best sources of a certain breed she had decided to try next. In 1961 Anna imported Hawaii's first Charolais – a French breed of cattle. Again she was a pioneer in introducing a new kind of cattle to the islands.

She purchased her Charolais from the top source recommended by the Chamber of Commerce – the Keith Mets ranch in Holtville, California. As in her earlier cattle buying days, Anna made the 1961 trip over on the 'Lurline'. At Holtville, she bought three of Mets' prize bulls and some heifers. On the return trip out of Wilmington she traveled on the same freighter as the Charolais. Each Matson freighter had accommodations for only twelve passengers, usually two to a cabin. Only twice did Anna ever have to share a cabin. Once was when her cabin mate had been a Christian Scientist. It was, Anna recollects, the one crossing where she can remember the ocean being so rough that for the first time in her life she became seasick. When she returned to the cabin from checking on the crewmen who were tending her cattle, she looked and felt ill.

"What's the matter?" asked her roommate.

"I'm sick!" said Anna, collapsing into her bunk.

"Oh, no! You aren't sick!" insisted the lady in an aggressively positive manner. Just then the ship began to pitch and roll in a violent fashion.

As the woman rushed to the head to throw up, Anna couldn't resist saying "Oh, no! You aren't sick, are you?"

On this trip home from purchasing her first Charolais, Anna found that once again she was not to have a cabin to herself. She had to share a cabin with an officer's wife and a woman who sat up all night drinking. Anna and the officer's wife would walk the deck most of the night in order to get away from the drinker and fill their lungs with fresh air, their ears with the quiet of the open sea.

Anna was relieved to reach Honolulu and see that her beautiful Charolais were put on Young Brothers' barge for Kawaihae. When she stopped at the Royal on her way home, Honolulu businessman George Murphy heard what Anna had done and he too went to Holtville to buy Charolais for his ranch on Molokai. Anna was amused years later when Monty Richards and Pono Von Holt gave a party celebrating 'the importation of Charolais by Kahua'. One of the cattleman there said to Anna, "Remember how we all criticized you for introducing these French cattle?" "People have short memories!" was Anna's comment.

The summer of 1961, Anna donned her beautiful red velvet *pa'u* costume to ride as Queen of Hilo's Kamehameha Day parade. She led a contingent of 150 riders and many beautiful floats, marching groups, and bands. Grand Marshal of the parade was her friend Richard Penhallow, the new manager of Parker Ranch. The June 4th account of plans for the parade, reported in the *Hilo Tribune Herald*, tell how "Mrs. Perry-Fiske, an accomplished rider since she was a young girl, is an unexcelled *pa'u* rider, having participated for years in parades in Honolulu and the Big Island. As a youngster she repeatedly rode her grandfather's race horses to victory," the reporter recalled – not mentioning Anna's racing triumphs during the twenties and thirties in Hilo.

That 1961 Kamehameha Day parade was the largest ever held in Hilo. Former Hiloan James Kealoha, longtime Big Island county chairman, was then the Lieutenant-Governor under Anna's close friend Governor Bill Quinn. Lt. Governor Kealoha led the parade in William Nobriga's Cadillac. The Hawaii County Band and color bearers came next, then parade marshal Penhallow. Queen Anna was escorted by her husband, her nephew Richard Lindsey, and by Albert and Thomas Lindsey. The photograph of Anna accompanying the newspaper article of June 4th shows her – not in *pa'u* or riding clothes but looking every inch the Queen in a regal satin holoku. Her shoulders are bare, one hand holds the edge of the long train, and on her head is a diamond tiara. "She prefers to be called a cowboy, and not a cowgirl," the reporter comments.

Back at the ranch, before and after the parade, Anna worked hard getting her new cattle used to their new home. She was sure that her Charolais would produce beef equal to the flavor and texture of her Brahma-Hereford crossbreeds. Already the Charolais gave her great esthetic pleasure. Every evening they would walk along the ridge above and behind the ranch house. To Anna, those white cattle, silhouetted against the blue sky with a foreground of bright green pasture sloping down to her white ranch house was one of the most beautiful sights imaginable.

It was not long before Anna Ranch had only Charolais and Hereford. Her prize Brahma bulls were sent to market. "They made good money!" says Anna. "All that weight!"

What were they used for? Steaks from a bull would be tough as their hide. "They're used for sausage. They made great sausage!" Anna explains.

Once again, as when she began her crossbreeding experiments in the early fifties, in the early sixties Anna's critics said how foolish she was to bring in Charolais. A breed from France? Why fool around with anything but Hereford, they sneered. And once again Yutaka Kimura and veterinarian Dr. Wally Nagao were about the only ones that applauded Anna's decision. "You know something? She's still way ahead of you people!" Wally Nagao reiterated whenever criticism of Anna's importing Charolais reached his ears.

Her French breed of cattle turned out to produce beef as flavorful and superior in texture as Anna had anticipated. Marketing was no longer a problem for her. Her ranch business was doing extraordinarily well. Thanks to her willingness to experiment in ways others were reluctant to try, Anna's pastures were in top condition. She had controlled emax, a plant that choked out grass. Emax was, along with the equally destructive lantana and guava scrub, the plague of most Waimea and Kohala area ranchers. Back in 1959, when use of herbicides was almost unheard of, and aerial spraying of fertilizers in its infancy, Richard Frazier had sat next to Anna at a dinner party. He had recently lost vision in his left eye due to an overexposure to the herbicides he was pioneering on Honokaa Plantation. This had not lessened his enthusiasm for what aerial spraying of herbicides could do to get rid of emax, lantana, and guava scrub.

Since 1957 Frazier had been leasing a small plane and personally accompanying the pilot to supervise the aerial spraying of herbicides on Honokaa's plantation acreage. He had tried to interest Parker Ranch in using this technique but their agriculturist was unwilling to risk doing anything so new. At the dinner party Anna listened to Dick Frazier's frustration. "Nobody will give it a try!" he complained. "And it works. It really works, Anna!"

"I'll try it!" Anna volunteered. "I'm ready to experiment, but not with a helicopter or an airplane. It would spook my cattle." She gave Frazier one of those keen, quizzical looks that meant she had just had a very bright and original idea. "Why can't we use a truck to do the same thing?" she asked.

"Why not!" said Frazier, delighted.

Over the next few weeks he and Anna worked out a system that she was sure her cattle would tolerate. Two trucks were fitted with tanks and spray arms through which a pump pushed the tank's mixture of 2-4-5T and 2-4D. It was the first such mass pasture spraying in Hawaii – and it worked. Anna's pastures were soon rid of emax, lantana, and guava scrub. Every inch grew grass on which her cattle could feed.

Talking about this experiment of Anna's, and about her gutsiness in being willing to experiment, Dick Frazier remarks, "None of the men would try anything new. It took Anna to lead the way!"

A few years later Anna found that helicopters would not spook her cattle as she had thought, so she began using helicopters to apply fertilizer to her pastures. The pilot she hired to do the job would fly in from Hilo, land at Waimea airport to pick up sacks of fertilizer, and then make low passes over Anna Ranch, spreading fertilizer from an enormous airborne bucket that was suspended from the helicopter by a length of cable.

"It sure was less work and faster than my spreading fertilizer from horseback!" says Anna. She likes to tell the story of the first time she hired a helicopter to spread fertilizer in this way. She and her nephew Richard Lindsey drove up to Keawewai to watch the operation. To her consternation, Anna saw the helicopter fly on over her boundary and spread some of her fertilizer on Kahua Ranch. She jumped out of her four-wheel drive vehicle. As if the pilot could surely hear and see her, she waved her arms at the helicopter, shook her head, and shouted, "No! No! Put it on *my* land!"

For some reason that neither she nor Richard Lindsey could figure out, the pilot had stationed a man down in the pastures. Every time the big spreader bucket would descend, Anna would shout to this man to stay out from under it.

"If that cable holding the bucket ever gives way, he'll be killed!" she told Richard.

Not five minutes after she said this, with the man fortunately a safe distance away, the cable did break and the heavy bucket came crashing to earth. Had Anna not shouted her warning, "It would have killed him for sure!" exclaimed Richard.

In 1962 President John F. Kennedy appointed Martin Pence to a federal judgeship in Honolulu. For a number of years Pence had been Anna's attorney. "Anna didn't trust most lawyers," recollects John Ushijima. "But she trusted Martin Pence, who took me in as his partner when I got out of law school." Ushijima, who later became a prominent political figure in the Hawaii State Senate, likes to remember how Anna drove to Hilo through one of the Hamakua Coast's torrential downpours, and slogged through the mud in downtown Hilo to attend the opening of the firm's new offices. "She didn't have to come. We didn't expect her to come. But she did!"

Much of her legal pursuit of such matters as defending her ownership of the water rights to the stream that ran behind her ranch house was done by Anna herself. This stream was very precious to her so she was initially relieved when an attorney sent from Honolulu by the state assured her that her ownership of the water rights to that stream, and the waterfall that fed it, would not be questioned. This attorney, a Honoluluan named Ashford, sat at one end of Anna's koa dining table, consulting long legal lists and assuring her she had no problem. Anna was indignant and alarmed a week later when she received a letter from Ashford telling her she did *not* have legal ownership of the water rights, and that the state would be entitled to take water from her stream to be channeled into the new reservoir to be built for Waimea's water supply. Her stream, with its good water, was essential for Anna to provide adequate water for her cattle.

When she wrote back to Ashford that she protested his decision, he asked her to meet him in Hilo at the office of her attorney there. Anna wanted Ashford to come to Waimea to see her instead. Her intent was to walk the rather corpulent attorney up the steep hill, behind her big waterfall, and show him the courses of the old Hawaiian *auwai* – the irrigation ditches that proved her claim to water rights. She wanted to walk him down across her ranch, following these *auwai* to the sites of several ancient taro patches. Instead, against her wishes, Anna was prevailed upon to come to Hilo to meet with Ashford and her attorney on the matter. At this meeting, a top State Engineer, Bob Chuck, accompanied Ashford. Anna's attorney was there, but simply as a silent presence. It was Anna who defended her water rights.

Verbally, and with diagrams, she explained how the *auwai* proved her ownership. As he listened, Bob Chuck exclaimed, "Anna's right! Those are hers!" With him on her side, Anna was finally able to convince Ashford of what he had confirmed at their very first meeting – the legal ownership of those water rights was hers.

Although she had been a Republican in the 1949 legislative campaign, by 1962 Anna was an ardent supporter of the newly elected governor of the state of Hawaii – Democrat John A. Burns. Her enthusiasm for the Burns regime was great, but so was her rigorous criticism when she felt some wrong needed to be redressed. From 1962 on Anna Lindsey Perry-Fiske was known as a strong and constructively critical supporter of Governor Burns' plans for developing a new base for the prosperity and growth of Hawaii. She had also become a strong supporter of Shunichi Kimura, a young Hilo attorney who in 1965 was the popular Democrat elected as Hawaii County Chairman, the name by which the Mayor of the Big Island was then called.

Anna had long since met the rigorous expectations she had set for herself – to succeed as a man would succeed, to be at the same time a great lady, to give generously to the community causes that she felt most important, and to continue to be a strong political voice in Waimea, in Hilo, and in the state capitol.

In addition, she was fulfilling what she considered one of her most important roles – being a good mother to Weston.

At nineteen, Weston graduated from the University of Hawaii with honors. For a graduation present Anna gave him a condo in Seaside Towers, one of the handsome new high rises in Waikiki. It was a corner unit, with a view of Diamond Head.

Weston, who had majored in business, was eager to start out in a job but Anna advised him that it might be best if he first got his military service obligation out of the way. "You're right!" said Weston. He flew home to Waimea to do just that, but the day before he intended to drive to Hilo to volunteer, his draft notice arrived in the mail. The Army sent him to Fort Ord in Monterey California for basic training. Anna visited him there. During his army service in the early sixties, Weston was stationed as a chaplain's assistant at the U.S. base in Ethiopia. When he left the army three years later, Anna met him in New York. Together they enjoyed more than a month exploring the great places of Europe. They visited cities like London, Paris and Rome and traveled through charming country villages and hamlets. Weston was as enamoured of travel as was Anna. "Someday," Anna promised her son, "we'll take a trip around the whole world!"

During Weston's three years in service, Anna was recognized with a number of awards and honors. In 1963, because of her yearly prize-winning of the Easter Seal spring fashion show's hat contest, she received an engraved certificate from the Millinery Institute of America. It read: "in recognition of her consistent and tasteful selection of millinery" the Institute "is pleased to acknowledge Mrs. Lyman Perry-Fiske as one of the best-hatted women in America." In 1964 she was presented with the Heart Fund Certificate of Merit "for outstanding service in advancing the heart program and stimulating public support in the fight against the diseases of the heart and circulation."

It was a very special certificate of merit, given in recognition of Anna's exciting original fund-raising project, 'Old Hawaii on Horseback.' She had racked her brain, lying awake nights trying to think of something different, more exciting and unique that might draw more people and raise more money than did her annual coffee-fests. Suddenly the right idea struck her. Why not a pageant of Hawaiian history – a pageant on horseback that she could stage on the expanse of lawn fronting her ranch house. At once Anna got busy. She wrote a script. She asked the best riders on the island to bring their horses and participate. She designed the costumes. She directed rehearsals. She produced the show. And she herself was part of it. 'Old Hawaii on Horseback', one of the most successful and colorful pageants ever produced in the islands, was launched by her in 1964.

The amount of work involved was far more than she had done in preparing for and hosting her coffee-fests, but she felt it was well worth it in results. Soon not hundreds but thousands of people were flocking to see each year's 'Old Hawaii on Horseback'. All who attended made a donation to the Heart Fund. For each show, Anna wrote a new script, produced, directed, designed costumes, made the special period hats and was a star performer.

1964 was the year marking another major beginning in Anna's life. From that year on, she never again traveled to the Mainland to buy her prize bulls. She now had an annual source of purebred, champion stock available to her at the Hawaii Cattleman's Horse and Bull sale in Waimea. At this first of what was to become an annual sale, Anna set her own twenty-year pattern for the future by making the top bids for both the grand and reserve champion bulls. "Much less expensive than paying for a round trip to the Mainland plus the cost of the bull plus the freight bill for shipping him to Hawaii!" she enthused.

The one annoyance in Anna's life at this time was the way the influx of new people into Waimea were identifying her native village as Kamuela – the name given to the Waimea post office when Hawaii became a U.S. Territory. "They never changed the name of this place – they only re-named the post office!" she told newcomers. Her annoyance became indignation when she heard some of the teachers at Hawaii Preparatory Academy referring to Waimea as Kamuela. Whenever she heard such remarks, she set the person straight. During the sixties she had increasingly stronger ties to HPA both as a member of its Board of Governors and as mother of an alumnus. In 1961 the upper school had moved to a handsome new campus, a broad swath of bright green Kohala Mountain slopes just above the juncture where one road leads down to Kawaihae and another over the mountain route to North Kohala.

The new campus, and the new landscaping that would grow into rows of handsome windbreaks, were among the changes at HPA that Anna was eager for Weston to see when he came home after three years in uniform. Returning from service, he did not remain long with her and Lyman in Waimea, but settled in Honolulu, living in the condo she had purchased for him, and working in a good job at Sears. Even though Weston was now earning a living, Anna continued her pattern of the indulgent mother – showering him with affection, gifts, and cash. Lyman grumbled about her giving their son so much. After a year or two working at Sears, Weston went to an even better job, teaching at Cannon School of Business in downtown Honolulu, one of the oldest and finest private schools of its kind in Hawaii.

It was while he was teaching at Cannon's School of Business that Weston met the man who changed his life. It was a casual encounter. Both of them were out watching one of the big Honolulu parades. Before long they had introduced themselves. Bob was a public school teacher. Weston was teaching at Cannon's. They found each other most congenial and Bob became a frequent visitor at Weston's condo. When, during the summer, Bob left for Alaska, Weston missed him. When Bob returned, it was not to his own place but to Weston's. Anna surmised this was the case when she came on one of her trips to Honolulu that fall. To support Weston by paying all his condo expenses and buying him expensive clothes was something she enjoyed, but she was not about to support this fellow Bob. "Is he going to be living here with you? I don't think I like that," she told Weston. In answering her, Weston lied to her for the first time. "He's not staying here Mother. Don't worry!" Weston said.

At first Anna shut her ears to the rumours that began to reach her about Weston and Bob partying at the condo, and the questionable friends they were entertaining there. Since Weston had been under age when she gave him the condo, the deed was in both his and Anna's name. She continued to pay the maintenance fees, taxes and other bills even after it became obvious that Bob was sharing the place. When complaints began to reach her from the condo manager, and condo neighbors, Anna still was reluctant to believe what was being said about her son. Wasn't he just young and sowing some wild oats? she asked herself. "People always find something to talk about," she decided and for a time she let the rumours and complaints float on by.

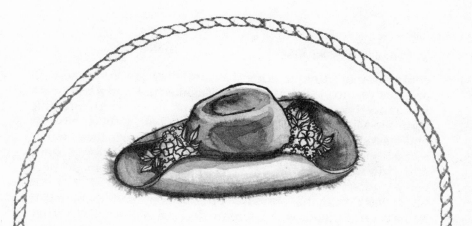

What's In A Name?

IN 1965 LAURENCE Rockefeller invited Anna and Lyman to spend four days and three nights during the opening festivities at Rock Resorts new world class luxury resort – Mauna Kea Beach Hotel. As did Mr. Rockefeller's other special guests for the grand opening, Anna received the gift of a 14-carat gold chain with a locket of the Mauna Kea Beach Hotel logo. Lyman was given a pair of gold cuff links. It was a spectacular beginning to the growth of West Hawaii's South Kohala coast as the prime luxury resort development in Hawaii – a development that was to take more than twenty years. Such a time frame was an advantage, for South Kohala has not yet suffered the density and overbuilding that has been the fate of Waikiki, of many of Maui's resort areas, and of some on Kauai.

Anyone who has seen Mauna Kea Beach Hotel's breathtaking site, atop a low bluff overlooking a perfect, long crescent of white sand beach, agrees it is assuredly one of the world's most beautiful. For local people, the transformation of dry, brown, *kiawe* covered slopes into a Robert Trent Jones oceanside eighteen hole golf course for the hotel was a small miracle. So was the lush tropical landscaping, the green lawns, the soaring coconut palms that not only surrounded the three hundred room, low rise hotel but also made its central open-roofed courtyard into a unique tropical atrium. Big Islanders came with awe that year to view the handsome architecture, and the art work that ranged from exquisite Japanese antiques and Thai temple drums to Michael Rockefeller's collection of New Guinea carvings and masks. On the upper floors, on the wall between the entrance to each guest suite hung a Hawaiian quilt in traditional colors and patterns, each one different, and each hand made by a contemporary Hawaiian quilt-maker.

It was during the four days of the hotel's grand opening that Anna became friends with Laurence Rockefeller and his wife. They were also to be her neighbors, for they had purchased the Parker Ranch Manager's house, a huge rambling white structure set back from the road, as was Anna's beautiful home, by vast stretches of green lawn. Known as the 'White House' after the Rockefellers acquired it, the home for a time was used as an annex where very special guests of the hotel were housed. Among these was Jacqueline Kennedy, widow of the President, and her two young children.

Plans for the hotel had sparked a boom in real estate in the area, and once the hotel opened, property in Waimea soared in value. The combination of Waimea's cool mountain air, its peaceful setting of green hills and big sky, and the educational advantages of Hawaii Preparatory Academy were enhanced by the accessibility of the Mauna Kea Beach Hotel Beach Club which offered access to the hotel beach, pool, tennis, and charge privileges, plus use of a pleasant dressing room and showers for an initially modest membership fee. Always attractive as a retirement area for older Honoluluans, Waimea now began to draw young couples who were affluent enough to be able to buy a home in one of the handsome new subdivisions of the village. For those less affluent, there was the attraction of new kinds of employment, and more modestly priced developments like Kawaihae Village which was originally designed for hotel employees.

For men and women in Kohala, Waimea, and Honokaa, jobs were no longer limited to Kohala or Honokaa plantations or Parker or Kahua Ranch. On the payroll at Mauna Kea Beach Hotel were to be five hundred employees – about as many as Kohala Plantation had on its payroll when the hotel was opened. Many of these hotel jobs were service jobs, but the hotel also hired engineers, maintenance experts, accountants, phone operators, and computer programmers. Top chefs were imported from Europe. Many of these were single men who soon married Waimea girls and brought a European flavor into the community.

Such amenities as concerts by the Honolulu Symphony Orchestra, art shows, and a variety of cultural offerings began coming to Waimea. Anna loved entertaining friends at the Mauna Kea's fabulous buffet luncheon, or at dinner in one of its two fine dining rooms. She and Lyman still enjoyed frequent stays at the Royal Hawaiian Hotel, but with neighbors like the Rockefellers, and a hotel like Mauna Kea nearby, there was no longer an urgent need to go to Honolulu for recreation.

Anna continued to make frequent business trips to Honolulu, and occasional trips to the Mainland. During one of her trips soon after the Rockefellers became Anna's next door neighbors, Lyman invited realtor Tom McCormack and banker Alfred Vierra to visit him. When she returned home, Anna was appalled to see what the three men had done in her absence. Red flags were flying along the stone wall boundary and up the drive. As Lyman drove Anna home from the airport and they reached Anna Ranch, she took one dismayed look at those flags and gasped, "What's all that about!"

"We're going to build a road and have a subdivision!" enthused Lyman.

Anna angrily reminded him that this was her land. She wanted no road and definitely no subdivision. She was too tired from her trip to talk about the matter that night. Next morning she directed Bull to remove those flags. Undeterred, Lyman showed her the maps that had been drawn, the course of the roads to be built and the outline of the lots to be sold. "We'll make money!" he exclaimed. At this comment, Anna decided she had best get to her lawyer, her old friend who was now a Judge – Bill Heen.

Off she went to Honolulu to see Judge Heen. As usual she stayed in her suite at the Royal Hawaiian Hotel. Early in the morning, as was also her custom, she left her room to go down to breakfast. By chance, in the same elevator was one of Rockefeller's top men. "Anna!" he exclaimed, delighted to have run into her. "Can you have breakfast with me?"

"Of course!" she answered.

During breakfast Anna listened to the executive describe how upset Mr. Rockefeller was about the projected subdivision on Anna Ranch. "He wants to stop it!" Anna was told.

Something told Anna not to speak out about her own objections, and how she was in town to see Judge Heen and prevent the subdivision from ever becoming a reality. What Mr. Rockefeller had in mind was a plan he thought Anna might like as an alternative to the subdivision. Would Anna talk to Mr. Rockefeller's lawyer, whom he would send over from Chicago?

Anna agreed.

Not long afterward, three Rockefeller men came to Waimea to see her. One was Walter Collins, the planner and developer, whom she knew well. He was dressed in a business suit, and so was the second man. It was the third man who confused Anna. He was dressed in old Army fatigues and she remembers that to her he looked "like a grease money". Anna had two four-wheel-drive vehicles. The three men wanted to be taken to the top of Anna Ranch – where, she told them, she one day wanted her ashes to be scattered. To make the trip comfortable for her guests, Anna used both of her jeeps. Bull drove one, with the 'grease monkey' and the second man. Anna drove Walter Collins.

During the trip up across the ranch, the 'grease monkey' leaped out at every stop, rushing about, exclaiming over the view. Anna had been wondering why they brought him along today. "He's certainly lively!" she thought.

To her surprise, the 'grease monkey' turned out to be Rockefeller's Chicago lawyer!

He asked her to come to Honolulu to discuss an offer from Mr. Rockefeller, which he thought might be attractive to her. They arranged for the meeting to be held in Judge Heen's office so that, if necessary, Anna might consult with him. When the day for this meeting arrived, the Chicago lawyer was no longer wearing army fatigues but he was, Anna noticed, still a very casual man.

"Mr. Rockefeller much enjoys the peace and quiet, the open space around the White House," said the lawyer. "He is anxious that the noise and bustle of a subdivision not ruin this lovely tranquil environment. Therefore, he has asked me to offer to buy the land you had intended to subdivide."

"No, no! I won't sell it. That land is very precious to me. It was my father's ranch, and those pastures are the best in Waimea."

"Then if you won't sell, Mr. Rockefeller wants to know if he can lease some of the land from you."

All this while, in each of their encounters, Anna had not mentioned her own personal opposition to the subdivision. As far as the Rockefellers and their representatives knew, since it was Anna's land they assumed the subdivision had been her idea.

Next, the lawyer from Chicago mentioned the amount Mr. Rockefeller was willing to pay for an annual lease. It was a substantial figure. He also would pay the tax on the land.

Intrigued, Anna asked, "What does Mr. Rockefeller intend to do with these pastures he wants to lease from me?"

"Nothing. Nothing at all!" said the lawyer.

"If I can use the land to run my cattle, and keep my cattle pastured there, then I might be willing to give him the lease–," said Anna. "I'd be willing to take care of the fences!"

"Of course! Of course!" the lawyer agreed. And so the deal that pleased Mr. Rockefeller, and did what Anna had intended to do from the beginning, was drawn up by Judge Heen and signed by both parties. Lyman grumbled for a time about how much more money he could have made for her on a subdivision, but with the substantial lease arrangement there was really not much for him to say. The boom in Waimea continued, but Anna's lands were not sacrificed to it. "Anna's one shrewd business woman," said Tommy Rodenhurst, who with his wife, Julia Waterhouse Damon Rodenhurst, are among Anna's dearest friends. Anna and Laurence Rockefeller were both pleased by the new arrangement which kept Anna Ranch, and the 'White House', secluded by the open space that both of them were determined to preserve.

During this decade, when Anna was in her sixties, the *Honolulu Star-Bulletin* and *Advertiser* in their combined Sunday edition ran a full page feature about Anna Lindsey Perry-Fiske. *Advertiser* Staff-writer Mary Cooke described Anna as having "the strength of an athlete, the precision of an artist and a will of iron". Anna was, said the article, "a raven-haired dark-eyed dynamo." Anna was a dynamo indeed, with an iron will when it came to something as important to her as using the correct, traditional Hawaiian name for the place where she lived. What's in a name? For her, when it came to Waimea, the very preservation of the Hawaiian-ness, the history, and the original meaning of the name – "reddish waters" – meant that everything unique, important, and historic in Waimea was involved.

Her passion for restoring the proper usage of Waimea erupted into a political and personal cause one day when she and Lyman were about to fly home from a trip to Honolulu. As they boarded the plane, the stewardess announced, "We will be taking off for Kamuela in five minutes."

It so happened that Anna had recently prevailed upon the manager of the airlines to print boarding passes that read 'Waimea'. Since the airline still had some 'Kamuela' boarding passes, they were using both on today's flight. Anna, Lyman, and several tourists had been given passes that read 'Waimea'.

When the stewardess made her announcement that the flight was about to leave for 'Kamuela', Anna called out – "Hold it! Hold it! I'm on the wrong plane! I'm not going to Kamuela. I'm going to Waimea!"

With this the tourists who had 'Waimea' boarding passes stood up and scrambled to get their hand luggage out of the overhead storage bins. The poor stewardess was beside herself. Lyman was pink with embarrassment. "Oh, Anna!" he protested, shocked. She had had no time to tell him what she was going to do for hers had been a spontaneous outburst.

"No problem!" urged the stewardess. "Kamuela and Waimea are the same. You are on the right plane. No difference! It's okay!"

With this, Lyman began to smile. He knew what Anna would say now!

"Kamuela is the name of the post office. Waimea is the name of the place," Anna said in a loud firm voice. "It's not the post office where we're landing, is it?"

The poor stewardess looked baffled. She was still looking confused when the plane landed in Waimea and Anna and

Lyman disembarked. When they got into their car, and drove out past the 'Kamuela Airport' sign, Anna's annoyance, her indignation, and her determination fused into one. "Lyman!" she announced. "I'm going to see that this name business is settled for once and for all. And first, I'm going to see to it that the airport is renamed. Waimea-Kohala airport, that's what it ought to be. That's what it's got to be!"

For Anna the restoration of Waimea's rightful name became a crusade. With new people and young people either ignorant of or forgetting the past, Waimea was more often than not being called Kamuela – which, as she kept reminding everyone, was simply the name given to the Waimea post office when Hawaii became a United States Territory. *Advertiser* staff-writer Mary Cooke's impression of Anna as a "raven-haired dark-eyed dynamo" was also the impression received by the county supervisors, Mayor Shunichi Kimura and the Hawaii State Government as Anna fought for legal recognition of the name Waimea-Kohala for the airport, for the village itself, and for its usage on all highway directional signs.

In March 1967 Anna wrote to the County Board of Supervisors putting the 'what's in a name' question in its proper Hawaiian perspective. She was politely scornful of the recent comments of state statistician Robert Schmitt, chairman of the Hawaii State Board of Geographic Names, who had informed the supervisors by letter that the post office had indicated a preference for keeping the name of Kamuela for the community. "The name Kamuela is not Hawaiian," Anna wrote to the Hawaii County supervisors and Mayor Kimura. "Before, during and after the Great *Mahele* the name of this area was Waimea, meaning reddish waters because of the champagne color. Kauai has an area called Waimea, and they will want to keep it Waimea. Oahu has an area called Waimea and they would not want it changed. Hawaii has a Waimea and we, of Hawaiian ancestry, also want to keep our Waimea. It's a beautiful name with a definite meaning. If you understand the Hawaiian language you could learn much of its history, its lore and attraction of this area, Waimea, from the old song, 'Waimea.'" She discounted both the recommendations of the post office and of Robert Schmitt, adding, "What is there about Kamuela, (which is Hawaiian for

Samuel) that has anything to offer. It has no meaning to the Hawaiians whatsoever." She concluded, "I strongly suggest that we discard the name Kamuela and let us use the rightful name Waimea, such as Waimea-South Kohala, Hawaii 96743. We now have a zip code to signify the particular post office. So, by the zip code the sorting of mail should not be confused with Waimea, Kauai or Waimea, Oahu." She further suggested that Kauai adopt the hyphenated name, Waimea-Kauai, and Oahu the name Waimea-Oahu, following the recent example of the renaming of the Oahu and Big Island communities both bearing the name Kailua. The official name for the latter was now Kailua-Kona.

The letter had one immediate positive effect. Three weeks after she wrote it, Jack Bryan, *Honolulu Star-Bulletin* reporter on the Big Island, wrote an article headlined "A Rose by any other name . . . is Waimea". He filed the story from "Waimea (Kamuela?) Hawaii" leading off with the statement that "This proud old community on the high plain between Mauna Kea and Kohala Mountain is more concerned with proper geographic recognition than with the prospects of a four-year college." Governor John A. Burns' statement the previous week that he would rather see the next four year campus of Hawaii's community college system located in Waimea instead of on Oahu "caused barely a ripple of public comment" in the village. "Yet," wrote Bryan, "letters continue to pour into County Chairman Shunichi Kimura's office stating emphatic preference of residents, old and new, for the name Waimea rather than the official post office designation of Kamuela for this community."

On Tuesday April 4, less than one month after Anna's letter to the Board of Supervisors, there was a front page story in the *Hilo Tribune-Herald* reporting that Yoshito Tanaka, Hawaii County Attorney, "after an exhaustive research, says Waimea is the proper name for the community on the high plain between Mauna Kea and Kohala Mountain". That settled the matter as far as the Police Substation, the Public Works Station, and other county entities were concerned. The tax key maps continued to carry the name of Waimea – but then, they had never used the name Kamuela! Anna's one remaining problem was the State of Hawaii's airport sign, and its state highway signs.

She was incensed to see that the Honolulu papers, and to make it worse their Big Island Bureau Chief Walt Southward, were still using the name Kamuela in a half page feature on Waimea in the Sunday paper for October 29, 1967. "Kamuela, Hawaii" was how Southward described the place from which he filed his news story on the changes that Mauna Kea Beach Hotel and the real estate boom had brought to the Waimea area.

"Kamuela! Did he write the story at Kamuela Post Office?" asked Anna. She phoned the reporter to remind him that the subject of his story, and its origin, was not 'Kamuela' but Waimea-Kohala." However, she congratulated him on the story itself, and endorsed all that he said about the changes in Waimea, changes about which she was as excited and enthused as anyone.

On the plus side, there had been a 25% increase in the number of Hilo Electric Company's residential and commercial customers, with an even greater increase of 39% in the kilowatt hours used in the Waimea area. Residential property that sold for 60 cents a square foot before Laurence Rockefeller chose South Kohala for his hotel site was now going for $1.25 a square foot. This alone meant that within a five year period the real property value of Anna Ranch had more than doubled. And the village which had had a minimum of shopping and restaurant facilities now had three new eating establishments, two new small hotels, and a shopping center with SureSave Supermarket and the Ben Franklin Store ready to move in as soon as the buildings were completed. There was to be a pharmacy. Plans were under way for the Lucy Henriques Medical Facility which was to offer twenty-four hour emergency medical service to a community which had always had to make the long drive either to Kohala or Honokaa hospitals for either regular or emergency medical care.

The banking business shared in the boom. "We've seen a 35% increase in overall bank business in the past five years," Joseph Andrews, manager of the Bank of Hawaii's Waimea branch was quoted as saying. Joe Andrews was Anna's banker, and her personal friend whose investment advice and counsel she was to rely upon for many years. First Hawaiian Bank was opening a Waimea branch and two savings and loan associations were planning to open branches– one in the shopping center and one across the street from it.

By the time this feature story appeared Anna was in high gear on her push to restore the name of Waimea to the airport and the state highway signs. The previous month, September 9, 1967, she had received a letter from Mayor Shunichi Kimura saying "Our friend, Supervisor Willie Thompson has relayed to me your request to change the Waimea Airport sign. As you know, I was very disappointed that the State Department of Transportation refused our request to change the name to Waimea Airport. I shall have our Chief Engineer look into this matter to see what further can be done in this area."

In November 1967 Aloha Airlines was initiating service to the airport whose sign still identified it as 'Kamuela Airport'. Anna received a special invitation, in her name alone, to the inaugural and dedication ceremonies to be held by Aloha Airlines at 'Kamuela Airport' on November 1st. Following these airport ceremonies she was to be the guest of the president, officers and staff of Aloha Airlines at cocktails and a luncheon at the Waimea Steak House – one of the three new restaurants in the village. In her acceptance of this invitation, Anna reminded the president of Aloha Airlines, Kenneth Char, that the airport should correctly be designated 'Waimea-Kohala'. To that end, she finally went to the very top – her good friend, Governor John A. Burns. "You made your point, Anna. I agree! You are correct!" said the Governor, who had himself bought a home in Waimea to which he hoped one day to retire.

With the Governor backing her, Anna knew she had won. Waimea was officially and for all time Waimea. As she had suggested, the airport sign was changed to read: Waimea-Kohala. Highway signs today give the distance to Waimea, not Kamuela. And as Anna always has on her letterheads and her distinctive calling cards, Hawaii Preparatory Academy began listing its mailing address as 'Kamuela Post Office, Waimea-South Kohala'.

Oddly enough, Anna's successful 'Waimea' crusade on behalf of the Hawaiian-ness of her community was not a factor in the Hawaii Federation of Business and Professional Women naming her "Career Woman of the Year" in 1968. The newspaper account of this award describes Anna as "Big Island rancher and cowboy par excellence", and stresses that she had been chosen from many fine candidates proposed by clubs throughout the islands. The reason Anna was chosen? That year's statewide Federation president, Charlene Leonard of Captain Cook, Kona, explained.

"It was felt Mrs. Perry-Fiske is worthy of the honorary award as she gives unselfishly of her time and effort, not only for her own island, but the entire state and elsewhere." She cited Anna's years of participation in the Easter Seal (formerly Crippled Children and Adults) Society benefit luncheon and fashion show at the Royal Hawaiian. For ten years, said Miss Leonard, "Mrs. Perry-Fiske took first prize for the most beautiful hat worn by women in the audience. Each year she has donated her hat for auction, the proceeds of several hundred dollars benefiting the Easter Seal fund." But the judges for the BPW award considered Anna's 'Old Hawaii on Horseback' her greatest achievement, describing it as an "original Hawaian pageant" which she "originates, directs, and produces – and for which," says the news article, "Anna is being recognized by a further award from the Heart Association."

The Business and Professional Women's statewide convention was held in Hilo that year. They honored Anna with a dinner at the Hilo Yacht Club. Their award, a handsome monkey pod bowl with brass plaque, and the special certificate from the Heart Association, recognized the unique contribution Anna was making to Hawaii with her annual pageant, 'Old Hawaii on Horseback'. That year she had scheduled her show for March 20 but, as Maxine Hughes wrote in the May 12th edition of *The Orchid Isle*, a visitor guide for the Big Island, "the show has been postponed until May 25th, due to unseasonally heavy rains on the earlier date." The elements were beyond even Anna's remarkable ability to sway and persuade. "Although" wrote Mrs. Hughes – "every last detail of the historical, outdoor presentation was in complete readiness on the original date, including hundreds of leis for riders, their horses, and special guests, the show will be even better this month." It was!

In 1968 Waimea's Civitan Club manned a booth to sell lunches to the crowds who came to see the pageant. A percentage of the proceeds went to the Heart Fund and the remainder was donated to the Big Island Association to Help Retarded Children. Anna's charitable hands were extending farther and deeper, to help more and more people.

By November, she was already writing the script for the 1969 pageant. In 1968, the Fourth Annual Hawaii Cattleman's Horse and Bull sale was held on Saturday, November 23rd. Howard Brown of Chico, California, a well known auctioneer was back again with his fast moving banter. Anna always bid through Monty Richards. "When I sit and cross my legs, that means – 'Keep going! Bid!' If I put my leg down, he knows that means stop bidding! Otherwise," adds Anna, "if I bid they are going to push the prices way up!"

In 1968 Anna took home the champion bulls, bidding a successful $2000 for the reserve champion and $1500 for the grand champion, the latter a somewhat older bull. She also beat out her competitors on another Parker Ranch Hereford bull for which she paid $1500. 300 buyers, sellers, and spectators were at the 1968 auction. The bleachers at the Parker Ranch race track were filled to overflowing. November weather can be gorgeous or not in Waimea. To protect those attending from either too much sun, or from rain, a gay red and white striped tent had been erected. Those against whom Anna successfully bid for her champion bulls were the top ranchers in Hawaii – all of them men!

The Big Parades

ALL THE SUCCESS Anna was enjoying, the sweet taste of her victory at restoring official use of the name Waimea, all the awards and honors she had won were of no use in diminishing the heartache she suffered when Weston suddenly left Hawaii and broke off all contact with her.

One day Weston wrote Anna, saying, "Mother, I'd like to own my own home." Reading this, Anna went into her bedroom to phone Weston. She knew that if Lyman overheard the conversation it might upset him. Now in his seventies, Lyman was much incapacitated by emphysema and in addition had suffered several mild heart attacks. Anna tried to keep life free of stress for him. The last thing she wanted was any argument with Weston bringing on another heart attack for Lyman. But in the privacy of her room, Anna herself became upset as Weston asked her to send him $10,000 so he could put earnest money down on a house in Hawaii Kai. One of his friends was in real estate Weston explained. He and Bob were eager to give him some business.

"Mother! Send me over $10,000 right away. I want to make a down payment to hold the place!"

"Weston," said Anna. "I have just paid my taxes. I have other expenses to meet. I don't have the $10,000 to send you. Be happy with what you have, Weston! Enjoy your condo!"

But Weston was not about to take her advice. A short time later he wrote her, again asking for money. This time it was so he could buy an apartment he and Bob had fallen in love with. It was on the ground floor at the Diamond Head Ambassador. Anna handed Weston's note to Lyman. "Please Lyman. You write such beautiful letters. You answer him – I cannot." When she read the letter Lyman wrote in reply to Weston she was deeply touched, and she was sure Weston would be also. In the letter, Lyman with much sensitivity pointed out to Weston the difference in lifestyles between the one Weston seemed to have chosen, and the lifestyle Lyman and Anna followed.

Weston was in no mood to either listen to his parents or to do as they wished. Evidently Anna's refusal of the $10,000 and Lyman's letter infuriated him. To Anna's hurt surprise, when she flew to Honolulu several days later, she found that Weston had already left Hawaii with his friend Bob. He had given his condo keys to the manager. "Give these to my mother," he had told the woman. She told Anna that she thought Weston and Bob had gone to California. From Cannon's School of Business, Anna was able a short while later to obtain Weston's forwarding address.

Anguished over his having left Hawaii without speaking or writing to her, apprehensive that he might need money and be too proud to ask for any, Anna went to Bishop Trust, asking them to manage the condo as a rental and send the income to Weston. She then had her lawyer write Weston telling him of the arrangement. Anna had been pleased to hear that in the California mobile home community where the two men were, Weston had a small garden. "He loves flowers!" Anna thought. "He'll be so happy having a place to grow things."

When the lawyer called her saying Weston's reply to her concern had been a curt, "Tell her to keep her money. She may need it!" her son's blunt rejection of all she had ever meant to him or done for him broke Anna's heart.

"Forget him! All he's ever done is take advantage of you," advised Lyman.

Anna could see this, but it was still hard for her to try to accept such a reality. As she had when everything was so difficult after her father's death, when she had had so many debts to pay and

Anna takes a dare. Fisher Ranch, Blyth, California, 1950's.

Anna greeted by Captain of Lurline on bull-buying trip, 1950's.

Anna honors Richard Penhallow at an aloha *pa'ina* on his promotion to Parker Ranch Manager.

Anna buying Hartwell Carter's champion bull at Hawaii Livestock Show and Sale, Waimea.

Anna purchases prize Parker Ranch bull at first Hawaii Livestock Show and Sale, Waimea.

Anna and Les Wishard, Sr. show off her crossbred calves at 'baby luau', 1950's.

Judge Luman Nevels, Anna, HPA Headmaster James Taylor, Mrs. Nevels and Lily Lindsey at one of Anna's 1950's coffee fests.

Anna and Lyman at entrance to her ranch.

Weston at University of Hawaii graduation.

Courtesy Budger Ruddle.

Anna's long-time friend Eben Low– 'Rawhide Ben'.

only $150 in the bank, no cattle in her pastures, and a ranch to run, Anna put on her most dynamic smiling front. To watch her at parties, or on her trips to Honolulu, no one would guess she was a mother devasted by her son having turned his back on her. With that iron-willed courage which never deserted her, Anna carried on as if she were the luckiest, happiest woman in the world.

In April, as usual, she went to the Easter Seal fashion show luncheon and carried off first prize for her stunning white hat, which was decorated with varied pink flowers to match her pink lace dress and coat. She admired the Monarch Room's traditional Easter display of blooming tulips flown in by Canadian Pacific Airlines from Holland. She laughed and joked with her Honolulu friends as if nothing in her life was anything but perfect.

That same month the Honolulu Sunday papers featured close-up pictures of Anna on horseback, expertly twirling her lasso. She startled *Advertiser* photographer Gordon Morse when, as he snapped the last in this series of pictures, she dropped her lasso firmly around his shoulders with the same deft precision as she used to lasso a calf for branding. Mary Cooke, the reporter who visited Anna for a Waimea interview, gave readers the details of the schedule Anna was following in April 1969.

"In three hours, between 5:30 and 8:30 A.M.," wrote Ms. Cooke, Anna "gets all her housework done. Then it's 'to horse and away'. Daily she rides miles, checking fences, counting herds, moving calves and sometimes riding through thick forest lands following the tracks of cattle that get lost when fences are broken." What the reporter was not told was that in addition Anna was caring for an ailing fast-aging husband.

Anna told the reporter that "If I haven't found trouble I'm usually back by 3:30 in the afternoon. But sometimes not until after dark."

The interview was held in Anna's ranch house. "We were," writes the awed reporter, "having afternoon coffee at the family dining table. The cool Waimea air was steeped in the scent of yellow freesias. The coffee was dark, rich, and steaming hot and slices of cake were offered on gold and white china plates set on mats of embroidered organdy. My hostess (Anna) served from the highly polished silver coffee pot, sugar bowl and creamer. Her hands moved quickly and gracefully and though small, they are as strong as steel, with long tapered finers that curve up and back at the tips. Her voice range is wide and unfailingly dramatic, and the lady has a lively narrative sense."

What Mary Cooke never knew was that at the time of this interview, Anna's steel will hid a deep sorrow. Her energy, her vivacity, her animation and drive masked an undercurrent of sadness at Weston's refusal to communicate with her. In May, as the day of Anna's 'Old Hawaii on Horseback' neared, the *Honolulu Advertiser* ran a special half page story, with a panel of photographs in which Anna is demonstrating the proper draping of a *pa'u* riding costume on her young friend, Pat Hall, a Waimea artist who is the wife of one of the faculty at Hawaii Preparatory Academy. Anna's face in the photographs is very serious, for she is intent on draping the *pa'u's* fourteen yards of fabric. "First," says the article, "the fabric, held tightly, must be secured to the waist with six kukui nuts." Anna needed an assistant to hold up the immense stretch of material so she could fold, tuck and drape the costume so that the folds of the material would fall down gracefully once the rider mounted her horse.

This 1969 "Old Hawaii on Horseback" was attracting many Honoluluans who were taking advantage of a special one-day excursion tour which had been arranged for those who wished to fly over for the occasion. The event was the most successful of all the pageants Anna had produced. A full page story in the *Advertiser* shows her in a velvet riding costume, matching hat, beautiful lei, and a lovely, vibrant smile. Her figure is that of a young girl, and so is the grace with which she is sitting on her horse. Her beautiful face is ageless. "Horsewoman with Heart" says the subhead under the large headline which is simply "Anna Perry-Fiske". "Everyone attending the pageant, including tourists by the busload," says the article, "seemed caught up in the spirit of Old Hawaii."

After describing in detail the numerous riders portraying such characters in Hawaii's history as Captain Cook, Queen Liliuokalani, King Kalakaua, and Anna's great-grandfather, Thomas Weston Lindsey, the reporter concentrated on Anna's tremendous output of creativity in producing, directing, and taking part in this pageant. "Not only does the grande dame of

Anna Ranch supervise every last detail of 'Old Hawaii on Horseback' which she conceived five years ago, but she is up at the crack of dawn." Kapua Heuer and her daughter Pudding Lassiter drape the island princesses and queens. Anna herself drapes the *pa'u* of the Princess Kaiulani riders.

Only at the close of this fifth, and most successful of all of Anna's pageants so far did she break down. The news article in the *Advertiser* closes with "The standing ovation which Mrs. Perry-Fiske received at the conclusion of Master of Ceremonies Kelcy Isenberg's accolade brought tears she couldn't hold back. There was no doubt in the mind of anyone on the lawn of the sparkling white house at Waimea that 'Old Hawaii on Horseback' represents a heart full of love and aloha . . . that of Anna Lindsey Perry-Fiske." No one there guessed that Anna's tears were not only that of a heart touched by the warmth of thirty-five hundred people applauding her. They were also tears of an anguished mother's heart. The hanai son she had raised with such love and indulgence was not here, no longer caring to share in his mother's triumphs and joys. Although there were thirty-five hundred people watching Anna's magnificent pageant that lovely May afternoon, her heart ached for there to have been just one more.

In 1970 Anna bought a beautiful thoroughbred horse from Parker Ranch, which had become famous for its fine horses – quarter horses, Morgans, and polo ponies. Their horses were shipped to discriminating customers throughout the world – including the Shah of Iran. Anna's new horse was a big gelding whom she trained herself. "He was tame!" says Anna.

One morning as she mounted the gelding and settled herself in her saddle, the horse suddenly screamed and gave a rodeo buck. Anna stuck to the saddle, as her father had taught her, but what she did not realize was that this was no ordinary buck and rear. The gelding was suffering a massive heart attack. He fell over backwards, dead.

"Boss! Boss!" shouted Bull Awaa. Without a moment's hesitation he lifted that huge, heavy dead gelding while Lyman pulled Anna out from under. She was badly hurt but conscious. An ambulance was called. "Take me right to Hilo hospital! Call Dr. Mitchel!" she ordered.

She was conscious all the way from Waimea to Pepeekeo, an old plantation community close to Hilo. There the ambulance broke down and she finally fainted away from the intense pain. When she came to, she was in Hilo Hospital. Dr. James Mitchel, an outstanding surgeon who had trained at Mayo Clinic, was examining her. "Anna, you have a broken pelvis. And it's a bad break," he told her.

Anna had guessed that was what had happened. "I don't want a pin, Doctor! I don't want a plate put in there either!" All she could think of was that if they either pinned the bone, or put in a steel plate, she would never ride again.

Dr. Mitchel had both skill and compassion. He did as Anna asked, warning her that if the break did not heal naturally he might have to operate again. Then there would be no option of not having a plate or a pin.

It was a long, long stay for Anna in the hospital. Once a week Richard Lindsey, on his day off, would make the long trip to Hilo to bring his Auntie Anna an orchid corsage. He would pin it to her bedjacket, then visit with her as long as he could. Among Anna's first visitors were Judy Hancock and her sister Pat Hall. Anna was only allowed one visitor at a time. Judy, who like her sister was an artist and married to a faculty member at HPA, had just returned from the mainland. At the airport she heard of Anna's accident and immediately came to see her. This was, Anna recalls, the beginning of her close friendship with this young woman who, like Anna, loves horses and riding and ranching but who is at the same time most feminine in her dress and manner.

At first Dr. Mitchel was frank to tell Anna that because the break had been so bad she might never walk again.

"Oh," said Anna. "Well, Dr. Mitchel, do you mind if I try to walk sometime?"

"After a while you can try," said the surgeon, a gentle man who was killed six years later, in 1975, rescuing a group of Boy Scouts from a tidal wave.

"How fortunate I was that he was alive when I had my accident!" says Anna. She grins, telling how the day after he told her she might try to walk 'sometime', he repeated his warning that she might not be able to walk ever again. "I told him, don't worry about that, Doctor. I can! I walked around my bed three times this morning!"

One day Martin Pence came to see her. "I've been in here long enough," Anna told him. "I need to get back home and take care of business. I'm worried about the ranch."

"Be patient!" Pence advised. "You know, Anna. You and I are not as young as we used to be!"

"That doesn't matter. We're strong people, Martin. And my faith is going to pull me through. This will come out all right! I'll be back on a horse as soon as the bones are knit. A horse can fall on any cowboy–!" she said.

To her surgeon's amazement, the broken pelvis was healing. Anna's faith did pull her through. For one year she stayed off a horse as Dr. Mitchel warned her she must until the break in the bone was completely repaired. In 1970 she did not even attempt to stage 'Old Hawaii on Horseback'. She kept her strenuous activities to a minimum. Her patience, her persistence, her determination and faith in God and in herself paid off. She fully recovered. A year later, on April 1, 1971, the full-length portrait of Anna in *West Hawaii Today* was that of a beautiful, youthful woman, slim and straight in a fitted silk holoku. "It was designed by Pauline Lake, who had an artist decorate the silk with paintings of night-blooming cereus. No picture can do it justice," Anna reminisces.

The picture had been taken the previous weekend at the Hawaiian Civic Clubs' annual Holoku Ball, held that year in Kona. The caption under Anna's portrait informed readers that in the holoku parade, a traditional feature of the ball, of all the beautiful holokus and stunning women there, Anna won first prize for the most outstanding holoku. In her dining room that prize is still proudly displayed – a unique monkey pod serving stand with three tiers of scallop edged bowls.

Her broken pelvis mended, and her anguish over Weston lessening as time went by and he never tried to contact her, life again rose to a high point for Anna. Her intense energy seemed boundless. On May 15th she staged Old Hawaii on Horseback for a record crowd of 5,000. A highlight of the 1971 pageant was the presentation to Anna of her portrait, done by artist Diana Neville of Honolulu. Anna is painted in a flowing Hawaiian *pa'u* wearing flower leis and a crown of flowers. Her spirited horse is also draped in fresh flower leis. Anna loved that portrait and hung it where it still hangs today – in a prominent place in her living room.

Six months later, in October 1971, Anna was in Honolulu to ride in the twenty-fifth annual Aloha Week parade. As in the days when her dear friend Eben Low had been Grand Marshal, she rode as Queen of the *pa'u* riders. Unbeknownst to her, one of the men watching as she rode by in her royal blue velvet *pa'u* was Virgil White, president of the Tournament of Roses Association, from Pasadena California. The final date for applications of entry into the New Year's Day 1972 parade had passed, but one look at Anna and Virgil White decided to break the parade rules if he could coax her into coming to Pasadena to ride in her *pa'u* costume and pikake leis as Hawaii's Queen. An hour after Anna returned to her suite at the Royal Hawaiian Hotel that day, Mr. White called her from the lobby and urged her to say she would come to Pasadena in January.

Anna gave him a tentative yes. She promised to make her final decision in November. On the 22nd of that month, for the seventh consecutive year, Anna – according to the *Hawaii Tribune-Herald* was the "mainstay of the annual Bull and Horse sale" in Waimea. Once again she bought both the grand champion and the reserve champion. Altogether she purchased three bulls at the auction. The newspaper account lists the price she paid for the three champion animals as "over $7000''. The grand and reserve champion bulls this year came from Hartwell Carter's Homestead Farm. The third bull, a two-year old Hereford, was produced by Kauai's Kipukai Ranch. It brought the second highest price in the sale – $2300.

On the same day that the story about Anna's purchases at the November 1971 Horse and Bull sale appeared in the Hilo paper, Governor John A. Burns was writing a letter that asked Anna to serve as the official representative of the state of Hawaii at the Tournament of Roses Parade, to which he had learned she was invited. How could Anna refuse this honor from the Governor? She immediately finalized her plans for going to Pasadena and received a call from Virgil White. Not only was he proud she could ride as the Governor of Hawaii's official representative, he wanted her to ride as marshal of one section of what is certainly one of the world's biggest and most exciting parades.

On December 14, 1971 Mary Cooke of the *Advertiser* wrote an article announcing that "When the Tournament of Roses Parade gets under way New Year's morning in Pasadena, a grande dame of Hawaii will be the marshal of one section of the pageant." Ms. Cooke reported that "in royal Hawaiian style Mrs. Perry-Fiske will travel to Pasadena with a dresser, a lei maker and thousands of island flowers."

"For the parade," Anna had told Ms. Cooke, "I will wear a royal blue velvet *pa'u* with 50 strands of pikake (jasmine) and a crown of pikake blossoms. We hope to get white crown flowers for the lei for my horse." Those who would accompany Anna to Pasadena were to be Lyman, and Judy and Will Hancock. Judy, said the reporter, "will help dress Mrs. Perry-Fiske and drape her *pa'u* at parade time." Honolulu florist Eileen Townsend was to fly to California with boxes of island flowers and make the leis to be worn by Anna and her mount. "The island rancher has chosen a palomino horse and her saddle and bridle will be mounted with sterling silver." The article ended with a brief account of Anna's Old Hawaii on Horseback pageants and the information that the 1971 pageant which Anna wrote, directed, produced, and held at Anna Ranch in Waimea had been the most successful Heart Association fundraiser held anywhere in the nation. In June the American Heart Association, for the third time, had presented Anna with a distinguished service medallion, the highest award accorded a volunteer.

On December 22nd Anna and Lyman abandoned their usual holiday stay at the Royal Hawaiian Hotel to fly to Pasadena. Their reservations were at the Huntington-Sheraton there. Judy and Will were in California to spend the holidays with their families at Newport Beach and were delighted to be on hand to help Anna with preparations for riding in the Rose Bowl parade. With Weston now out of her life, Judy filled a void for Anna as did Richard Lindsey who gave her unstintingly of his affection and support. "Both Richard and Judy are always there when I need someone!" says Anna. The Hancocks, like Judy's sister and brother-in-law, Pat and Howard Hall were part of the HPA 'family' of which Anna was an invaluable and much loved member. During the sixties there had been a fairly large turnover of teachers who came from the Mainland to teach a while, and then left. The rigorous teaching schedule, the challenge of academic excellence, the rural atmosphere of the school's Waimea campus, and the extra duties and hours expected of teachers at a boarding school, is not to everyone's taste or ability. Howard Hall and Will Hancock were among the exceptions, both leaving promising careers on the Mainland to come and teach – a life they and the sisters whom they had married found fulfilling, exciting, and – as the Hawaiians put it – *no ka oi:* the best. This alone endeared them to Anna. Early on she had begun to treat them, and feel for them, as part of her extended family – her ohana. She was elated to have Judy and Will with her in Pasadena.

"Understandably," wrote Maxine Hughes in a half page account in the December 26th issue of *The Orchid Isle,* "Mrs. Perry-Fiske is pleased and excited she has been selected for the honor of being the first *pa'u* rider in the famous parade."

Early in December Anna asked Hilo police chief Ernest Fergerstrom for an introduction to the Chief of Police of Pasadena. Lyman couldn't understand why she did this, but Anna had her own very good reasons. She had learned from Tournament of Roses president Virgil White that at the end of the parade route, no autos were allowed – only those with special press or police passes. So, when Anna checked into the Huntington Hotel on December 22nd, she immediately called Pasadena's police chief. "Yes," he replied, "I have a letter from Chief Fergerstrom of Hilo asking if I'll assist you in every way possible. What can I do, Mrs. Perry-Fiske?"

With the same care as she pre-planned every moment of a cattle drive and each step of her 'Old Hawaii on Horseback' pageant, Anna had pre-planned every detail to be settled before the day of the big parade in Pasadena. Under her royal blue velvet *pa'u* she would wear slacks of the same color. "I need a way to get from the end of the parade route back to my hotel so I can change. We have tickets for the Rose Bowl game. I don't want to be late for that, so I thought perhaps you could send down a policeman to meet me at the end of the parade route.

I could ride on the back of his motorcycle from the Naval Station to the hotel," Anna told Pasadena's police chief.

His immediate response was a startled silence. The official Queen from Hawaii, draped in fourteen yards of velvet riding costume, hitching a ride on the back of a police motorcycle? Anna never realized how audacious her idea sounded to him, or how intrigued he was by a Hawaii Queen riding *pa'u* in the Tournament of Roses Parade. "I'll see what I can do, Mrs. Perry-Fiske. Let me call you!" said the chief.

It was several days before Anna heard from him again. When he finally did call, he said "I'm coming to see the parade just because I want to see you!" Then he told her he had arranged for the car she had rented to be marked with a special police pass. She would have no trouble getting to or from the parade route.

The rest of the details of getting prepared for the big day did not at all go with such ease. Anna had been asked by Tournament of Roses officials if she had a silver-mounted saddle. She had told them early on that she did not. Before she left Hawaii they had called saying she must rent one from them, and that the rental fee for the parade would be $300. With some annoyance, Anna assented. She was already paying her own way and that of the florist, in addition to the expense of shipping all the flowers to make the leis. A few days later they called to say they couldn't rent her the saddle. She would have to buy it, and the price was $2000.

Renting a palomino horse presented another problem and much anxiety. Anna always made it a practice to acquaint herself with the horse and the horse with her as a new rider before any parade. She went to Pasadena a week ahead of time just for that reason. But every time she called the owner of the horse, wanting to go ride him, she was given a variety of excuses. It was too muddy out at the horse farm. The owner wasn't feeling well. It was raining. Day after day Anna called, but by New Year's Eve she had not even been able to get a glimpse of the horse, or of the saddle!

On New Year's Day morning, Anna was at the parade site by 4:30 A.M. with Lyman, Judy and Will. They all sat in the car, waiting for Anna's horse to arrive. Worry increased as horse trailer after horse trailer discharged mounts for other riders and still Anna's had not appeared. Feeling desperate, Anna sent Lyman and Judy to look for the parade chairman, who had arranged the horse and saddle rental for her. They had no sooner left to find the chairman when Anna saw a trailer with a palomino that she knew was hers. It was jumping up and down, a nervous and spirited animal. The owner, Anna discovered, was a jealous person who, having heard of Anna's reputation as an expert horsewoman, had decided Anna would not – or could not – ride the palomino. It was, she told Anna, a 'one-woman' horse.

When Lyman and Judy came back, to her chagrin Judy saw that the woman was milking the horse. "It has a young colt. That's why it's so unruly!" Anna explained. They had a difficult time saddling the palomino. "Toss me up!" Anna said to Lyman, and with a worried look, Lyman boosted her up to the saddle. The velvet *pa'u* which Judy had draped under Anna's direction hung in elegant long folds down over the palomino's flanks. Anna looked stunning, with a crown of pikake flowers worn like a tiara on her dark hair.

The immediate problem now was how to reach up to drape the leis around Anna's shoulders, and over the head and shoulders of the nervous palomino. "Get on that truck bed, Judy!" directed Anna. "I'll just keep this horse going around and around in a tight circle and each time I come past, you toss a lei on one of us."

At 6:00 A.M. on New Year's Day in Pasadena, the sun is far from up. In the pale pre-dawn gloom, Anna tested the horse she was riding for the first time. She would have to manage the fiesty mare the entire long route of the parade. Judy stood on the bed of the truck and somehow, during the next hour, she threw thirty leis of crown flowers and 50 strands of pikake (jasmine flower) leis on Anna, and fragrant green maile and white carnation leis on the horse. Just before the parade was scheduled to begin, the owner of the palomino rode up on another horse. "Oh! you are going to be able to handle her!" she commented in amazement.

The next problem was a delay in the starting time of the parade. Here in Pasadena, Anna was discovering, the Tournament of Roses Parade did not operate on the tight and efficient time table on which she always ran her Old Hawaii on Horseback pageant. There is an old joke in the islands about 'Hawaiian time', which means "always late". What Anna found was that Pasadena ran its parade that year on 'Hawaiian time'.

She had to keep the horse moving, and before the parade began, the horse – who had never felt the weight of flowers on her neck before– managed to break the carnation lei. A passerby picked it up, handed it up to Anna, who put it over the horse. When the mare shook it off a second time, Anna let it lay. The palomino was still wearing the green strands of fragrant maile. That would have to do.

At last Anna's section of the parade received the starting signal. She had no trouble keeping her horse moving. In addition to riding as Hawaii's Queen, and being the first *pa'u* rider ever to be in the Tournament of Roses Parade, as Maxine Hughes had told Big Island readers in December, Anna was marshal of one section of the parade this New Year's Day, 1972.

A man behind her kept spurring his horse. Finally he rode up to Anna and said, "Get back here!"

"I have been asked to ride as marshal, which is what I am doing. Leading this section. Now you get back there and mind your business!" snapped Anna. She had no more trouble from that man!

Millions of viewers watched her as she passed the reviewing stand and the television cameras. She was every inch Hawaii's Queen that New Year's Day riding the frisky palomino past the crowds lining Pasadena's parade route.

On January 4th, Anna and Lyman returned to Honolulu. Two weeks later the 1972 legislative session opened in the new state capitol building. In the spacious chambers of the State Senate, on February 2nd, a Senate resolution was passed unanimously congratulating Anna Perry-Fiske "for her participation in the Tournament of Roses Parade" and commending "her years of dedicated service to the community." She had, the resolution stated, "brought honor to the State of Hawaii by her participation in the Annual Tournament of Roses Parade on New Year's Day 1972.''

Adventures Unlimited

IN 1972 ANNA fulfilled a lifelong dream – a leisurely two months trip around the world. She had put out of her mind the yearning she had once had that Weston and she might take such a trip together. It was Richard Lindsey, her beloved nephew, whom Anna invited to go along as her companion through 17 countries. Lyman was neither interested in the trip, nor was his health equal to keeping up with Anna on her fast paced itinerary. In his younger days Richard had made several cattle buying trips with Anna. He would be good company Anna knew for Richard had become the pleasant, enthusiastic, loving and thoughtful adult that his boyhood had promised. He was devoted to his Auntie Anna, always there whenever she needed him. He now had a family of his own, but his regard for Anna continued to be like that of a son for a much loved mother.

"Can you get a two months leave from the Police Department?" Anna asked him.

Richard Lindsey could, and did. It was to be, he knew, the trip of a lifetime for him.

They flew from Honolulu to New York, spent one week there seeing the sights and then flew to London. On each leg of the trip, the moment the plane took off, out would come

Anna's rosary. "Flying with you, we're in the hands of God!" Richard told her. Richard's favorite European country was Belgium. He also much enjoyed their five day boat trip on the Rhine River where they met a Chinese family who were on their way back to Singapore. A mother with two daughters and a son were traveling together, and in the course of the boat trip Anna and Richard became very good friends with this family.

"When you come to Singapore you must visit us! Please call as soon as you arrive there!" the Chinese woman urged. She gave Anna her card and extracted a promise that Anna and Richard would surely come to see her when they reached that stop on their round the world journey. The five days on the Rhine were followed by an unforgettable stay in Barcelona, Spain. There Anna found the Spanish bullfights were quite a different experience from the one she had had in Mexico. "No rain – and my dress didn't shrink!" she laughs, remembering the fiasco of the bullfight in Mexico City. Both she and Richard loved the bullfights in Spain.

"It was a real eye opener," Richard Lindsey recollects. "Before the bull fight we went to see the chapel where the matadors prayed before each fight, and the hospital where they were taken if the bull gored them. There was a slaughterhouse too, for the bulls that were killed in the ring."

Anna watched with appreciation the skill of the young matadors who fought the bulls from horseback. The horses were all scarred from being gored. "That night," remembers Anna, "eight bulls were sent to the slaughterhouse!" She kept worrying about the small boys, no more than twelve years old, who kept jumping into the bull ring, racing around, provoking the bulls, until the police came after them. Usually, Anna was told, these daring youngsters grew up to become top matadors. She could see why such a dangerous profession tempted them. After a matador made a kill, goatskin containers of wine and beautiful bouquets of flowers were thrown to him by adoring fans.

In Vienna Anna and Richard were enthralled by the Lippenzaler horses, and with Anna's connections, they were able to see the stables and were taken into the show area itself. In 1972 the Middle East was not yet a battleground and terrorism not yet a threat to travelers. Anna and Richard stayed at a plush waterfront hotel in Beirut. One afternoon, as they relaxed in the pool area of the hotel, they were fascinated to see a belly dancer entertaining the guests at a wedding reception being held on a lower level. Lebanon was also where they visited a casino which had a live show with horses on the stage.

In the Holy Land they visited Old Jerusalem and Bethlehem, and went to mass on the knoll where Christ was crucified. The weather was ideal everywhere until they reached India. It was monsoon season when they arrived in Jaipur. Their reservations were in that city's finest large hotel, but they arrived to find the place closed. The hotel employees were on strike. The 'rinky-dink' hotel to which they had to be shifted was most unpleasant. The only item on the dinner menu was mutton stew – and the stench of the mutton was so strong that neither of them could eat it. Anna lived on tea and lemon the short while they were in Jaipur. Because of the heavy monsoon rains, they had to cancel their flight to Agra, and so they missed seeing the Taj Mahal. The day they made the flight from Jaipur to New Delhi, the rains were torrential. Just as they were about to land, the pilot suddenly pulled the plane back up into the sky. "It was a close call!" says Anna. An hour later, they tried another landing and this time, they made it. Everyone congratulated the pilot as they deplaned.

Anna and Richard checked into the Oberoi Hotel in New Delhi. Next morning the headlines of the newspapers in New Delhi told them how lucky they had been on their flight. The following flight from Jaipur had overshot the runway and crashed, killing eighteen passengers.

"See Auntie? You saved us with your rosary!" said Richard.

"I keep God very busy–" was Anna's comment.

The next stop was Singapore where their Chinese friends from the Rhine River trip lived. "I wonder. Should I call them?" Anna asked Richard. "Of course! They meant it, Auntie Anna!" he encouraged her. When Anna made the call, their friend invited them to come that afternoon to her home, and sent a chauffer and limousine to the hotel to pick them up. Only then did Anna and Richard learn their modest Chinese mother of the Rhine River trip was the Tiger Balm heiress – owner of a large estate in Singapore, of the famous Jade Palace and of the Tiger Balm Gardens. They were given a personal tour of the gardens and of the Jade Palace. Their hostess then took them to her home for an exquisite

Chinese dinner.

From this high point of their unexpected 'Tiger Balm Connection' in Singapore Anna and Richard flew to Djakarta, spent a few days at a beach hotel in Bali, and then went on to Hong Kong. Richard especially enjoyed their cruise by junk in Aberdeen Harbor but when they went to have dinner on one of the restaurant barges, he noticed the fish net, and the floating pond of dirty river water from which the diner's choice on the menu was taken to be cooked. "That doesn't look healthy to me!" agreed Anna. At that restaurant, one of Hong Kong's best, they did not order fish.

In Hong Kong, as they had everywhere, Anna and Richard attended mass. "It was offered in Chinese!" Anna marveled.

Their next, and last country before flying home was Japan. They flew from Hong Kong to Osaka, took a limousine to Kyoto and stayed at the Kyoto Hotel while they took in the sights of that ancient city. Having heard so much about the *onsen*, the famous spas built around hot springs in the mountains of Japan, they went up to one in the mountains near Kyoto. "It was great! So relaxing!" says Anna.

From Kyoto they rode the famous Bullet Train, the *Shinkansen*, to Tokyo where they remained five days, taking side trips to Nikko and the beautiful lake country above Nikko. There is a Japanese saying, "Once you have seen Nikko, you have seen the best of everything!" And Nikko seemed a fitting climax to two months of superb adventures. It had been a wonderful trip around the world, but they were glad to return home to the green hills of Waimea.

That fall Anna again bought the champion bulls at the Waimea Horse and Bull sale. She was concentrating on purebred Herefords now, and her herd was among the best in the state. Lyman was no longer able to be very active. He rarely rode anymore, though he still enjoyed being on horseback. As he grew older, he liked having Anna take him for long drives in the car, especially to Kohala. Every two weeks she took him on a trip they both looked forward to – spending the weekend in the cool elevation above Keehi, Kona at the home Anna bought from a cousin of her father.

It was a beautiful redwood house complete with lovely old

furniture. There was an acre of land on the place. The garden was that lush Hawaiian style that is characteristic of upland Kona. Every two weeks Anna would send Bull over in the truck with three or four yard men to keep the lawn mowed and the flower beds weeded and trimmed. She had acquired the Keei property while Weston was still in school. As the years went by she and Lyman used it more and more frequently. Anna had the place painted all white, as was her ranch house. "When I come here I have new life. I love it here!" she exclaimed when she first acquired the property.

Lyman, who was good at Hawaiian names, after hearing Anna say this, named the house Hanuola – 'breath of life'. From Hanuola, they could look down and see Captain Cook's monument off in the distance, on the far shore of Kealakekua Bay. Anna still loved Keawewai, but it was an integral part of her ranch. At Hanuola she was removed from all sight and sound of her many responsibilities. There she could really relax.

It had been too much of a strain to put on 'Old Hawaii on Horseback' every year. Anna realized that after her broken pelvis forced her into a year of inactivity. It was during that period she decided in the future to put on the pageant as a biennial event. It was still a demanding schedule. In 1972, after returning from her round the world trip, Anna began writing the script for her May, 1973 'Old Hawaii on Horseback.' During the spring of 1973, she designed costumes and began rehearsals with the 119 riders who were to participate. She chose a long, gold colored English riding habit for this year's pageant, and rode side saddle accompanied by Richard Smart, owner of Parker Ranch, whom she had asked to be that year's marshal. Anna's pageants were never repetitious. She always had something new and exciting to offer the crowds who came from all over the island, and from throughout the state. There were tourists who planned their Hawaii vacation especially to be able to see 'Old Hawaii on Horseback'.

No longer was there room simply for people to sit on the lawn. Bleachers were now erected on three sides of the arena. People began arriving early to get a good seat. And Anna added to the attractiveness of her affair by arranging pre-pageant entertainment for those who came hours ahead of time. Throngs of early arrivals were entertained by the Hilo hula troupe of Edith Kanakaole, one of Hawaii's most revered hula instructors. The Hawaii County Band was on hand, under the direction of Andres Baclig. The Civitan Club had its lunch booth set up and ready, selling plate lunches of stew and rice – Waimea's traditional cowboy fare.

The 1973 pageant was even more spectacular than Anna's previous shows. She had each horse and rider adorned with a fresh lei made of pansies, ferns, maile and an assortment of Waimea flowers. That year's pageant was a two-hour extravaganza which had been so carefully planned and rehearsed that Anna was sure it would go forward without any delays.

There was always something new and different about each pageant. This year the master of ceremonies announced to the crowd that a 'mystery rider' had just arrived by air from Molokai. "She has come from the backwoods of Molokai to appear in this pageant!"

All eyes were on the 'Hawaiian woman from Molokai' riding across the lawn on a white mule. Her saddle bags were full of ferns, as if she had just come down from the mountains. Her feet were bare. She wore an old fashioned black holoku. On her head was a lauhala hat, its big floppy brim pulled down tight over her ears so that her face was hidden. With her was what appeared to be an old Hawaiian man, dressed in palaka shirt, a bandanna neckerchief, and also riding a mule.

Who could the mystery rider be? Julia and Tommy Rodenhurst, sitting in the front row special seats Anna always reserved for them, were stymied until Julia exclaimed "Look at those legs! They're white! And those dainty feet! That must be Anna, the rascal!"

By the third round everyone guessed who the mystery rider was – Anna!

She and Lyman had thought up the stunt. An old print had given Lyman the original idea. Recently he had bought a mule from Alika Cooper and Anna put that fact together with the idea of the old couple portrayed in the print – and had her special 'mystery rider' for the 1973 pageant. Her mystery escort was Frank Vierra, a Parker Ranch cowboy. "I sure had to hustle to change from my fancy gold riding habit to that black holoku and then back again. I fooled everybody all right!" Anna laughs.

The one hitch of the afternoon, and that only a momentary one, was something no rehearsal could have foreseen. Even the best of bulls are unpredictable! One of Anna's prize bulls gave the crowds at the pageant a new thrill that May afternoon. Anna had asked Dr. William Bergin of Kona to play the role of Captain George Vancouver. To carry out Vancouver's historic part in bringing the first cattle to Hawaii – and of seeing Waimea as an ideal pasturage – Anna arranged for a prize bull to be led by Dr. Bergin. At first all went beautifully. The bull, whom Bergin led by a rope, and Bergin's horse were in perfect step as they made the rounds before the packed bleachers. But once they had made the first trip around the arena, the bull decided he did not want to leave all these people, and all this excitement. He spooked, refusing to be led away.

He slipped off his halter and, completely free, the huge bull stood facing the apprehensive crowd. There were a few anxious moments before a cowboy slipped the halter on again and led the bull off and away.

The crowds attending the 1973 pageant, and the money Anna raised for the Heart Association again broke all national fund raising efforts. It was her expertise in this that led Bernard Nogues, longtime teacher and admissions director of Hawaii Preparatory Academy, to come to Anna with a proposal, and a request. The school, whose tuition even for day students was expensive, wanted to set up a scholarship fund to benefit Waimea boys and girls whose families were unable to afford to send them to HPA. The fund was also to offer scholarship assistance to boarding students whose families needed or requested such aid. James Taylor, long time HPA headmaster, was determined that the student body not be just an elite group from socially prominent and wealthy families. His hope was to have a fund from which scholarships could be given to an increasing number of day and boarding students who were of varying ethnic and socio-economic backgrounds.

Bernard Nogues, a native Frenchman who originally joined the HPA faculty in 1966 as a French teacher, had heard of Anna, of course. For him, before 1973, she was a distant and somewhat formidable figure living in her big ranch house, someone he saw at great events but had never yet known personally. He was aware that Anna was someone "you didn't mess around with", but also that she was known as "generous, with a good heart, and helpful."

"I was not in Anna's orbit," Nogues recalls, "but in 1973 I went to the Hawaii School for Girls auction in Honolulu. They called it HOOPLA, and it was a big success. They were one of the first to raise money this way. It hit me that here might be the answer to the problem for which I had practically no budget. As Director of Admissions at HPA, I had been given the charge to develop a foundation or endowment fund for scholarships. Why couldn't HPA hold such an auction? We might have a dinner in an elegant place with good food and wine, donations which could be catalogued, a top auctioneer. But what I really needed to go forward with this tentative germ of an idea was somebody with a big name, a name with instant statewide recognition to head the auction. As I thought about it, just one person could do it for us. Anna Perry-Fiske! I knew if she would accept such a responsibility, her dependability would be phenomenal. The problem was, how do I approach this great lady whom I do not really know!"

Finally Nogues decided to take his courage in his hands and go face Anna with his idea. He prepared his presentation with great care. He arranged an appointment through Judy Hancock, who had become increasingly close to Anna. On the day he was to call on Anna he dressed in his best – blue blazer, gray flannel trousers, shirt and tie. "I never forget Anna receiving me in that fabulous living room!" says Bernard Nogues. "She was sitting there in an elegant straight backed chair, in a charming outfit." To him Anna is a grande dame in the European style. "I saw in Anna this same regal appearance, the oblivion to things trivial or vulgar, traits of great European ladies which many Americans may not well understand but to me are extraordinary."

That afternoon Bernard was exceedingly nervous, facing Anna. To his great relief, when she heard that he was asking her to help with a scholarship fund – not with raising money to build a new building or pay off an old debt for the school – she looked keenly interested.

"I like what you are telling me, but as you know, I'm a busy woman," said Anna when Bernard finished his presentation. "I don't want to commit until I think it over. I'll call you."

He left that afternoon, not knowing whether to be hopeful or discouraged. By the next morning, Anna rescued him from his indecision. "Let's begin planning!" said Anna. "But I don't want a committee. Just you and I will do this. We'll target the auction for next fall, 1974."

That December of 1973, when Anna and Lyman left for their two weeks of holiday festivities at the Royal Hawaiian Hotel, Anna had plans for the November 2, 1974 first HPA auction already detailed. There was much to do, she informed Bernard Nogues, and the spring and summer of 1974 were to be exceptionally busy ones for her. Two big events were being held in Canada that summer: the Calgary Stampede, and the Lethbridge, Alberta Centennial Celebration of the Royal Canadian Mounted Police. Anna had been invited to ride in both. At first the two cities argued over which of them would have Anna, the *pa'u* rider who would grace their parade as Hawaii's Queen. "How could I expect to choose one and not hurt the other?" asked Anna. "I told them both I would go – after all, the Calgary Stampede parade was scheduled for July 4. The parade in Lethbridge was not until July 15. I could easily do both!"

In May of 1974 Governor George Ariyoshi wrote congratulating Anna "on behalf of the people of the State of Hawaii on your selection as Hawaii's Queen in the centennial celebration at Lethbridge, Alberta, Canada." He was delighted that she had been invited to Canada, spoke with appreciation of her having been the first and only woman to represent the state of Hawaii in the Tournament of Roses parade in Pasadena, and, like his predecessor Governor Burns, under whom Ariyoshi had served as lieutenant governor, he told Anna that "your participation in such events has enriched your stature and the stature of Hawaii immeasurably. For that, I am grateful." He wished her "aloha" on her July trip. As she had been asked to do in 1972 in Pasadena, in the two Canadian parades Anna was to represent the state and people of Hawaii.

She knew she must ship the flowers, take along a lei maker

to string them just before the parade, and have a dresser who could help drape her properly in her velvet *pa'u*. Her Kona friend Irene Caldwell offered to do this. Anna paid the way for Irene and her husband Jim to accompany her and Lyman to Canada. "I'll wear a different outfit for each parade," Anna decided. For Calgary, she decided upon the royal blue velvet *pa'u* she had worn in Pasadena but rather than trying to ship fragile pikake blossoms she took along the longer lasting white crown flowers which also made a distinctive lei. For Lethbridge she decided upon a red velvet pa'u with which she would wear ilima leis. The ilima was another of the rare Hawaiian leis reserved for wear by the alii in ancient times. This deep golden yellow flower, strung into a lei, has the same appearance as the gold feather leis with which Hawaiian royalty adorned themselves. Ilima is so delicate that to take or ship the fresh flowers was not feasible. Anna was delighted to find Mrs. Jesse Hanna an expert in making silk ilima flowers that were almost impossible to tell from the real ilima blossoms. "No one would know that the closed buds I wore and the more open ilima flowers on the horse's lei were not freshly shipped in from the islands!" Anna recalls.

On arrival in Calgary, a celebrity's welcome waited her. Television cameras from the news stations of that Canadian city were there to record her entry into the airport where Jim A. Taylor, one of the Stampede chairmen, was on hand to personally welcome Anna and her party. Tom Dawson was assigned as Lyman and Anna's personal representative for all events. Courtesy cars and drivers were put at their disposal along with reserved seats at all stampede activities. Brunches, luncheons, dinner parties and receptions swept Anna and Lyman, and the Caldwells, who were former Canadians, into a whirl of activity before and just after the mammoth parade.

Anna had to use all her equestrian skills to handle the fiesty Apaloosa they gave her to ride in Calgary. Those at the stampede were, many of them, ranchers like herself, and people who knew horses. They appreciated how hard that Apaloosa was to handle and Anna was applauded every mile of the long route. Few Canadians had ever seen a *pa'u* rider, or a woman who could ride as Anna did. Lyman was as thrilled as was Anna to be at the famous Calgary Stampede. Their Canadian hosts could not do enough for them there but soon it was time to go on to Lethbridge.

Just before they left Calgary, Anna received a phone call. "This is Wes speaking," said her son's familiar voice. "I want to see you in Lethbridge. We are on our way to Alaska, Bob and I." He told her they had planned their trip and fixed the date in order to see her. "Grandma Lily wrote me about your being in the big parades there and in Calgary," he told Anna.

Like any fond mother Anna invited Weston to have dinner with her and Lyman that evening in Lethbridge, giving him the name of the hotel where they would be staying. She could hardly wait for the plane to land in Lethbridge, and for the dinner hour to arrive. How will he look? she kept wondering. How has he been? "Oh my goodness!" Lyman kept saying. "Oh my goodness!"

At the hotel in Lethbridge Anna learned they were honoring her with a party that night. "I'm going to invite Weston to come along!" she told Lyman.

When Anna met Weston down in the lobby that evening she was shocked to see her son in such cheap looking clothes – poorly cut jeans, a shabby black cowboy hat, seedy looking boots, ill fitting shirt. Always, before he left Hawaii, she had bought him expensive clothes in which he looked so well.

During the dinner party, Anna felt no emotion beyond that of pity to see how down at the heels Weston and his friend looked. At the table, Weston suddenly broke down and cried and cried. People began asking Irene Caldwell, whom they knew was well acquainted with Anna and her family, "What's wrong with the young man?"

"He hasn't seen his mother in a long time" Irene told them.

Even seeing Weston weeping so uncontrollably, Anna did not cry. "I didn't feel like crying!" she remembers.

The next day, since the group was one car shy of taking guests around Lethbridge on a sightseeing jaunt, Irene Caldwell suggested to Weston that he take his mother. It was on this ride, alone with Weston, that Anna had a chance to hear how it had been for her son. "I didn't want to leave California," Weston confessed to her. "But my friend Bob did. We got into a terrible fight over it. He even broke some of our furniture –"

Over the next several days Weston shared in the festivities for his parents. The Hawaii group were guests of the Royal Canadian Mounted Police one night at a dinner party in the Flying Inn, a renowned restaurant in the nearby town of Claresholm. Harold Leppard was the person directly responsible for entertaining Anna and her group in Lethbridge. Leppard was a rancher himself. He and his wife entertained the Perry-Fiskes in their home as well as taking them out to their ranch.

"We Canadians are a shy people, really reserved and not given to demonstrate how we feel. So don't be alarmed if there is little applause along the parade route. It won't mean we don't appreciate you – it's just that in Lethbridge we don't usually go in for things like applause," Leppard told Anna.

In the Lethbridge parade, Anna had the great pleasure of riding what she described as "one of the finest horses I've ever seen or ridden." It was a stallion, a 17-hands high Tennessee walking horse owned by Ken Hudson. Against the glossy dark chestnut color of this horse, Anna's vivid red *pa'u* and her gold ilima leis were most striking. "Never did Anna look so beautiful!" recollects Irene Caldwell.

One of the things that had touched Anna on her arrival in Lethbridge was a greeting by the mayor and other city officials. She felt so at home when a young Canadian-Japanese woman, dressed in a kimono, presented her with a bouquet of red roses at the welcoming ceremony at the airport.

The day of the centennial parade was clear and pleasant. "The greatest thrill of my life was the applause I received all along the two-mile-long parade route!" Anna reminisces. After what Harold Leppard had told her, she was totally unprepared for the warmth and Hawaii-style aloha of the Lethbridge crowds. Many, she learned later, had driven hundreds of miles to see this Hawaii Queen in her *pa'u* riding costume. Anna doubled the distance of the two mile route as she kept riding from one side of the street to the other to wave to the cheering crowds. People lined both sides of the street. Many were standing on top of buildings. There was a continuous bank of children seated along the curbs. She kept waving and calling "Thank you! Aloha!" until her arm ached and she was hoarse. Lethbridge and its people captured Anna's heart that day.

Having seen her ride in Calgary and at Lethbridge, another group of Canadians tried to persuade her to ride in the Klondike Days celebration, but Anna refused. She had a pre-arranged schedule to keep. One was a rare luncheon invitation to a group that seldom invited outsiders – the New Elm Hutterite Colony at Magrath, Alberta. Anna and Lyman went on from there to be guests of Mr. and Mrs. Richard Blasco at Beauvais Lake. Another day they were honored at a luncheon in a chateau at Waterton Lakes national park. And while they were in western Canada, Anna and Lyman also visited Lake Louise, Banff, and Victoria, B.C.

When she returned to Waimea, Anna went into high gear on preparations for the HPA Scholarship auction. Bernard went along with her to Honolulu, amazed by how Anna could walk into the offices of top bankers and business people and come out with substantial donations which were often far more than the donors had originally intended. "She just has a special way with her!" Bernard says. "These captains of industry always seem super-thrilled to see her. When she begins talking, they forget about time and I never think to worry about making our next appointment on schedule. She has everthing under control. And when she asks what they can give – and they say $1000 – she'll often tell them – that's not enough. We need more." Bernard gives his characteristic and very charming French shrug. "And they give her more!" As Martin Pense had long ago observed, Anna could not only sell men cattle they didn't need or want, she could get from them more charitable donations than they had ever intended to make.

It was Anna who prevailed upon Honolulu's most successful auctioneer, Steve Rosen, to come for the auction. "No charge," he offered. "I'm doing this for you Anna, and for HPA."

Early on, Anna had arranged with Mauna Kea Beach Hotel for use of their very special dining room, the Batik Room. The dinner was to begin with shrimp cocktail au courvoisier. Complimentary Mouton-Cadet Rothschild was to be served the guests throughout the meal. The entree was the hotel's very special prime rib with Yorkshire pudding, and the dessert Vacherin Chantilly with fresh strawberries. Tickets were fifty dollars a couple, for dinenr and the evening. Guests of course were expected to bid generously for the items Steve Rosen was to auction off for the scholarship fund.

The Batik Room is a dimly lit, intimate room which was fine for the dinner, but turned out to be disastrous for those wanting to view the items that would be auctioned off that night. "No one can see!" Anna informed the hotel manager. Immediately the manager had powerful projectors brought in, and focussed on the items to be auctioned – and the auctioneer.

It was, unfortunately, the hottest night in years. The air conditioners in the Batik Room were unable to absorb the heat from all the bodies. "Everyone was gasping, wilted, mopping their faces – but not Anna!" says Bernard. "She is absolutely unflappable and looked gorgeous as usual although she was in the hottest spot in the room – right under the lights, next to the auctioneer."

Jack Lord, star of the popular t.v. show, 'Hawaii Five-O' had given Anna his Arizona roper saddle to be auctioned off during the evening. Paintings, antiques, furniture, and Anna's choice freezer beef were among the items listed in the auction catalog provided each guest. To Bernard Nogues' relief neither the heat nor the lighting problem diminished the spirited bidding. Anna's vibrant presence kept interest high and Steve Rosen's inimitable auctioneering brought top prices for each item.

Dr. and Mrs. Mitchel of Kona were successful bidders for the rare Howard Hitchcock painting. A painting by Madge Tennent went to Raymond Salley. Dr. Alex Miles outbid everyone for half a steer and an antique obi. W.K. Woods of Pauuilo, sportsman, yachtsman, and rancher was high bidder for the ancient fish board from the Tuamotu islands, a Waterhouse family antique donated by Anna's dear friends, Julia and Tommy Rodenhurst. The Jack Lord saddle went for a high price, to Paul DeDomenico of Honokaa. Altogether, to Bernard Nogues' amazement and Anna's quiet satisfaction, this first of its kind HPA scholarship benefit auction brought in a total of $29,000.

We'll do better next time!'' Anna assured the delighted Nogues.

Anna was radiant that evening in a strapless satin evening gown. At the close of the auction, she was given a standing ovation. ''Fitting tribute to a very great, very hard working lady!''

commented Bernard Nogues. Earlier, the Academy had presented her with a pansy lei, the Bank of Hawaii with a lei made of hundred dollar bills – which she promptly donated to the scholarship fund. Lyman's brother Al Kealoha Perry and his wife Katherine and Mauna Kea Beach Hotel Manager Bob Butterfield and his wife Charlotte presented multi-strand pikake leis to Anna. "It was the team effort which made this auction successful and encourages us to consider another!" Anna said after telling the people there how grateful she was for their presence tonight, their participation, and their support.

It was an evening Lyman much enjoyed, and where he was one of the most enthusiastic bidders.

Crises

AFTER THEIR REUNION in Lethbridge, Anna and Weston
kept in touch by mail. To each of his letters she wrote a fond
reply. In May 1975 she wrote him about the success of her 'Old
Hawaii on Horseback'. A crowd of more than 5000 had
converged on her spacious lawns to watch 136 riders in
costumes that Maxine Hughes described "as colorful as the
rainbow, hats with great feathered plumes moving with the
breeze, brilliantly hued pa'u rippling against the horses
haunches". For the first time in one of Anna's pageants a group
of heart patients rode as a team. Among them was Lyman, now
80. He had had a series of increasingly severe heart attacks.

"This time," said Maxine, who had become the editor of
The Orchid Isle. "to a far greater extent than ever before, the
tireless director-producer of the outdoor tableau, Anna Lindsey
Perry-Fiske, was hailed, decorated with leis, presented gifts and
acclaimed both for her efforts in preserving island heritage and
for 10 years work in raising many thousands of dollars for heart
research and equipment."

One of the resolutions that Anna most prized was one read
that day by the Association of Hawaiian Civic Clubs honoring
her "as a descendant of those Hawaiian people who have their
roots deep in the ranch country of Waimea" and praising her

171

as "an outstanding Hawaiian for her contribution to the well being of all the people of Hawaii." The resolution was accompanied by presentation to Anna of a gold medallion embossed with the seal of Hawaii.

Maxine Hughes reported to readers of *The Orchid Isle* that at the conclusion of the 1975 pageant, Anna had announced that half of the pageant's proceeds this year would go for equipment to treat heart patients at the Hilo and Kona hospitals. The other half, as usual, was to go directly into the Heart Association fund for research. The May 17, 1975 extravaganza was Anna's sixth 'Old Hawaii on Horseback'.

This year of 1975 Anna added another first to her long list of achievements. On October 18, she was the first woman marshal of the big Aloha Week parade in Honolulu. She shipped her favorite mount, a registered quarter horse called 'My Bert' to Honolulu to ride that day. Judy Hancock, dressed in white trousers, blue cape and a specially designed cap, was Anna's page. She rode ahead of Anna, carrying her banner. Escorting Anna as parade grand marshal were Lyman, who insisted he felt well enough to do so, Richard Lindsey, and friends Morgan Brown and Jack Baird. An Oahu man, Buddy Gibson, was also a mounted escort. It was a nostalgic event for Anna. How well she remembered the first Aloha Week parades in which she had ridden when Eben Low was grand marshal.

All through 1975 Anna was much concerned for her friends and neighbors in North Kohala. The closing of Kohala plantation, which Castle and Cooke had announced four years earlier, was about to be finalized. Twenty thousand acres of Kohala agricultural land would lie idle. The 3500 people of North Kohala were losing the economic backbone of their district – over five hundred jobs. In many ways, like Hana-Maui, North Kohala had retained its old fashioned Hawaiian atmosphere. The boom that escalated land values in South Kohala after the opening of the Rockefeller resort at Mauna Kea Beach had not traveled the seventeen miles over the tortuous mountain road to North Kohala. Akoni Pule, the Democrat who had won the 1948 election in which Anna was a candidate for the West Hawaii seat in the legislature, had remained in office. In 1968, due to his efforts a beach road – a new link between South and North Kohala– had been built from

Kawaihae to Mahukona. Despite everyone's hopes, the Akoni Pule Highway, as it was later named, by 1975 still served only to cut travel time of Kohalans driving to work at Mauna Kea Beach Hotel.

Anna had been relieved when the plight of the economic disaster facing that district was immediately addressed by Hawaii's State government. In 1971 Governor John A. Burns had appointed a joint state-county Kohala Task Force to use government funding for new ventures that might offer employment to Kohala's people and find new profitable uses for the cane acreage. For the first time in more than a century, the famous winds of Kohala would not ripple shades of silver and green across fields of sugar cane. The precious sweet water supply of millions of gallons collected daily in the Kohala Ditch, where Lyman had had his first job as a construction crew supervisor, was to be allowed to run out into the sea.

Anna's old friend Dick Frazier was one of Governor Burns' 1971 Kohala Task Force appointees. Chairman of the task force was then Lt. Gov. George Ariyoshi. Other members were John Bellinger, president of First Hawaiian Bank, Eddie Tangen and Ah Quon McIlrath of the ILWU, Robert Cushing, Robert Gordon, Big Island Mayor Shunichi Kimura, John Farias, Sunao Kido, Shelley Mark and Fred Erskine. It was a prestigious and able group. In 1974, when George Ariyoshi assumed the governorship after cancer prevented Jack Burns from completing his third term, former Big Island Councilman John Farias was appointed Task Force Chairman. He was also Ariyoshi's Director of the State Department of Agriculture. McIlrath, Cushing, Tangen, Bellinger and Frazier retained their membership when Ariyoshi took office. New appointees in 1974 were Hawaii County Mayor Herbert Matayoshi, long time Kohala councilman Ikuo Hisaoka, Hideto Kono, Jess Boyers, and Chris Cobb.

Because one of its projects was to be a feedlot Anna was an early supporter of the Task Force idea. In concept she knew a Kohala-based feedlot would be a tremendous economic advantage to ranchers such as herself, and to the small individual ranchers such as those on the 300 acre Hawaiian Homes Land farm lots that Anna, together with Hartwell Carter and Richard Penhallow had been instrumental in doubling from the original 150 acres proposed. "You can't make a living running cattle on 150 acres," Anna had long ago told the Commission, "To make a go of ranching – which is what most of Hawaiian Homes lands applicants in Waimea intend to do – you need at least 300 acres." Letters signed by her, by Hartwell Carter and Richard Penhallow had exerted steady political pressure until they succeeded. As a result, in the years since statehood, Hawaiian Homes Commission Land grantees like Kalani Schutte, a former policeman from Honolulu, had been awarded 300 acre tracts.

Kalani Schutte, who later became a Big Island Councilman, joined with Anna in 1975 in supporting Biogenics, the feedlot proposal. It took the Kohala Task Force some time to approve the loan to enable that enterprise to begin construction. Anna well understood that the responsibilities given the Kohala Task Force were those no private lending institution would assume. The plantation economy of large-scale sugar cane acreage that had been profitable and popular for more than a century was being phased out by declining sugar prices in the world market and by foreign competitors with immeasurably cheaper labor and operating costs. By 1975 it was clear that economic resuscitation for North Kohala would not be an easy venture. The Kohala Corporation, the initial project by which the Task Force had hoped to provide new jobs for Kohala and stimulate new industries in the district had been a disaster. Biogenics seemed to Anna much more feasible.

For a number of years she had recognized the economic advantages of a local feedlot. She hoped that once one was established there might eventually be a slaughterhouse operation in either North or South Kohala. Cattlemen had always suffered from having to ship their steers to Honolulu on the hoof. The twenty-four hour trip by barge resulted in considerable weight loss by each animal and the expensive necessity of fattening the steers in the feedlots on Oahu. To have a feedlot close by, on their own island, to have a slaughterhouse and be able to ship their dressed carcasses by refrigerated barge from Kawaihae would mean considerably more profit accruing to each rancher. Anna urged that it was an advantage to have Biogenics feedlot even though cattle must be trucked to Hilo to be slaughtered.

The site selected for Biogenics was a dry area close to the Mahukona end of the district, only twelve miles along the new

Akoni Pule beach highway to the deepwater harbor at Kawaihae. The man at the head of Biogenics had credentials that were impressive. Jack Caple was a likeable man. His wife Polly was most personable. The Caples, who quickly made friends with Anna, seemed both affluent and trustworthy.

At the beginning, says her old friend Dick Frazier, "Anna could overlook gossip regarding the Caples, who were in charge of Biogenics, and could see the vision which she felt they tried to bring to the operation." With initial enthusiasm she sent her cattle to Biogenics as did numerous other ranchers in both North and South Kohala. When they reached an optimum marketable weight, Anna then trucked her cattle to Hilo to Richard Devine's Hilo Meat Company slaughterhouse. For her it was a good arrangement. Though she was distressed by the poor construction of the interior of Biogenics' Barn Number One, she continued to be supportive.

From the outset she had problems with her heavier, larger cattle suffering broken legs. The wooden grids of the feedlot barn floor were so poorly spaced that the cattle sometimes got one leg caught in a grid. The enormous concrete barn, a structure designed and built to last 'a million years' said one unenthused observer, had had poor construction supervision of such interior and far less permanent features as the slatted wooden floor. As the cattle being fattened in the barn dropped their manure, it fell through these slats into a pit from which – so Biogenics manager Caple proposed – it would be transported to Barn Number Two, which had not yet been constructed and for which he would need to borrow an additional $200,000.

Cattle excrete 65% of the nutrients in the grain fed to them. Grain is a most expensive item in Hawaii since it must be shipped in from the Mainland. The homogenized cattle manure, fed to pigs, would – said Caple – result in 90% usage of the expensive grain nutrients. The problem was that the initial loan had been used to build silos and Barn Number One, and to set up an office in Hawi which was as magnificently furnished, according to those who saw it, as affluent corporate offices in downtown Honolulu.

There were, Anna knew, operational problems in Barn Number One. The huge silos built as part of the initial operation held sileage that was put fresh into the troughs of the barn each day.

"They're putting in the fresh sileage without cleaning the troughs!" Lyman observed when he and Anna visited the feedlot one morning. She had been concerned about some of her cattle getting sick there. "No wonder!" she exclaimed. "In this climate fresh sileage will putrify fast if any old sileage is left to contaminate it!" She was assured by Biogenics management that they would 'look into' the problem.

Anna kept a careful check each week on the cost of the feedlot services and the weight her cattle gained. Then she compared these figures with prior similar costs at the Honolulu feedlot of Hawaii Meat Company. A few weeks of such comparative analysis and she was assured that as far as her own economic advantage, per pound cost of weight gained by cattle, using Biogenics feedlot, was a much better deal for her. When rumours of Biogenics being a potential failure began to circulate, Anna brought in Yutaka Kimura to check what was being done. He endorsed Anna's positive impression that conceptually Biogenics was on the right track, but that Barn Number Two was critical to the success of the operation.

As she had been asked by Caple, Anna tried to free up the loan for Barn Number Two, and to stave off the bankruptcy proceedings that were imminent since payments on the original loan had not been made as agreed and the enterprise was heavily in debt. As always loyal to friends, she did Caple the favor of using her political clout to try to help them. Together with Monty Richards and Dick Frazier she went to see the governor, to give Ariyoshi the facts in support of the feedlot enterprise. Anna's feeling was that Governor Ariyoshi had been misled as to the viability of Biogenics and the whole idea of its feedlot operation including a piggery to use all of the nutrients in the grain. Not until headlines in the Honolulu and Hilo papers began printing allegations about Biogenics and its poor management did Anna drop her support. By then the Caples had left,– "without even calling me to say goodbye!"

Looking back, she agrees with the assessment of Anderson D. Black, a former Castle and Cooke executive who in 1979 was faced with having to do an audit of the Kohala Task Force

Anna on her favorite horse, 'My Bert' at Old Hawai on Horseback pageant, 1970's.

Anna with Waimea Civitan members at Old Hawaii on Horseback pageant, 1983.

Anna with Diana Neville portrait in the elegant living room of Anna Ranch.

Photo by Kanemori, Modern Camera, Hilo.

Anna receiving Hawaii Federation of Business and Professional Women's Clubs award as State Career Woman of the year, 1968.

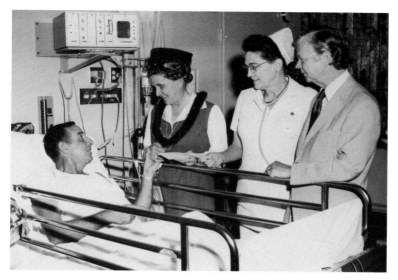

Cardiac unit at Hilo Hospital receives another check from Anna's Old Hawaii on Horseback proceeds.

Anna's favorite parade horse, Kulumanu, shows off for crowds at Old Hawaii on Horseback.

Hawaii Preparatory Academy 1985 Scholarship Auction gala at Mauna Kea Beach Hotel – Anna and Bernard Nogues.

Anna and Headmaster Ronald Tooman at April 1985 auction.

projects when he became Mayor Herbert Matayoshi's Director of Research and Development. County and state funds had gone down the drain in failures such as Biogenics. "The problem facing the Kohala Task Force was really insurmountable," reflects Black. His insider assessment of the feedlot Anna had tried to salvage was that as she had said, it was conceptually sound but operationally too much had gone wrong. "With one exception," says Black now, "the Task Force companies such as Biogenics had not realistically assessed marketing, transport, and other basic problems."

For Anna it was back to either shipping her cattle to the feedlot in Honolulu, or when occasion demanded still continuing to do her own butchering in her slaughterhouse. "Well," she says philosophically, "Things don't always go as you wish they would!"

However, as to Weston, things were again going as she wished – she was about to enjoy a much closer relationship with her hanai son. The Christmas of 1975 Anna and Lyman flew to Honolulu to spend the holidays in their suite at the Royal Hawaiian Hotel. To her surprise, when she arrived, Anna found a tape waiting for her. It had been mailed to her, in care of the hotel. "Probably from your friend Mary," said Lyman.

Up in their suite, Lyman settled himself in the living room with a book. Anna took the tape into the bedroom, where her listening to it would not disturb him. She put the cassette into her player, thinking perhaps it was from her friend Mary. To her delight, astonishment, and then concern it was from Weston. Things had gone from bad to worse for him in Alaska. Weston began to cry as he related how he and Bob were broke. At first they had had enough to afford sleeping at the Y. Lately, Weston told her, they had been sleeping in their truck.

When the tape was finished, Anna went into the living room. "Lyman," she said, "the tape was from Weston. I think he'd like to come home. And I'd like him to. You know, Lyman, lately I've been feeling like a traveling mama-san – always on the road from Keawewai to the ranch house to Hanuola. I tell you what. Weston keeps things up so nicely. Why don't we let him have Hanuola."

"If that's what you want for him –" agreed Lyman. And so

Anna sent a tape back to Weston telling him of her plans should he wish to return, and offering him Hanuola.

As soon as he received her tape, Weston called. Would she send him $2000 which he and Bob would need to pay for plane tickets to Hawaii and to ship their possessions? She promptly did so.

When the day of Weston's arrival came, Anna had her surprises ready for him. She had bought him a sporty new Bronco. She had had the title to Hanuola conveyed to him. With her to the airport to greet Weston and Bob she took the deed to Hanuola, the keys to the new car, fresh flower leis, Weston's grandmother Lily Lindsey, and Irene and Jim Caldwell. From the airport in Kona Anna took everyone to dinner at a fine French restaurant near Disappearing Sands beach. After dinner, when they drove on to Hanuola, Weston's friend Bob was elated to see what a beautiful home his mother had given Weston. Anna had filled the refrigerator and cupboards with food. She had fresh flowers arranged throughout the house. "This is great! Just great!" Bob kept exclaiming.

There followed a few intensely happy months for Anna. Every Sunday Weston and Bob would come to Anna Ranch for lunch and a short visit. Often Anna would take them down to the buffet at Mauna Kea Beach Hotel. Once in a while she and Lyman would drive to Kona to see them. Weston had been able to get a good job right away with the Sears store in Kona. For Bob, teaching jobs were not easy to come by. There was an oversupply of qualified teachers for the few jobs open in Hawaii's public schools in 1976. Anna, at Bob's request, went to see Ken Asato, supervisor of the Kona Schools to see if she could persuade him to hire Bob. "We are required by law to give first preference at jobs to local teachers who have been born and raised in Hawaii," Asato told her. "For mainlanders now, finding a job is almost impossible. At least it is here in Kona."

"I hear it is everywhere in the islands," Anna conceded. She understood and agreed. Hawaii's jobs must be reserved for Hawaii's young people to have first chance at them. That was only fair. But when she reported this to Bob, he was furious. "I thought you had so much influence around here!" he snapped.

Anna snapped right back at him. "I can't get the moon

because you ask!"

Other than that small flare-up, for several months all went well. Weston loved the yard at Hanuola, and kept it looking its best. He and Bob seemed to be happy with the house and Kona. It was around this time that Lyman suffered his ninth heart attack. Anna rushed him to Hilo hospital. He was there for some time in intensive care before she could bring him home. After this attack Lyman was so feeble that Anna had to be stronger than ever. When he got up at night to go to the bathroom, she accompanied him, letting him lean on her arm and actually half carrying him. From the bedroom they must walk through the living room, through the dining room, and then to the bathroom for the ranch house had been built in the days when bathrooms and bedrooms were not adjoining.

That first Saturday after she brought Lyman home from the hospital, Anna called to ask Weston a favor. "I need an extra lamp in the living room to turn on so that I can see to guide Dad to the bathroom during the night. There's one dark place for which I have no light, and where I'm fearful he might stumble and fall. When you come over tomorrow, could you bring the Tiffany lamp from Hanuola. That will be just right for the light we need here."

Anna was shocked to hear Weston's curt refusal.

"But you have three lamps already in your living room there!" she reminded him. "And the Tiffany lamp is no good for a reading light anyway!" Then Anna said, "Also, Weston. Can we have lunch tomorrow at one instead of at twelve. I won't be able to get my roast ready before one."

"We're not coming tomorrow!" said Weston, and with that, he abruptly hung up.

A few minutes later, when the phone rang, Lyman answered. It was Weston's friend Bob. When he told Lyman he wanted to speak to Anna, Lyman said no – she didn't want to speak to him. At this Bob said, "You go to hell, both of you!" and hung up.

The following day Irene Caldwell phoned Anna from Kailua-Kona. Weston and Bob had just been to see her. Both were covered with bruises. They told her they had had a big fight over Bob wanting to leave Kona, and Weston wanting to stay. It was,

Bob had told the Caldwells, Weston's temper that had started the fight.

During that night, Weston and Bob had evidently driven to Waimea bringing Anna's mother's picture – which had been at Hanuola, the Tiffany lamp Anna had asked for, and a number of blankets they had borrowed from her. Next morning Anna found all this dumped on her porch. She had no sooner taken everything inside when she had a phone call from Lily Lindsey. "Weston and Bob called to tell me goodbye just now. They're leaving Hawaii." Lily said she had urged Weston to call Anna, but he had told her, "I'm not going to call my mother and dad. I'm through with them! I've put Hanuola up for sale!"

Anna was still reeling from the impact of Lily's call, worried over whether this would cause Lyman to have another heart attack, when George Brito called her from Hilo. Brito was the car salesman from whom Anna had purchased Weston's Bronco. Brito wanted her to know that when he heard Weston was leaving, he'd called Budger Ruddle, asking him to buy the car and give it back to Anna but Weston had already sold it.

Heartsick, Anna got in her car the next day and drove to Kona. She phoned Nancy and Dick Frazier to come to Kona Surf Hotel to have lunch with her. At the hotel dining room, Anna was well known. Lunch time a certain section was closed off. "Could we have a table over there. I msut talk very privately about some things." she asked the manager.

"Of course, Mrs. Perry-Fiske!" was the reply.

Anna sat undisturbed in that closed off section of the restaurant, talking with the Fraziers from noon until four p.m. She told Nancy and Dick all that had happened with Weston and Bob leaving, Weston's putting the house up for sale, and selling the car, refusing to call her to say goodbye or even tell her he was leaving. "I've suffered, but that's okay," Anna concluded. "What Weston does or does not do cannot hurt me anymore. He has succeeded in completely killing any feelings I still had for him. No broken heart this time around! I just don't feel anything at all – except that I hate to see the furniture in Hanuola, and the fine china and things I put there, be sold to strangers."

"Also, I think I want to buy the house back, for myself," she added.

Luckily, her deed of Hanuola to Weston had not mentioned furnishings. She got hold of Richard Lindsey, asking him to bring his friends and several trucks to Kona. "You can have everything in the house, Richard," she urged. "Use it. Give it away. Whatever you want to do with it."

It took Anna two days to strip the place. She did it without a tear. The first time Weston had turned his back on her had been agonizingly painful. This second time was not easy by any means but it jolted her into realizing that Weston had moved far, far away from all the things he had been and meant to her. "I don't ever want to hear from him, or about him again," she told her closest friends. She had fully discharged her promise to Weston's dying mother. Weston's father, John Silva, had never remarried. He was fond of his son, and from time to time had wished to see him but Weston had turned his back on his father too.

As to Anna's buying back Hanuola, which Dick Frazier found Weston had put in the hands of a real estate salesman who was a friend of his and Bob's, Anna began to have second thoughts. Weston's real estate friend came to tell Anna the house was being advertised for $80,000. As to her buying it, if she gave him a round trip ticket to the Mainland, he would try to get Weston's permission to sell it to her.

The whole business gave Anna a strange, reluctant sense that perhaps she did not really want Hanuola back. She kept praying and the answer she seemed to hear more and more clearly was "Don't buy it!"

She did not.

At Lyman's suggestion, Anna rewrote her will. "Otherwise he'll come back like the prodigal son to get whatever he can!" Lyman warned.

As if none of this had happened, with her usual aplomb, Anna carried off the second HPA dinner-auction on May 8, at Mauna Kea Beach Hotel. The lighting was just right. Steve Rosen was at his best as auctioneer. Articles donated for the evening's bidding ranged from rare pieces of art, jewelry, antiques, gowns, dressed beef and rare Hawaiian books to a three-wheel Tri-Sport motorcycle, a power mower, needlepoint pillows and first class hotel accommodations at a dozen hotels around Hawaii's prime resorts. There was a standing ovation for Anna. She was heaped with leis until she could not see out above the flowers. Bernard Nogues was ecstatic. Thanks to Anna and her hard work, the affair added more than $50,000 to the HPA Scholarship fund.

That evening, to those who did not realize what she had just been through, it looked as if Anna Perry-Fiske had had the easiest of lives, with never a care. "That," says Bernard Nogues, "is the core of her being a European style very great lady!"

Never Give Up!

THE FACT THAT, at eighty-five, Lyman could still manage to mount a horse for very special occasions gave him great satisfaction. He was essentially a romantic, a mystic, a person who at times thought he might live forever. Yet, his breathing difficulty worsened. Each heart attack left him weaker. The last year of Lyman's life, Anna devoted herself to caring for him. When he had an attack, she rushed him to Hilo's cardiac intensive care unit, staying with him until the worst was over. When he improved, she was so happy to be able to bring him back home.

In May, 1977, while Anna was finalizing that spring's 'Old Hawaii on Horseback' production, Lyman had another severe attack. She rushed him to Hilo and stayed at his side until he began to show some improvement. She was ready to cancel the pageant but Lyman insisted she go ahead with her plans. "Everyone's waiting for it!" he reminded her. "I'll be o.k.!"

Honolulu Advertiser writer Mary Cooke, who had written so many fine features about Anna, had already published a feature about this year's pageant. Reminding readers the event was scheduled for May 21 at 1:00 p.m., Ms. Cooke went on to say that the mounted pageant "is history, showmanship, artistry, local color, and expert horsemanship displayed by some top

Big Island riders. Props and costumes are spectacular. And authentic." This year 130 horses were to be ridden by "descendants of early Big Island ranchers, famous Hawaiian cowboys and missionaries" portraying the role of their ancestors. "The setting," said Ms. Cooke, "is the heart of Waimea's ranch land. Gentle-rising hills, chartreuse-green pastures, lava rock fences, eucalyptus trees, ti hedges and tall tree ferns."

Anna was lauded as originator, writer, director, producer, costumer and star. "The whole upstairs of my house is nothing but 'Old Hawaii on Horseback' costumes," Anna told Ms. Cooke. At the pageant there was to be a five dollar admission charge. Heart barrels were set out at each entrance for donations from those attending the pageant. "People would come up to me as I rode out to the pageant and hand me checks for the Heart Fund!" Anna recalls.

One half of the proceeds from the 1977 pageant were to be earmarked for the purchase of more cardiac equipment for Big Island hospitals. The other half would go directly to the Hawaii Heart Association for research. The Advertiser article stressed that "all time, labor and materials are donated." Ms. Cooke quoted Anna's emphatic, "Not one cent is deducted for expenses or services!" Anna was adamant that "every dollar we take in goes to the heart fund or the hospitals". It was a relief to Anna that her pageants had already installed the kind of cardiac equipment at Hilo hospital that enabled Lyman to survive so many heart attacks. "You must put on this year's show!" he persuaded her.

Annd did, but it was far from easy for her. She rode that day with a heavy heart, worried about Lyman. "This is my last pageant. I will not be doing this show ever again," Anna told the crowd as they paid tribute to her with leis and thunderous applause. Toward the end of the pageant, Pat Hall ran up and gave her a welcome message. "The doctor just called. He says for you to relax, Anna. Lyman is doing well today!"

A few days later, Lyman was well enough to be moved from intensive care to a private room. Each day Anna made the long trip back and forth to Hilo. Just before his tenth and fatal attack, Anna was sitting talking to him. She remembers him lying there, his hand on his chest, talking to her about Weston. "You've borne the brunt of all this, Anna!" Lyman lamented. "How could he do this to you!"

As Anna drove home late that afternoon, she could not stop worrying about how agitated Lyman was when he talked about Weston and his rejection of them. Next day, she decided, she would stay on in Hilo overnight so she could visit him in the evening too. But when she returned to Hilo the following morning, she was told by the nurse that Lyman had been returned to intensive care. She hurried to that unit. "The doctor is with him, Mrs. Perry-Fiske. Please wait!" the nurse in charge there told her.

Anna waited until the doctor came out. "He's very bad, Anna," said the Doctor. "You may go in now, but he is not conscious. This was a bad attack!"

Lyman was in a coma. They had drained the fluid from his lungs so that the terrible struggle for each breath was eased. He looked peaceful, Anna thought. Perhaps the doctor is wrong! Perhaps he'll survive this tenth attack. But this time the heart fund equipment, and her prayers, were of no use. An hour after she was allowed in to be at his bedside that morning of June 3, 1977, Lyman died. He was eighty-five years old.

For more than fifty years, Lyman had been active in the Masons and active as a Shriner. The first service held after his cremation was in Hilo at the Masonic Lodge. Then, with Lyman's brother, Al Kealoha Perry and Al's wife Katharine accompanying her, Anna drove Lyman's ashes back to Waimea. "Al held the urn on his lap the whole way. I drove," Anna remembers, tears flooding her eyes.

The kind of funeral she had for Lyman in Waimea was one that Anna had always said she wants for herself when that time comes. It was held in St. James Episcopal Church, which Anna had attended in recent years. Since her marriage to Lyman in 1943, she had been unable to receive communion as a Catholic. As a student at the Priory, long ago, she had been confirmed an Episcopalian and for a number of years this had been her church affiliation.

The morning of the funeral Bull Awaa went up into the mountain forest to pick maile for the garlands of maile and pikake that draped Lyman's urn. Long before the service was scheduled to begin, the church was packed with people. Many stood outside. The traditional Episcopal funeral service was held. Some of

Anna's favorite prayers were read. Eva Perez, Sarah Ruis, and Elaine Flores sang one of Lyman's favorite songs – *"Ka Makani o Kohala"* (The winds of Kohala). When the service ended, a motorcade of four-wheel drive vehicles formed behind the mounted escort taking Lyman's ashes to the place where they were to be scattered.

Anna, in black riding coat, black hat, and white trousers was escorted by her beloved nephew Richard and a big group of cowboys on horseback. Parker Ranch had sent all their four-wheel drive vehicles to be used that day. Each car had been washed and polished until it was spotless, and each had a driver dressed in black and white. The cowboys who were escorting Lyman to his last resting place all wore white hats and white shirts. Anna and the riders led the way from St. James through town, and on past Anna Ranch. They turned through Pako pasture and rode up the slopes of the Kohala Mountains to Waiohau Falls on Waiauea Stream. Looking down Anna could see a ribbon of vehicles following in what seemed an endless procession.

On a grassy knoll overlooking the falls, above a cliff to which ferns and ohia trees clung, the riders stopped. Below them, the vehicles parked wherever they could and passengers climbed the last half mile on foot. When everyone was assembled, Rev. Guy Piltz conducted the final Episcopal rites. The three Hawaiian women who had sung at the service in town sang *"Aloha Oe"* as the urn was opened and Lyman's ashes were cast over the precipice. He had rejoined the soil of the Kohala Mountains, which he had known and loved so well.

The anxiety over Lyman in his last illness, the push he had encouraged her to make to put on 'Old Hawaii on Horseback' less than two weeks before his death, the lingering anguish over what she felt Weston had done to Lyman, took their toll of Anna's health. Her pressure was alarmingly high. She had become very thin. She was exhausted. Yet, as always, work was her panacea. She saddled her horse and rode out each morning to do what had to be done on her ranch. She kept a careful eye on how her business was going. Richard helped her dispose of Lyman's personal things but she could not yet bring herself to go through all the papers in the small room that he had used as an office.

It had become the custom of Thelma Parker Smart's son Richard to hold special Parker Ranch races each fourth of July, and to entertain his very special guests that day at a luncheon at Puuopelu. One month after Lyman's death, July 4, 1977, Richard Smart paid tribute to Anna, making her the guest of honor at the races that day.

Slowly she began to regain her strength, and her verve, to settle into living alone in her big ranch house. There was so much that kept her busy and high on her list of interests was her service on HPA's Board of Governors. In October 1978 she was on the interview committee assessing Ronald Tooman, former headmaster of St. Stephen's, an international school in Rome, Italy, who was applying for the position of headmaster of Hawaii Preparatory Academy.

"I had no idea what to expect in that interview," says Tooman, a tall, good looking man with a tremendous sense of humour. "At first sight of the committee I was intrigued!" he remembers. At one end of the long table sat Anna Perry-Fiske dressed in a fashionable suit, a hat, and color coordinated gloves, hose, shoes and handbag. At the other end sat University of Hawaii Regent and Kahua Ranch manager Monty Richards in dungarees, cowboy boots, and a rumpled sweatshirt. "This looks like an interesting place!" was Tooman's assessment. The range in appearance, background, age, and professions of the interview committee represented, he could tell, the broad spectrum of the community. Anna's particular question of him concerned his thoughts on students at HPA attending chapel and church.

"I really couldn't answer her except to say I thought hers an important question," recalls Tooman. "I told her that if I became HPA's headmaster, I would do things at the school to get the kids back into chapel more often." After nearly ten years as headmaster he ruefully comments, "And I'm still trying!"

The big question Ronald Tooman asked of the Board of Governors that day was answered in a positive and reassuring way by Anna.

"I want you to know right away that I'm married to a Chinese girl," Tooman told them. "If that will make a difference, I don't want to continue this interview."

"Mr. Tooman, you're in Hawaii!" said Anna. "We're all

kinds of people living here together, working together, and as far as we're concerned there are no differences!" The days when her Chinese-Hawaiian first husband was socially ostracized by Hilo society were long gone. The war had been a great leveler of prejudice where it did exist. There were islanders with racial biases in one direction or another, that Anna knew well, but in Waimea, and at HPA, there was no obstacle to the Toomans being welcomed by everyone everywhere.

Ronald Tooman soon found out that Anna Lindsey Perry-Fiske was an HPA supporter whose ardor and energy never flagged. He was much taken by the fact that although she had been through so much the previous year with Weston's departure and Lyman's death, she never allowed her private suffering to surface in public. Hearing how, as a young woman, she had always put on the same brave face and affluent appearance even when she was so desperately poor and trying to rescue the ranch from failure, Tooman was reminded of a saying he'd seen written on the walls of a small church in Italy. "Our respect for our Lord is too great to permit us to show our poverty."

"Italians," says Tooman, "are very concerned with outward appearances – how they look, how they dress. No matter how tired or weary or upset she may be, when Anna leaves the house to go anywhere she is always beautifully dressed. To me this is out of respect for herself and where she's going. She's very European in this."

By the time Tooman became Headmaster, Anna had the biennial auction for the school's scholarship fund in high gear. "Anna has the 'I'm going to win' spirit," admires Ronald Tooman. "Some people think her difficult to work with. They don't understand! Anna is the easiest person in the world – just do what she tells you! She's not a committee person. She does it her way and it's always a terrific success."

Tooman grins, telling how he has often heard Anna on the phone to someone, telling them the HPA auction is coming up. "'If you can't give me anything, give me a big fat check!' she tells people. To those who say, 'I've already given to HPA this year' Anna retorts, 'I know you have but this time you're giving to me for HPA!'"

As are Anna's friends Will and Judy Hancock, Ronald and

Vivian Tooman are among the guests annually invited to Anna's traditional New Year's Eve party at the Royal Hawaiian Hotel. Anna reserves a room for each family near her suite at the hotel. She hosts them to a buffet lunch in the Surf Room New Year's Eve day and at brunch New Year's morning. But the gala New Year's Eve party in the Monarch Room is her greatest treat to her friends. Anna has the best table, right at the edge of the dance floor. She looks every inch the Queen, an ageless beauty year after year presiding over the evening with the zest of a twenty year old. Each year she wears one of her stunning formal gowns, her diamond tiara, and a white fox fur on her handsome bare shoulders.

"How Anna loves to dance, and what a good dancer she is!" says Bernard Nogues, who with his wife Mary Alice is another of Anna's frequent guests. For Bernard Nogues, who is Anna's non-committee of one for HPA's scholarship benefit auctions, since 1974 his acquaintance and working relationship with Anna has evolved into what he describes as "friendship, mutual respect, and genuine affection".

Over the years, native Frenchman Nogues has been Anna's escort to many parties. "I'm always impressed by her elegant fashion, her ability to talk to men, her tremendous wit and humour." Nogues recalls one evening when he and Anna were at the home of Bob Griffin, then Director of the Honolulu Academy of Arts. "Anna told him about the time in Mexico City when she went to the bullfight looking so gorgeous – then it rained and while she was rushing out of the place, her expensive, ankle-length purple dress shrunk to her knees. The way she told this was so hilarious that Griffin rolled on the floor with laughter."

"For me personally," says Nogues, "Anna Perry-Fiske has been a source of inspiration in how to courageously face life with all its ups and downs. Her form of life is based on the kind of commitment one has to onself." He often used to wonder. What makes Anna tick? After working with her for twelve years he says, "I think it's an image of what her potential is, which is another way of describing her commitment to values and to God. When Anna tells you she speaks to God, I know what she means. Prayer is powerful for her."

For him, raised in the European culture, Anna's commitment to the dignity of living 'humanly' is expressed by the French phrase *'noblesse oblige'* which, he explains, means that for the noble person there are obligations. To Bernard it is this sense of inner commitment, this strong core of *noblesse oblige* that has fueled and continues to fuel Anna's amazing energy. His mental view of her very positive self-image is: "I am Anna Lindsey Perry-Fiske. I've come through countless catastrophes. I've survived. I've made it. I'm a person who has always had God at my side."

"Hers," adds Nogues, "is a refusal to give in to the vulgarities of life – a refusal to be a stereotype. She has aches, pains, disapointments of course but she is not going to give in!" Anna's courage and fortitude remind him of the motto of a famous European family, "Je maintenerai" – I shall maintain.

Maintaining in the usual sense of the word is, however, not Anna's style. She shakes herself free of the past, free of the fears that are the 'what if' preoccupations of so many of her contemporaries. She enjoys her own company. Solitude refreshes her but she balances it with the gregariousness that she also needs and enjoys. The offspring of her two brothers, and of her father's branch of the Lindsey family alone give her an extended family with grand-nieces and grand-nephews who are often her worry and concern. As close to her as if they too were her own family are Judy Hancock, her husband Will, and their children. Thane, born in 1975, is one of Anna's godchildren. The birth of her godchild Theana Hancock the November of the year of Lyman's death gave Anna special solace. So, alone, Anna is really never alone. Each morning her nephew Richard calls her on the telephone and rarely a day goes by when he does not see his Auntie Anna. In the same way Anna talks to Judy almost every day, and for the Hancock children, Anna is their Auntie too.

After Lyman's death Anna's lifestyle, her philanthropic interests, her family network did not change. Her religious affiliation did, however. Now that she was again single, she could return to being a Catholic as she had long wished. Other of her contemporaries as they approached their eightieth year began to decrease their activities, left their business interests in other hands, and settled into quiet retirement. Not Anna! If anything, she became more active than ever.

In 1982 she had a run of hard luck with her cattle – losing three champion bulls. One had a split hoof. One suffered an injury to his *uli* which meant the end of his ability to sire calves. The third was attacked by two horned bulls. This was an accident for Anna had been about to take the horned bulls out of the pasture when she happened to see a cow that she assumed was lying down to deliver a calf. She rode over to take a close look and saw that it was a dead animal, cleverly camouflaged. Someone had shot the cow, dressed her out, taken the meat, but left the head intact and then pulled the hide back over the bones so that from a distance the cow looked alive.

Temporarily distracted from moving the horned bulls as had been her intention, Anna rode home to report the shooting and pilfering of her cow to the police. Next morning when she returned to take the horned bulls out of the pasture, she found they had fought and killed one of her champion bulls. "I live in a man's world where you don't cry about such things. Just go out and buy another bull!" was Anna's practical reaction.

By 1982 Anna had switched to concentrating on Herefords. "I can register each animal in my herd!" she says proudly. She has kept upgrading until she has all good healthy calves. The Parker Ranch cowboys whom she relies on as occasional helpers told their boss to buy Anna's heifers. "They're heavy!" they told him.

When their boss called, Anna said, "Buy my steers too!" Her business strategy is, "To make money you've got to spend money. I do!" She is forthright about acknowledging her success. "I'm brave!" she asserts. "My banker gets a kick out of me. I always make back more money than I spend!" The lesson Anna's father taught her about risking her winnings in marbles was one she had thoroughly learned.

Joe Andrews of the Bank of Hawaii was not only Anna's banker but the man who has become her trusted advisor. When Big Island Mayor Dante Carpenter talked Joe Andrews into becoming a top aide in his administration, Anna called Andrews. "I'm happy for you. Dante picked the best when he got you – but save some time for me in your new job!" Anna reminded. Being advised is not Anna's style. "No one tells me how to run my business!" As her business made more and more money, and as she began to diminish the size of her herds and sell some of her surplus pastures, she had a great deal of capital to invest. It was in these financial investments that she sought the advice of Joe Andrews. "Only in investments – and then it's I who make the decisions!" reiterates Anna. "In my ranch business, no need to depend on anybody but myself for advice!"

Computerization of the ranch operation is something Anna has staunchly resisted. "I don't know about Kahua!" she says, referring to the highly sophisticated computer programming used by Monty Richards and Pono Von Holt to run their ranch. One day Anna went to see Monty Richards. "You still want to buy my feeders?" she asked.

When he heard her price, Monty protested. "Anna! I'll lose my shirt!"

Anna held firm. "That's my price!"

Telling this story, Anna chuckles. "With that," she says, "Monty went to his computer. He tried to work me down in price after he punched all those fancy buttons. No deal!" I told him. "Eddie Rice has offered me my price and with him there's no computers. His check is right there!"

But Anna liked doing business with Kahua. However when she offered her feeders to Monty next time around, he went through the same routine of pressing buttons on the computer in order to make his decision. "Look, Monty!" she interrupted him. "You're pressing those buttons to please you! The computer doesn't see my cattle. My stuff is good, Monty and I don't want to sit beside this computer every time. If you treat me right, I'll treat you right. I'd rather sell my feeders and weaners to you. Instead of haggling over price, how about going 50-50 on the profit each time!"

Monty agreed. And from then on that's how they worked. "No waiting on computers!" says Anna.

On April 24th, 1982, Anna was overjoyed when HPA's fifth biennial scholarship auction raised a record-breaking $138,500. Steve Rosen, the Honolulu auctioneer who always donates his services for this event, remarked that "There are many charity auctions in Honolulu. None even comes close to the total raised for HPA scholarships. There is no doubt in my mind that there is here a unique combination of quality, talent, and generous

Anna Ranch.

Photo by Peter French.

Mauna Kea looms behind the high green pastures of Keawewai.

Photo by Barry Fried.

The green hills of Waimea.

Anna working in rain slicker
at Keawewai.

Anna ropes and steadies a calf for branding, Waimea.   Lyman.

Anna roping at Keawewai.

Anna briefs cowboys before early morning branding, Waimea.

Anna and horse pull a calf out for branding at Keawewai.

Cross-bred cattle.

Photo by Douglas Davidson

Anna and Richard Smart.

Photo by Peter French.

Richard Lindsey brings in Hawaiian flag at Anna's mounted pageant.

Photo by Thomas Kunichika.

William Andrade and Judy Hancock. Old Hawaii on Horseback, 1960's.

and loyal support from the HPA Governors, parents, and friends. There is also this very unique and formidable figure: Mrs. Perry-Fiske."

As usual the dinner and auction was held in the Batik Room of Mauna Kea Beach Hotel. As usual also, Anna sat next to auctioneer Rosen throughout the bidding. Lighting was no problem – but temperature was! This year an unusually large number of items had been donated. It took three and one half hours to auction off the 168 items offered for sale. Among these was a regal grandfather clock made of curly koa by Lani Cabinets of Hilo. It had been donated by Mr. and Mrs. Fred Moore of Kona. Anna outbid several would-be buyers, paying $5,250 for this one item. Other fine koa pieces, a number of paintings, and a 25 carat topaz also brought top prices. It was a long evening, and halfway through the auction the room's air conditioning failed. No breeze from either mountains or sea. Everyone began to wilt. Eyes looked longingly at the exit doors. Anna was in the most uncomfortable position in the room, under the bright lights beside the auctioneer but, recalls Bernard Nogues, "She looked unflappable!"

As the audience grew more and more restive, Anna interrupted the bidding. She stood beside Steve Rosen and with a piercing gaze that seemed to personally engage each one of the roomful of people she enlisted their commitment to finish out the auction. "You're not going to leave me now, are you?" she challenged.

No one would. No one did. Perspiration pouring from them, wilted and uncomfortable as they were, not one person left the auction until the last item was sold after 1:00 A.M. Anna kept them one last moment to express her gratitude. "Never before have I felt such excitement and never before has the taste of success been so sweet. We certainly worked hard on our project. Yet, without our friends, the donors and bidders, nothing would have been accomplished. They are the ones who deserve the leis and congratulations!"

Bernard Nogues reported in the Hawaii Preparatory Magazine issue of Spring-Summer 1982 that "once again 'Anna's auction' has provided us with enough funds to sustain our financial aid program for the next few years. We cannot adequately express our gratitude to our friends, our Governors, and our parents without whom the success of this auction would not have been possible."

Ever since she had announced that the 1977 'Old Hawaii on Horseback' was to be the last one of these productions, Anna had been pressured to "do it just one more time!" What she described to the *Advertiser's* Big Island bureau chief, Hugh Clark as "tremendous demand" led her to start work early in December 1982 on writing, casting, and preparing for another pageant.

"We were surprised but pleased when Anna said she would do another one," said Connie Sensano, longtime administrator of the Big Island unit of Hawaii Heart Association. So, in the spring of 1983, Anna was a whirlwind one-woman production committee. Her May 21, 1983 'Old Hawaii on Horseback' was, for all who either attended or participated, an inimitable experience.

Against the back drop of Waimea's lush green mountains, under the great blue bowl of a sun-drenched Hawaiian sky, thousands gathered to pay tribute to Anna Lindsey Perry-Fiske. Her petite figure straight-backed and supple in the saddle, she opened a mounted pageant of island and particularly Big Island South Kohala history. This 1983 extravaganza combined Anna's innate flair for drama, the spirit of old Hawaii and its history, and the splendor of the Waimea ranch country with the aloha of its people.

Some of those who came to the Big Island to attend stayed at the newest of South Kohala's world class luxury hotels, Mauna Lani. Built on the former seaside estate of the famous international sportsman and former territorial senator, Francis Ii Brown, the hotel had been dedicated with lavish opening ceremonies in February. Anna was one of the guests invited to stay at the Mauna Lani during festivities which included a luau with helicopters dropping clouds of fragrant plumeria blossoms on the site. Hawaii's Governor Ariyoshi, dressed in a traditional happi coat, opened a cask of sake – Japanese rice wine – which was served to the guests in souvenir wooden cups.

Anna loved the elegance and excitement of Mauna Lani. Its manager, Nick Klotz, was her old friend. A few weeks after her successful May, 1983 'Old Hawaii on Horseback' Anna was about to have dinner at one of the Mauna Lani's fine dining rooms with friends when she tripped on an unlighted step leading to the hotel's porte-cochere. There was no way that Will Hancock, her escort, could break her sudden fall. It was another catastrophic accident like the one when the horse fell on Anna, breaking her pelvis. This time, however, it was not Anna the cowboy but Anna the grande dame in formal evening dress who was suddenly struck down.

"Don't move me. Something's broken. Call the ambulance!" Anna's face was contorted with pain. It seemed to her friends an eternity before the ambulance arrived.

"Take me to Lucy Henriques Emergency Room!" Anna directed the paramedic.

"No. They're closed now. We'll go to Honokaa hospital," he replied.

"Closed?" Anna gave him a stern look of reprimand. "What do you mean, closed! Young man, I donated money for that room and it was to be kept open twenty-four hours a day. Take me there!" As they lifted her into the ambulance Anna said to Will, "Call Dr. Dawson. Tell him to be waiting at Lucy Henriques for us!"

As the ambulance sped along the Queen Kaahumanu Highway towards the junction with the road that leads up to Waimea, the paramedic began asking Anna a number of those questions that seem so non-essential in an emergency. By now he had written her name down on his record sheet. Anna Lindsey Perry-Fiske. The next two questions would, he surmised, be equally easy. He surmised wrong!

"Mrs. Perry-Fiske. How old are you?"

"Young man," said Anna, "that's none of your business!"

The paramedic was startled. "But the doctor will want to know–"

"When we get to him, *maybe* I'll tell the doctor. And maybe I won't," said Anna. Pain had not altered her spunk – or diminished her sense of privacy.

With the next question the paramedic committed the inexcusable error of asking Anna what part of 'Kamuela' she lived in. At this Anna lifted her head to glare at him. "Young man I do not live in the post office! It's Waimea that's the name of the village and of the area where my ranch is!"

From Mauna Lani to Lucy Henriques Medical Center in Waimea is not more than a half hour drive. This modern facility, initially planned to provide twenty-four hour emergency care, professional offices, x-ray and laboratory facilities plus a small pharmacy, was built largely by community donations such as the generous amount given by Anna. That night the lights in the Emergency Room were on. Dr. John Dawson is one of the well trained medical specialists who settled in Waimea when Lucy Henriques was completed. He was there, awaiting Anna's arrival. An x-ray technician was on hand. An x-ray and a careful examination confirmed what Anna had suspected. She had a badly broken hip.

"Dr. Dawson, will you please contact the best orthopedic surgeon in Honolulu. Tell him to charter a plane if necessary. I'll pay for it. I want the very best waiting in Hilo to operate on me. Tell him I'm a rancher. I have to be able to ride horseback again!"

Shaking his head over Anna's tenacity and her determination that she must still live such a full and vigorous life, Dr. Dawson did exactly as she directed. She was taken by ambulance to Hilo. At Hilo hospital, by the time she was admitted and placed in a private room, a top orthopedic surgeon was there to examine her. As Dr. Mitchel had warned in 1970 when she broke her pelvis, Dr. Irvine told Anna frankly that the break was a bad one. She might never be able to walk again. Riding horseback? He just shook his head at that far-out possibility.

"There's no alternative. I must put in a steel plate and pins," he said. "How fully you recover, and how well you'll be able to get along afterward – that's up to you Anna. It won't be easy!" It was a long difficult operation. When Anna was wheeled back to the recovery room after several hours in surgery she had a pound of steel and three pins in one hip. "The pain was excruciating," she remembers. "Especially when I began physical therapy. I stood there between the support bars trying to learn to walk again. Each step was torture. The tears ran down my checks.

"Give up! It's too much for you, Mrs. Perry-Fiske!" said the therapist.

"I can do it. You wait!" Anna replied. Gritting her teeth, praying, and summoning all her reserves of courage, she kept on with the exercises.

Friends and family rallied to support her. Every day Richard Lindsey phoned her to see what she wanted done on the ranch and report to her how the pastures looked, and how the cattle were doing. He had had a heart attack and taken early retirement from the Police Force so he was able to be a great help to her. As he had when she was hospitalized with the broken pelvis in 1970, he drove in regularly to see her. So did Judy and Will Hancock who brought Theana and Thane in weekends to keep their Auntie Anna company.

Anna's private room was kept filled with flowers. Each day's hospital mail brought cards and notes from all over. Patiently, and yet impatiently, Anna waited for Dr. Irvine to say she could leave the hospital. She could walk a few steps now, but it was very painful. "If I keep up the physical therapy every day for a while, will that help?" Anna asked him.

"It would, but you have no physical therapy facility in Waimea," the surgeon reminded her.

"I know. That's why I've arranged to stay in Hilo for as long as is necessary," said Anna. From the hospital she moved into a pleasant room at the Naniloa Surf on Hilo Bay. The route leading to the Naniloa was along Banyan Drive. The trees planted by the Hilo Women's Club project which Anna had chaired in the '30's were now a half century old – magnificent broad-branched specimens with gnarled trunks and tangles of aerial roots. Many of the wooden plaques commemorating the famous people who had planted them were now gone. Their names, especially those of novelist Fannie Hurst and aviatrix Amelia Earhart remained fresh in Anna's memory as she drove by each of their trees.

For a total of five months, including her long hospital stay, Anna remained in Hilo. Penny Brito, the physical therapist, came once a week to give Anna a list of what to do. When Penny said, "Do this exercise ten times," Anna would ask, "How about if I do it 20 times!" "If you can–" Penny said, amazed. Within no time, Anna no longer needed the walker. She had graduated to a cane and she was determined to go beyond needing that, too. She concentrated each day all day doing her exercises. "I remember how she walked back and forth along the hotel corridor, so patient!" says Emily, one of the hotel employees who serviced Anna's room at that time.

"If I can't ride horseback right away, I'll drive my four-wheel drive Bronco out to the pastures!" Anna confided to Judy Hancock. Remarkably, by year's end, she was home doing just that.

At her December 31st, 1983 New Year's Eve party Anna was the vibrant picture of health as she laughed and joked with her guests at her table in the Royal Hawaiian's Monarch Room. When she rose to dance with Howard Hall, no one would have guessed that in July she had suffered a broken hip.

Now that she was home, running the ranch and busy as ever, Anna began to take on new responsibilities. In March, 1984 she was made a member of the Board of Directors of the Easter Seal Society of Hawaii. Her picture in that month's "Easter Sealer", the society's newsletter, is that of a lively, attractive woman who seems, perhaps, to be about sixty. Anna flew to Honolulu that spring to appear in the Easter Seal telethon. There were twelve prominent people on the panel on which she was to appear. Each took a turn before the camera, televising an appeal for funds that reached every viewer with a set turned to that channel. Anna had the largest response of her panel. Her plea for contributions elicited pledges of $25 and $50 a piece not only from her friends in Waimea but from throughout the state – as far away as Kauai.

In May 1984 Anna climbed back in the saddle to be photographed with her great grand-nephew Stemo Lindsey, a Rodeo champion. The Big Island newspaper *West Hawaii Today* in its issue of May 4, 1984 reported that "in appreciation for the many years she has proven to be their number one lady, the North Hawaii Western Athletic Association is dedicating their annual rodeo to her." The first annual Anna Lindsey Perry-Fiske Jackpot Roping was to be held in Hilo at Panaewa arena on Saturday May 5 and Sunday May 6. Top ropers from throughout Hawaii would compete in the ten steer and ten calf average roping contest.

One of the Big Island's most beloved ladies," said the news article, "Anna Lindsey Perry-Fiske has been a staunch supporter of the sport of rodeo from the beginning. She is interested in any kind of equestrian activities and her contributions, such as her annual sponsorship of the all around rodeo trophies on the Big Island, are legend." No longer was Anna riding and roping herself. She was still a working cowboy but like her Kahua ranch neighbors Monty Richards and Pono Von Holt she no longer rode a horse to work. Monty and Pono preferred dirt bikes to ride their range. Anna checked pastures and cattle from behind the wheel of her 4-wheel drive Bronco.

Hawaii's Incredible Anna

IN 1984 ANNA received two tributes that meant a great deal
to her. One was from the Hawaii Preparatory Academy, the
other from her fellow cattlemen throughout the state.

On Saturday, May 19, 1984, Anna was guest of honor at
the dedication of the Anna Lindsey Perry-Fiske Hall at Hawaii
Preparatory Academy. In April, the Board of Governors had
passed a resolution honoring her "for her long time support
of the school and her belief in the school's mission and purpose",
by renaming the girl's dormitory (formerly known as the Upper
dorm) the Anna Lindsey Perry-Fiske Hall. A bronze plaque now
marks that handsome building as such.

"Mrs., Perry Fiske's contribution to our school over the years
has been enormous," says Headmaster Tooman. "In a very real
sense we are her family and the strong conviction and faith she
holds for our school's mission has been an inspiration to
everyone in the HPA community." Anna is still demonstrating
that commitment by her unstinting support. When HPA began
to raise money for the new arts building and a swimming pool.
Anna gave three times the amount asked from each member
of the Board of Governors. Her contribution, in 1986, had
totalled more than $60,000 to that one project alone.

The past few years, she has also been generous to herself.

All work and no play has never been Anna's style. After Lyman's death she began to treat herself to an annual cruise, selecting the best of the luxury staterooms available. She enjoyed a cruise through the Panama Canal, and several trips through the Caribbean where she loved the shore excursions on islands so very different from her own. In 1984 she took a fall cruise up the east coast to Nova Scotia. Where she goes is not so important to her as traveling on her favorite Royal Princess line ship, renewing former acquaintances from other cruises, making new friends and seeing new and interesting places. As in the old days when she traveled on the Lurline, she sits at the captain's table, wearing a different formal gown for dinner each evening. One night, as she was escorted into the dining salon wearing her diamond tiara and a white lace gown she heard a fellow passenger exclaim as she passed their table, "She must be royalty from some European country!"

"I feel like I am on those cruises!" says Anna. They refresh and renew her. On the way she stops at the Fairmont in San Francisco to experience her favorite west coast city for a few days. If the cruise departs from an east coast port, she stops over to enjoy a few days in New York. In 1984 she scheduled her cruise so that she could be back in Waimea by October 15 to attend the Hawaii Livestock show and sale.

"Ranchers around the state are probably wondering whether their bull will be this year's winner," read an article by *West Hawaii Today*'s city editor, Sharon Sakai – daughter of Anna's old friend and former tax accountant, the late Sakuichi Sakai. "And ranchers are also wondering whether Waimea's Anna Lindsey Perry-Fiske will again purchase the champion. In the past twenty years Perry-Fiske, well known for her ranching expertise and her generosity in charity work, has purchased at least 18 champion bulls. In fact, she paid the highest price in the sale's history for an animal in 1970. Perry-Fiske, bidding against the government of Thailand, bid $6100 for a champion Hereford bull from Hartwell Carter's Homestead Farm." Young Ms. Sakai, an attractive and talented journalism graduate in her late twenties, had not yet been born when her father was Anna's tax accountant. "I don't think she knows how much I admired him, and how much he did for me in those early years," says Anna. She read the article with much interest. At its end, a spokesman for the Hawaii Cattleman's Association was quoted as saying that "Perry-Fiske's continuing support of the sale is one of the reasons the event is celebrating its twentieth anniversary this year.

Anna was not only there for the 1984 Horse and Bull auction. She was the day's honored guest, presented with a plaque honoring her twenty years of support. "The sale carries out one of my ideals for Hawaii's ranch industry," Anna reminisces, showing the plaque with just pride. "It gives all ranchers the chance to buy stock which will improve the bloodlines and performance of their cattle."

Because of Anna's having broken her hip in 1983, HPA's 1984 scholarship auction had had to be postponed. It was, like the Horse and Bull sale, an event that no one felt would be at all the same without Anna there. Not only her presence but her direction and planning were crucial to the scholarship auction. It was an affair that everyone agreed could not be held without her actively at the helm. Since 1974, through this biennial dinner-auction, Anna had raised more than $600,000 for HPA's scholarship fund. In addition, she had personally paid – and continues to pay – the tuition for a number of Waimea boys and girls, among them several of her grand-nieces and grand-nephews.

"Many who break a hip give up, but Anna is always super-courageous," comments Bernard Nogues. "In 1984 she immediately took on the hard job of preparing to hold the auction in April, 1985." Nogues marvels at her as he tells the story of how this commitment was number one in Anna's mind when she had another fall in March, 1985. She had been carrying a heavy silver bowl of roses into her living room when she tripped on one of her oriental rugs. Nogues was stunned to receive a phone call that day telling him Anna was in the Emergency Room at Lucy Henriques Medical Center. There was a possibility that she might have broken her hip again. "Come to Lucy Henriques. Anna wants to see you!" Bernard was told.

When he arrived there, Richard Lindsey and Judy and Will Hancock were already with Anna. She was lying on a stretcher, pale and drawn, evidently in great pain. She had fallen on the steel pin that was in her hip. "I can't move my leg," she told the doctor.

As Bernard walked in she turned to him and said,. "Oh Bernard! Don't worry! I'll be there for the auction. You can count on me!"

"How extraordinary for her to transcend pain and fear to reassure us about the auction!" Nogues is still overwhelmed by this and by how, despite her obvious pain, as she waited for the ambulance that would take her to Hilo Hospital, she joked with her nephew, with Judy and Will, and with him.

When Bernard drove in a few days later to see her at Hilo Hospital, he had his doubts about the auction. Anna was in traction. Luckily her hip had not been broken but the pin had given her a bad bruise. She was in a great deal of pain still.

Until two weeks before the April 13, 1985 auction, Anna was still suffering. She could walk only with the aid of a cane. "She knew her presence at the auction was all-important. She never gave up her determination to be there!" says Nogues.

On the morning of a scholarship auction there is always a large crew of people who come down to Mauna Kea Beach Hotel from Waimea to carry things. Anna lends all her vehicles to transport donated items. She has Bull Awaa helping with the heavy work. Such delicate, very precious items as fragile porcelain, crystal, gold, silver and jewelry items she takes down herself. Always an early riser, Anna likes to get to the Batik Room by 6 a.m. on the morning of an auction – and to have everyone helping her there at that hour to unload the items.

It is Anna who decides how and where each should be displayed. Before, she and Bernard did this final display alone. For the 1985 auction, Anna still drove down at 6 a.m. but this time she acccepted the help of a crew of George Watson, HPA maintenance superintendent who at her direction set out the display of items to be auctioned.

On the night of April 13th, to everyone's surprise and delight Anna was there at the entrance of the Batik Room, regally dressed, standing beside Headmaster Tooman. "She was in pain still – great pain – but she gave no sign of it beyond leaning on her cane," recalls Nogues.

After dinner, at the start of the auction, he seated Anna in a splendid peacock chair next to the auctioneer, Steve Rosen, who as usual was donating his time and services to HPA.

Like a queen on her throne, Anna sat there for three and one half hours. The muscles damaged in her fall froze. The pain was intense. But she carried on as if she were in the best of health. One hundred sixty-five items were auctioned off that evening in the Batik Room. With Tooman's guidance, HPA had rapidly become a well-known international school with boarding students from around the world. The overseas component of HPA was highly visible at the 1985 scholarship auction. The collection of native art sent by parents from Papua-New Guinea brought $5450. Special donations sent from parents in Japan under the leadership of Board of Governors member Kotaro Hori included a fine pearl necklace, a gardinian coral necklace, and opal and diamond rings, the latter given as a joint donation with Jim Bill's 'Gemfire of Kona'.

There was the usual collection of fine paintings, custom koa furniture, plus SureSave certificates donated by Anna's old friend Tom Okuyama, lamb from Kahua and Ponoholo Ranches, carcasses of choice beef from Anna Ranch, and innumerable vacation packages in leading hotels around the islands. By the end of the evening this sixth HPA scholarship auction had raised the unprecedented sum of $193,000 – a record-breaking amount for auctions in Hawaii. Everyone was overjoyed – except Anna. "If I'd only known how close we were I'd have worked harder! Just a few more items, just $7000 more in donations and we'd have hit the $200,000 mark. Next time we will!" she vowed.

"Anna has the memory of an elephant," observes Ronald Tooman. "At that April 1985 auction, one of those most helpful to her was HPA's superintendent of maintenance, George Watson. Maintenance people don't get a lot of glory. Anna realized that to put on such an auction a lot of people count and she remembers and recognizes them. For example, after the 1985 auction she told me that she must thank George Watson for all his help. She said she planned to take him to lunch at Mauna Kea Beach Hotel."

Tooman grins, telling the story. "A year went by. Anna at last recovered from her bad fall. In April 1986 she took George Watson to lunch at the hotel. He told me afterward how much he had enjoyed it." When Tooman called Anna to thank her for doing this, Anna said, "I'd had that in mind all this time. I hadn't forgotten what George Watson did for me!"

"You see?" says Tooman. "She never forgets. The mind of

an elephant!"

Not only did Anna have the mind of an elephant with her tenacious memory of commitments and obligations from the past. She also has a keen sense of the future and a shrewd business acumen. "People are not eating much beef anymore," she says. "Even I eat only fish and chicken. It's best for your health. I knew it was time to sell off my cattle and some of my land."

She prepared to do so in 1985 and 1986. Keawewai, that choice 300 acres for which she had carried the purchase price in gold dust in her saddle bags when she was ten years old, was sold for 1.5 million dollars to Doris Duke, who purchased it as a gift for a friend. Anna rose at three a.m. and worked hard until eight at night getting her cattle out of the Keawewai pastures and negotiating to get the best possible price for them in a declining beef market. "I'm getting out at the right time!" she observed. Her intention is to raise only Charolais, those pretty white cattle she loves to see grazing on the green pastures above her ranch house, and in the pastures she has eight miles away in Waimea.

Selling the major amount of her pastures and most of her cattle did not at all signal Anna's retirement. She simply changed the focus of her activity. "I keep a few good horses to use when Judy and I, and sometimes Thane and Theana, want to go riding," she says. "I'm busy of course keeping track of my investments, but most of all I'm getting ready to set up Anna Ranch and my home as a museum of the period that exemplifies the title of my mounted Heart Fund pageants – Old Hawaii on Horseback."

It was Mauna Lani Bay Hotel's manager Nick Klotz, she says, who first gave her that idea. "Anna!" he told her. "Your home should become a museum. It's a treasury of how a lady rancher has lived in Hawaii since the early days of this century."

"You're right!" she told him. Immediately, with the same precise attention to details by which she had planned her cross-breeding experiments in the old days, and her Old Hawaii on Horseback pageants and HPA scholarship auctions over the years, she began to work in that direction. For now, the ranch house would continue to be her home, full of memories and memorabilia of an intensely active and most unusual life.

"It's for the future, when I no longer live there, that I will have my home set up as Anna Ranch Museum. There'll be changing exhibits to acquaint visitors with the history of ranching in Hawaii." What will be even more unique about Anna Ranch Museum is that it will display the lifestyle and trophies of a 'lady rancher' of this century, a woman who was a pioneer in being recognized as an equal partner in the human race – equal in potential and in achievement with any man.

Along with her involvement in selling land and cattle, in continuing to prepare for the 1987 HPA scholarship auction, and in moving forward with plans to set up Anna Ranch Museum, as Ronald Tooman of HPA expresses it, "Anna began to relax and be a little better to herself, to not work quite so hard." She would spend occasional weekends at the oceanfront condo she had purchased in Kailua-Kona, near that of her old friends Irene and Jim Caldwell. She made reservations for an August 1986 cruise, and for a cruise to Alaska in the summer of 1987. Occasionally she spends a weekend at Mauna Kea Beach Hotel and, occasionally also, she still returned to the Royal Hawaiian where she continued to spend the Christmas and New Year holidays. For years she had always reserved the same suite whenever she stayed at the Royal.

In 1985 the manager of the Royal asked her, "Anna, for many years now you have always stayed in this one special suite when you are with us. If you would be willing to have one painted, we'd like a portrait of you to hang in the living room of the suite."

"Of course!" said Anna, much pleased. She commissioned Herb Kane (Herbert Kawainui Kane), the well known Hawaii artist, to do the portrait which today hangs in the handsomely redecorated suite at the Royal Hawaiian Hotel.

In May 1986, a tsunami warning resulted in evacuation of all low lying waterfront areas in Hawaii. It so happened, on the afternoon that the tidal wave sirens wailed their warning, Anna was in Hilo where she was spending a few days at the bayfront Naniloa Surf Hotel. She was at the beauty shop, having her hair done, when the sirens began to shriek. Hilo has a history of being badly battered by tidal waves. The April 1, 1946 tsunami had killed some 300 people and taken out bayfront buildings and the railroad line that once connected Hilo and the Hamakua Coast. In May 1960 a massive wave had hit Hilo at one in the morning, taking 57 lives and destroying 500 homes and businesses in Waiakea, the section where Anna had lived in the early days of her first marriage.

In Hilo, when those yellow tidal wave alert sirens wail, everyone hurries to evacuate lowlying coastal areas. In May 1986 the possibility was that the wave might affect all of the islands. In Honolulu evacuees caused one of the biggest traffic jams in Oahu's history. In Hilo at the Naniloa Surf Anna dashed out of the beauty parlor, her hair still wet, to hurry to her room. Ordinarily she is the most meticulous of packers. Not during a tidal wave evacuation! "I threw my things into my suitcase. Any old way!"

Staff members Mr. and Mrs. Carter helped her with all this. "Please call Volcano House and tell them to reserve a suite for me for the night," she asked. It never occurred to her that the Volcano House might already be full. The tidal wave was expected to hit at sometime between 5:00 and 7:00 p.m. that evening. It was already late in the afternoon when Anna set out in her Lincoln Continental (she owns two – one powder blue, one a dark blue with a diamond insignia). It is a thirty mile drive from Hilo, climbing all the way, up to the Volcano House, a hotel built on the rim of the vast caldera of Kilauea, one of the world's most active volcanoes.

By the time Anna reached the boundary of Hawaii Volcanoes National Park, in which the hotel is situated, it was raining hard. She parked, and just in hurrying from her car to the hotel entry, she was soaked. At the desk she told the clerk, "I'm Anna Perry-Fiske from Waimea. The manager of the Naniloa called to reserve a suite for me tonight."

The clerk looked at his reservations chart. He frowned. He shook his head and checked a second time. "I'm so sorry, Mrs. Perry-Fiske. We don't have a suite for you tonight. They're all taken."

"Just a room will do then," said Anna.

Again the clerk shook his head. "We don't even have a room for you. So many from Hilo drove up here to wait out the tsunami–"

"Hmmmm," said Anna. She quickly surveyed the hotel lobby. Several comfortable couches were near the fireplace where blazing logs gave off a welcome warmth in the damp chill of this elevation. Anna smiled at the clerk. "If you'll just have someone bring in my bags, I'll spend the night on one of your couches over there by the fire."

"Of course!" said the startled clerk.

Anna ensconced herself by the fire. She was soon dried out and warming up. Presently a disconsolate looking older woman came along. "What is the matter?" inquired Anna. "anything I can help you with?"

"I can't get a room here," said the woman. "I've got to stay the night. I don't know what to do!"

"No problem," Anna encouraged her. "I'm spending the night on this nice couch. Why don't you take that one next to me. It will be good sleeping in here by the fire. And we'll keep each other company if we can't sleep –"

The woman looked at her, then at the couch, and at the blazing logs. Her downcast expression began to change.

"Look at it this way," urged Anna. "We really have the biggest suite in the Volcano House – this whole lobby! And the ladies' room is right over there. How lucky we are!"

At this the woman began to smile. "You're something!" she said. "And you're right!"

By the time word came later that evening that the alert was over and no tidal wave had reached Hawaii, it was raining too hard outside for Anna to want to risk driving back to Hilo. On such nights, she well knew, portions of the Volcano Highway were apt to be shrouded in heavy fog. By now she and the woman from Ka'u had become fast friends. They went into the dining room for the 10 o'clock sitting. "With our eating this late the night will go more quickly," was Anna's advice.

That evening a Hawaiian group was playing dinner music. They recognized Anna and played a special number honoring her. "When I stood up to thank them, and everyone clapped, they had no idea I was sleeping out in the lobby!" Anna laughs.

When she and her new friend returned from dinner, the night clerk brought pillows and blankets for the two women. "I really slept well!" says Anna.

Photo by Peter French.

Anna's cousin Nancy Kerr and her husband John in Old Hawaii on Horseback.

Anna rides *pa'u* at Lethbridge, Alberta, Canada.

Monty Richards, Anna, and Brian Caires with a champion Charolais bull Anna purchased at Hawaii Livestock Auction, Waikoloa.

Yutaka Kimura.

Anna rides as Hawaii's Queen, Rose Bowl Parade Pasadena, New Year's Day 1972.

Anna with Captain John Young on Princess Line cruise.

Photo by Douglas Davidson

Anna riding side-saddle

Lyman with Anna's godson, Thane Hancock. 1975.

Anna and her cowboys after last branding at Keawewai, 1985.

Anna on cruise.

Anna celebrating Christmas at the Royal Hawaiian Hotel.

Anna hosts gala New Year's Eve at the Royal Hawaiian. Left to right, seated– Pat Hall, Ruth Tabrah, Howard Hall, Anna. Standing – Hawaii Heart Association Executive Reid Morrison and Mrs. Morrison.

Anna Ranch. Living room.

Ice carving, roses, and elegant buffet at one of Anna's unforgettable parties.

Anna with chef Salvador and staff in her dining room, Anna Ranch.

Anna with her newly christened goddaughter, Theana Hancock, 1978.

At first light next morning she was up, freshened her make-up and tidied herself, thanked the clerk for the blankets, said goodbye to her friend, and by six was on the road home. Anna Perry-Fiske in 1986 was still an independent, self-reliant, resourceful cowboy, and a very great lady to whom adversity is only a spur generating solutions to whatever problems may arise. Like the century at whose beginning she was born, she has endured much, been a survivor, and never lost her faith, never stopped being optimistic about the future.

It was the same gutsy woman who had dared to mount the bull in Wayne Fisher's California corral, the same young woman who bet on herself in Hilo horse races, the same girl who confronted the nuns at Sacred Heart Academy about the foolishness of bathing fully dressed in a high-necked, long sleeved, full length Mother Hubbard that climbed behind the wheel of the Lincoln Continental that May morning. She was Anna Lindsey Perry-Fiske, the grande dame of Waimea, the lady butcher and truck driver, the successful businesswoman and cattle breeder, the very special human being in whom Bernard Nogues recognizes the innate grandeur of European nobility. She was and is in every way Hawaii's incredible Anna – an inspiration to all women young and old, a devout practicing Catholic who communicates daily with her God, an astute business man, a generous heart, and above all a Waimean who is still in every way a legend in her own time.

Index